Cisco 802.11 Wireless Networking Quick Reference

Toby J. Velte, Ph.D., and Anthony T. Velte

Cisco Press

800 East 96th Street

Indianapolis, Indiana 46240 USA

Cisco 802.11 Wireless Networking Quick Reference

Toby J. Velte, Ph.D. and Anthony T. Velte

Copyright®2006 Cisco Systems, Inc.

Published by:
Cisco Press
800 East 96th Street
Indianapolis, IN 46240 USA

Printed in the United States of America   1 2 3 4 5 6 7 8 9 0

First Printing October 2005

Library of Congress Cataloging-in-Publication Number: 2004116064

ISBN: 1-58705-227-X

Warning and Disclaimer

This book is designed to provide information about wireless networking using the 802.11 protocol and with Cisco equipment. Every effort has been made to make this book as complete and as accurate as possible, but no warranty or fitness is implied.

The information is provided on an "as is" basis. The author, Cisco Press, and Cisco Systems, Inc. shall have neither liability nor responsibility to any person or entity with respect to any loss or damages arising from the information contained in this book or from the use of the discs or programs that may accompany it.

The opinions expressed in this book belong to the author and are not necessarily those of Cisco Systems, Inc.

Trademark Acknowledgments

All terms mentioned in this book that are known to be trademarks or service marks have been appropriately capitalized. Cisco Press or Cisco Systems, Inc. cannot attest to the accuracy of this information. Use of a term in this book should not be regarded as affecting the validity of any trademark or service mark.

Feedback Information

At Cisco Press, our goal is to create in-depth technical books of the highest quality and value. Each book is crafted with care and precision, undergoing rigorous development that involves the unique expertise of members from the professional technical community.

Readers' feedback is a natural continuation of this process. If you have any comments regarding how we could improve the quality of this book, or otherwise alter it to better suit your needs, you can contact us through e-mail at feedback@ciscopress.com. Please make sure to include the book title and ISBN in your message.

We greatly appreciate your assistance.

Corporate and Government Sales

Cisco Press offers excellent discounts on this book when ordered in quantity for bulk purchases or special sales.

For more information please contact: U.S. Corporate and Government Sales 1-800-382-3419 corpsales@pearsontechgroup.com

For sales outside the U.S. please contact: International Sales international@pearsoned.com

Publisher John Wait	**Editor-in-Chief** John Kane
Executive Editor Mary Beth Ray	**Cisco Representative** Anthony Wolfenden
Cisco Press Program Manager Jeff Brady	**Production Manager** Patrick Kanouse
Development Editor Andrew Cupp	**Copy Editor** Deadline Driven Publishing
Technical Editors Bruce Alexander, John Elliott, Fred Niehaus	**Editorial Assistant** Raina Han
Book and Cover Designer Louisa Adair	**Composition** Mark Shirar
Indexer Keith Cline	

CISCO SYSTEMS

Corporate Headquarters
Cisco Systems, Inc.
170 West Tasman Drive
San Jose, CA 95134-1706
USA
www.cisco.com
Tel: 408 526-4000
    800 553-NETS (6387)
Fax: 408 526-4100

European Headquarters
Cisco Systems International BV
Haarlerbergpark
Haarlerbergweg 13-19
1101 CH Amsterdam
The Netherlands
www-europe.cisco.com
Tel: 31 0 20 357 1000
Fax: 31 0 20 357 1100

Americas Headquarters
Cisco Systems, Inc.
170 West Tasman Drive
San Jose, CA 95134-1706
USA
www.cisco.com
Tel: 408 526-7660
Fax: 408 527-0883

Asia Pacific Headquarters
Cisco Systems, Inc.
Capital Tower
168 Robinson Road
#22-01 to #29-01
Singapore 068912
www.cisco.com
Tel: +65 6317 7777
Fax: +65 6317 7799

Cisco Systems has more than 200 offices in the following countries and regions. Addresses, phone numbers, and fax numbers are listed on the **Cisco.com Web site at www.cisco.com/go/offices.**

Argentina • Australia • Austria • Belgium • Brazil • Bulgaria • Canada • Chile • China PRC • Colombia • Costa Rica • Croatia • Czech Republic Denmark • Dubai, UAE • Finland • France • Germany • Greece • Hong Kong SAR • Hungary • India • Indonesia • Ireland • Israel • Italy Japan • Korea • Luxembourg • Malaysia • Mexico • The Netherlands • New Zealand • Norway • Peru • Philippines • Poland • Portugal Puerto Rico • Romania • Russia • Saudi Arabia • Scotland • Singapore • Slovakia • Slovenia • South Africa • Spain • Sweden Switzerland • Taiwan • Thailand • Turkey • Ukraine • United Kingdom • United States • Venezuela • Vietnam • Zimbabwe

About the Authors

Toby J. Velte, Ph.D., MCSE+I, CCNA, CCDA is cofounder of Velte Publishing, Inc. Dr. Velte is an international, best-selling author of business technology articles and books. He is coauthor of *Cisco: A Beginner's Guide* and *Cisco Internetworking with Windows NT/2000*. He is currently part of Accenture's North American Consumer and Industrial practice.

Anthony T. Velte, CISSP, is cofounder of Velte Publishing, Inc. Mr. Velte is an Information Systems Security expert and has led a multitude of network, security, and disaster-recovery initiatives for large banking and healthcare institutions. In addition to writing and publishing a variety of technology books and papers, he dabbles in marketing and Internet ecommerce strategies.

About the Technical Reviewer

Fred Niehaus is a technical marketing engineer for the Wireless Networking Business Unit at Cisco Systems, Inc. Fred has extensive customer contact and is responsible for developing and marketing enterprise class wireless solutions using Cisco Aironet and Airespace Series of Wireless LAN products. Prior to joining Cisco, Fred worked as a support engineer on some of the first wireless implementations for customers, such as Wal-Mart, Ford, Hertz Rent-A-Car, and others. Fred has been in the data communications and networking industry for the past 20 years and holds a Radio Amateur (Ham) License N8CPI.

Bruce Alexander is a channel account manager for Cisco Systems central region, focusing on wireless and mobility technologies. Prior to becoming a CAM, Bruce was the technical marketing manager for the Cisco Wireless Networking Business Unit. Bruce joined Cisco during the acquisition of Aironet Wireless Communication, where Bruce was director of technical support. Bruce has 31 years in the RF technology area, he was the Chairman of the Wi-Fi Alliance's Technical Security committee during the development of the WPA and WPA2 programs, and he is the author of the Cisco Press Book, *802.11 Wireless Network Site Surveying and Installation*.

John Elliott, CCIE No. 2095 and CISSP, is a consulting system engineer at Cisco Systems where he's been employed since 1996. John's previous work with radio networks led him to specialize in Aironet products from the initial acquisition by Cisco. Previously, John was a software engineer for 10 years developing communications code for diverse systems including phone switches, minicomputers, and embedded systems, and later spent five years deploying large networks around the globe. He is a graduate of the University of Arkansas with a BS in computer science.

Dedications

This book is dedicated to Elizabeth (Lizzy), Connor John, and Joey (JoJo), three little people who have made a very big impression on our hearts and in our lives.

Acknowledgments

It is once again our pleasure to acknowledge those individuals who help put a book like this together and help get it from conception into your hands. First and foremost, we want to thank Mr. Robert (Bobb) Elsenpeter for all of his hard work on the project. He always does an incredible job and we offer our acknowledgments and thanks to him.

In addition, we'd like to thank Tom Seiberlich and Brian O'Malley from our local Cisco office, and associates John Berg and Rex Hale for their insight and assistance.

Finally, we'd like to acknowledge all of the good folks at Cisco Systems and Cisco Press who had a hand in completing this book. Turn back a page or two and you'll see all their names. Their hard work completes the package, and they made this project a pleasure to be a part of. We thank you.

— ATV and TJV

This Book Is Safari Enabled

The Safari® Enabled icon on the cover of your favorite technology book means the book is available through Safari Bookshelf. When you buy this book, you get free access to the online edition for 45 days.

Safari Bookshelf is an electronic reference library that lets you easily search thousands of technical books, find code samples, download chapters, and access technical information whenever and wherever you need it.

To gain 45-day Safari Enabled access to this book:

- Go to http://www.ciscopress.com/safarienabled

- Enter the ISBN of this book (shown on the back cover, above the bar code)

- Log in or Sign up (site membership is required to register your book)

- Enter the coupon code
  4XJ5-YVVK-4XVM-UNKH-BRF1

If you have difficulty registering on Safari Bookshelf or accessing the online edition, please e-mail customer-service@safaribooksonline.com.

Contents at a Glance

Contents

Command Syntax Conventions

The conventions used to present command syntax in this book are the same conventions used in the IOS Command Reference. The Command Reference describes these conventions as follows:

- **Boldface** indicates commands and keywords that are entered literally as shown.
- *Italics* indicate arguments for which you supply actual values.
- Vertical bars | separate alternative, mutually exclusive elements.
- Square brackets [ ] indicate optional elements.
- Braces { } indicate a required choice.
- Braces within brackets [{ }] indicate a required choice within an optional element.

Preface

In the maternity ward at a local hospital, the nurse wrote her telephone number on a dry erase board in the new mother's room.

"If you need anything, just pick up your phone and call," the nurse told her.

The patient's telephone didn't plug into the wall with a conventional telephone jack. Instead, it was connected to an Ethernet port—she would be using an Internet Protocol (IP) phone. The nurse didn't have a regular cellular or cordless phone on her belt; she was also using an IP phone. However, in her case, she was equipped with a Cisco Wireless 7920 IP Phone.

Throughout the hospital, nurses had these phones to keep in touch with patients. Along the hospital hallways, Cisco Aironet 1200 Access Points (APs) were strategically located to ensure the nurses could talk with their charges.

Wireless networking has exploded in recent years. What started out as a somewhat slow medium (capable of 1 Mbps at best) has—like so many other computer-related functions—increased in speed at an amazing pace. Speeds of 54 Mbps are common now, and speeds at twice that rate are on the horizon. But it isn't just the networks' speeds that are increasing. The ranges and distances that wireless networks can traverse have also increased.

With this technology seeing so much growth from a technological standpoint, there is an equivalent growth from an application standpoint. That is, more and more organizations and individuals are adopting wireless technologies. It's not just for the "cool" factor; it's also the sheer utility of wireless technologies that attracts people, such as the aforementioned nurses.

Because wireless networking is so prevalent, it's necessary to provide the tools to help set up, use, and maintain these systems. To their credit, engineers are building easier-to-use wireless networking devices. However, with so many people using the technology, it is asked to do much more. Much depends on the technology's reliability. It's helpful to have the answers you need in one, convenient location.

Introduction

If want to set up a wireless computer network—specifically a network based on Cisco devices and technology—this book gives you the quick-reference tools you need to design, construct, and maintain such a network.

This book examines Cisco wireless networking equipment—from APs to client adapters, and more—plus it covers some of the Cisco technologies that help develop and operate a first-class wireless network.

The book is aimed at more of an intermediate audience, but a beginner can get help too. The book assumes you have some experience with the command-line interface (CLI) and are comfortable navigating a given piece of hardware's graphical user interface (GUI).

In these pages, you'll find information about:

- **Specific Cisco products**—Cisco offers a variety of products including APs, wireless client adapters, wireless IP phones, and the company's newest line of Airespace thin APs.

- **Network design tips**—You learn the best places to locate your wireless devices and how to get the most out of your plan.

- **Configuration details**—After everything is in place, you learn how to set up the devices for optimal service.

- **Troubleshooting steps**—If your wireless network falters, you can determine what went wrong and follow the steps to fix it.

- **Network tuning information**—Although your network is up and running, you can still optimize it for best results.

- **Security**—Keeping networks safe is a huge concern and it's not less of a concern with WLANs. In fact, new issues are presented with WLANs.

As a quick-reference tool, this is a handy book you can keep with you and refer to for common wireless networking tasks, questions, and problems that might arise.

Chapter 1 Contents

Cisco Wireless Equipment

With the growth and popularity of 802.11 wireless networking (also known as Wi-Fi), dozens of companies have developed wireless networking equipment. In 2000, Cisco acquired a company called Aironet. Since its acquisition, Aironet has become the title of Cisco wireless technology devices. From access points (APs) to client adapters, the Aironet family is a name you will become familiar with as you work more with Cisco wireless products.

You might also know the Linksys family of wireless networking devices. Most likely, you have seen these products in your local electronics store, somewhere between the spindles of blank CD-ROMs and new computers. Cisco acquired Linksys a few years ago; its products are aimed at consumers. Although these are useful utilitarian products, this chapter focuses on the products Cisco makes that are aimed at business and enterprise markets. Recently, Cisco acquired Airespace and has added its devices to the Cisco Wi-Fi line up.

This chapter examines the Cisco Aironet line of APs, client adapters, and bridges. It also introduces the Airespace equipment, as well as other unique wireless devices (such as the wireless IP phone from Cisco)—all the tools that you might use to deploy and upgrade a WLAN. These devices are compared at the end of each section, so you can match a Cisco wireless device against your own wants and needs.

Cisco Aironet APs

APs are the devices that connect to the LAN, providing wireless access to the network. Wireless clients communicate with APs to access LANs or WLANs, as shown in Figure 1-1.

Figure 1-1 *Wireless Clients Connect to the LAN via an AP*

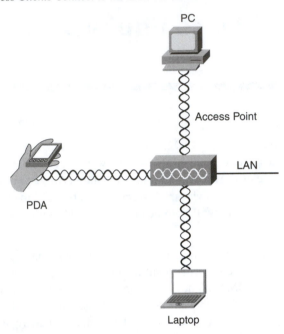

APs serve either as the core of an all-wireless network or as a point of connection between the wired and wireless networks. In addition, APs can be located throughout an organization to ensure access at remote locations in a facility.

Cisco features several models of APs. The model that fits best for your organization depends on a number of factors, which include:

- The number of wireless devices accessing the WLAN.
- The desired range.
- The desired speed.
- Your budget.

The following sections examine the Cisco Aironet APs, with specific details of each model.

Cisco Aironet 1100 Series

The Aironet 1100 AP (shown in Figure 1-2) includes a single radio and supports the 802.11g protocol. 802.11g is backward compatible to support the earlier 802.11b protocol. The most important distinction between 802.11b and 802.11g is the data rate—802.11b provides 11 Mbps, whereas 802.11g allows up to 54 Mbps.

Figure 1-2   *Cisco Aironet 1100 AP*

The 802.11b device can be upgraded to 802.11g capability. The 802.11g version allows wireless networks to leverage their investment on existing 802.11b equipment. It is also capable of 54-Mbps speeds with any new equipment. The Aironet 1100 AP allows the use of up to 16 virtual LANs (VLANs) and quality of service (QoS) functions. The AP also features hot standby and load balancing, which allow an organization to deploy intelligent network services and ensure network reliability and availability.

VLANs allow an organization to segment its users into their own discrete LANs. Thus, individual LAN policies, services, security levels, and QoS levels can be established for different groups of users.

The Cisco Wireless Security Suite manages the security for the Aironet 1100 AP. This product is based on the 802.1X standard for port-based network access, and makes use of Extensible Authentication Protocol (EAP) for user-based authentication. EAP and other security mechanisms are explained in more detail in Chapter 4, "Wireless Security."

The Aironet 1100 uses the Cisco Internetworking Operating System (IOS), which provides common command-line feel for Cisco veterans. Alternately, the device can be managed through a browser-based graphical user interface (GUI), such as the one shown in Figure 1-3.

The Aironet 1100 AP can be used as a single point of access to the WLAN, or several APs can be placed throughout the site to provide wireless access anywhere on the premises. Cisco offers various pieces of hardware to mount the device to the ceiling, the wall, or the edge of a cubicle.

Figure 1-3   *The Aironet 1100 Can Be Managed Using a Browser-Based Interface*

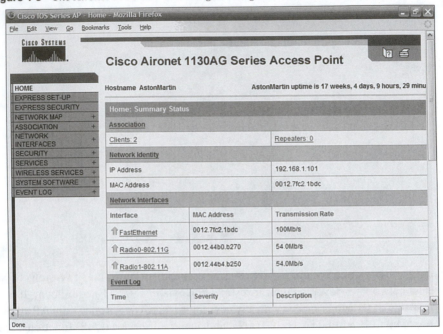

Aironet 1130AG Series AP

The 1130AG AP builds on the functionality and utility of the Aironet 1100 Series AP. This AP uses two built-in radios (802.11a and 802.11g) for optimal coverage and usability.

Shown in Figure 1-4, the 1130AG AP employs two internal antennas for omnidirectional coverage. The ring on the front of the device changes color, depending on its current state. For example, when nothing is associated, the ring glows a pale green. When one or more devices have associated, it glows blue. If an error occurs, it glows red.

Because the AP employs both 802.11a and 802.11g radios, it affords a capacity of up to 108 Mbps. In addition, because both radios are used, it can handle 15, nonoverlapping channels (12 from the 802.11a radio and 3 from the 802.11g radio). In a future firmware upgrade, this capacity will increase to 22 channels. This will ensure less interference with neighboring WLANs and fewer transmission errors.

NOTE: Because the AP uses an 802.11g radio, existing 802.11b legacy devices are supported.

Figure 1-4 *Cisco Aironet 1130AG AP*

For example, multiple 1130AGs can be installed in a ceiling to provide continuous coverage as users roam from room to room in a facility. As this device is somewhat of an "entry-level" model, it is easy to connect and deploy. Additional benefits include ongoing maintenance and an overall reduction of costs. To ensure security, the Aironet 1130AG uses the Cisco Wireless Security Suite, supporting 802.11i, Wi-Fi Protected Access (WPA), WPA2, and many types of EAP. In addition, the radio's power can be adjusted to fine-tune the device for operation in various environments.

Cisco Aironet 1200 Series

The big brother to the Aironet 1100 is the Cisco Aironet 1200. The 1200 series (shown in Figure 1-5) incorporates single or dual radios, and it allows connectivity in both the 2.4-GHz (802.11g) or 5-GHz (802.11a) bands. The device can be configured for optimal flexibility (as shown in Figure 1-6), and it can be set up to operate solely in the 802.11a, 802.11b, or 802.11g mode. Alternately, it can be set in dual mode, which allows connectivity for clients operating in two different protocols. Ultimately, it can be set in trimode, to offer simultaneous service for all three protocols. This functionality provides great flexibility and return on investment because devices using any of the popular protocols can be used.

Figure 1-5 *Cisco Aironet 1200 AP*

Figure 1-6 *The Aironet 1200 Allows Connections in Single, Dual, or Trimode*

Cisco Aironet 1200

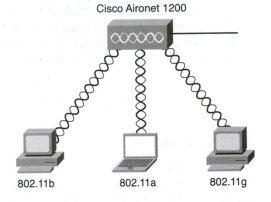

802.11b   802.11a   802.11g

Like the Aironet 1100 series, the Aironet 1200 offers up to 16 VLANs, QoS capabilities, and Cisco Wireless Security Suite manages its security set.

The Aironet 1200 series is an important component in the Cisco Structured Wireless-Aware Network (SWAN). SWAN is a framework for deploying, operating, and managing thousands of Aironet APs when using a Cisco infrastructure.

For 802.11a networks, the Aironet 1200 series offers a variety of antennas including one that can be configured omnidirectionally (in a circle surrounding the AP) or as a patch antenna that directs a hemispherical signal from the wall and across the room.

NOTE: Antennas are explained in greater detail in Chapter 2, "Cisco Antennas."

Like the Aironet 1100 series, the Aironet 1200 Series is managed either via the command line using IOS or via a browser-based GUI.

Aironet 1230AG Series AP

The Aironet 1230AG Series AP provides many of the same features as its younger brother, the 1130AG—chiefly dual 802.11a and 802.11g radios. However, the Aironet 1230AG is designed for environments in which omnidirectional antennas would be lacking. The 1130AG AP employs only internal antennas, but the 1230AG AP features connectors for external antennas.

This is ideal in environments such as factories, warehouses, or large retail facilities that require specialized antennas for proper functionality. Figure 1-7 shows this device.

Figure 1-7   *Cisco Aironet 1230AG AP*

Like other AP offerings from Cisco, the Aironet 1230AG AP is a component of the Cisco SWAN framework that delivers an integrated wired and wireless network.

Because the device uses both 802.11a and 802.11g radios, up to 15 nonoverlapping channels are available. This number will increase to 22 channels in a future firmware release.

The Aironet 1230AG AP is rugged enough to withstand high levels of heat.

Cisco Aironet 1300 Series

For outdoor wireless applications, Cisco offers its Aironet 1300 Series of APs, shown in Figure 1-8. These APs are encased in a tough, durable exterior, which makes them well suited for operation in the elements. In addition to its work as an AP, this device is also used as a network bridge (which is explained in greater detail in the "Cisco Wireless Bridges" section).

Figure 1-8 *Cisco Aironet 1300 AP*

NOTE: Although the Aironet 1300 is designed for outdoor environments, it can still be used indoors.

The Aironet 1300 supports the 802.11g standards, providing data transfer rates of up to 54 Mbps.

These APs are not just for employees to take their laptops outside during lunch breaks. A number of organizations that benefit from an outdoor AP include the following:

- **Campus networks**—For multibuilding organizations (schools, apartment buildings, hospitals, and so on), Wi-Fi makes interbuilding networks easy and inexpensive.

- **Nomadic users**—Networks and users are not just tethered to their desks, offices, or even buildings. Many users work in trucks, vans, cars, or ambulances and require connectivity to the network. To resolve this problem, outdoor, Wi-Fi networks come in handy.

- **Outdoor public access**—Wi-Fi hotspots pop up at many places, such as coffee shops, libraries, hotels, and now truck stops. As hotspots grow, devices such as the Cisco Aironet 1300 can be employed to provide Wi-Fi access to large outdoor areas.

- **Temporary access**—The Aironet 1300 is a good solution when a temporary wireless network is needed. For example, aid workers caring for victims of a natural disaster can employ this sort of device to provide easy, reliable connectivity among its users and devices.

The AP can manage 16 VLANs and 24 Voice over IP (VoIP) circuits on a point-to-point link. It also uses the Cisco Wireless Security Suite for its security chores. The Cisco Aironet 1300 can be easily managed as part of a Cisco SWAN solution (Chapter 3, "Cisco Wireless Technologies," covers SWAN in more detail). In addition, the command line or browser-based GUI can manage it.

AP Quick Comparison

When considering which AP is best for your organization's needs, a number of variables come into play. Table 1-1 through Table 1-5 compare popular traits of these Cisco APs.

Table 1-1 *Aironet 1100 Properties*

Network Standard	Speed	Range	Security	Channels
802.11b and 802.11g	1, 2, 5.5, 6, 9, 11, 12, 18, 24, 36, 48, and 54 Mbps	**802.11b Indoor:** 220 ft (67 m) at 11 Mbps 310 ft (94 m) at 5.5 Mbps 350 ft (107 m) at 2 Mbps 410 ft (124 m) at 1 Mbps **802.11b Outdoor:** 490 ft (149 m) at 11 Mbps 700 ft (213 m) at 1 Mbps **802.11g Indoor:** 90 ft (27 m) at 54 Mbps 95 ft (29 m) at 48 Mbps 100 ft (30 m) at 36 Mbps 140 ft (42 m) at 24 Mbps 180 ft (54 m) at 18 Mbps 210 ft (64 m) at 12 Mbps 250 ft (76 m) at 9 Mbps 300 ft (91 m) at 6 Mbps **802.11g Outdoor:** 250 ft (76m) at 54 Mbps 600 ft (183 m) at 18 Mbps 1300 ft (396 m) at 6 Mbps	Cisco Wireless Security Suite, which includes: Authentication: 802.1X (Cisco LEAP, PEAP, EAP-TLS, and EAP-SIM) MAC Addresses and basic 802.11 authentication tools Encryption: 40- and 128-bit WEP keys TKIP WEP enhancements (key hashing, message integrity check, and broadcast key rotation)	**Americas (FCC):** 2.4-GHz Band: 11 channels **China:** 2.4-GHz Band: 13 channels **ETSI:** 2.4-GHz Band: 13 channels **Japan (TELEC):** 2.4-GHz Band (OFDM): 13 channels 2.4-GHz Band (CCK): 14 channels **North America:** 2.4-GHz Band: 11 channels

Table 1-2 *Aironet 1200 Properties*

Network Standard	Speed	Range	Security	Channels
802.11a, 802.11b, and 802.11g This model must be configured for one or more network standards.	1, 2, 5.5, 6, 9, 11, 12, 18, 24, 36, 48, and 54 Mbps	**802.11b Indoor:** 220 ft (67 m) at 11 Mbps 310 ft (94 m) at 5.5 Mbps 350 ft (107 m) at 2 Mbps 410 ft (124 m) at 1 Mbps **802.11b Outdoor:** 1000 ft (304 m) at 11 Mbps 2000 ft (610 m) at 1 Mbps **802.11g Indoor:** 90 ft (27 m) at 54 Mbps 95 ft (29 m) at 48 Mbps 100 ft (30 m) at 36 Mbps 140 ft (42 m) at 24 Mbps 180 ft (54 m) at 18 Mbps 210 ft (64 m) at 12 Mbps 250 ft (76 m) at 9 Mbps 300 ft (91 m) at 6 Mbps **802.11g Outdoor:** 250 ft (76m) at 54 Mbps 600 ft (183 m) at 18 Mbps 1300 ft (396 m) at 6 Mbps **802.11a Indoor:** 90 ft (26 m) at 54 Mbps 225 ft (69 m) at 48 Mbps 300 ft (91 m) at 36 Mbps 350 ft (107 m) at 24 Mbps 400 ft (122 m) at 18 Mbps 450 ft (137 m) at 12 Mbps 475 ft (145 m) at 9 Mbps 500 ft (152 m) at 6 Mbps **802.11a Outdoor:** 170 ft (52 m) at 54 Mbps 800 ft (244 m) at 18 Mbps 950 ft (290 m) at 6 Mbps	Cisco Wireless Security Suite	**Americas (FCC)** 2.4-GHz Band: 11 channels 5-GHz Band: 12 channels **China:** 2.4-GHz Band: 13 channels 5-GHz Band: 4 channels **ETSI:** 2.4-GHz Band: 13 channels 5-GHz Band: 9 channels **Japan (TELEC):** 2.4-GHz Band (OFDM): 13 channels 2.4-GHz Band (CCK): 14 channels 5-GHz Band: 4 channels **North America:** 2.4-GHz Band: 11 channels 5-GHz Band: 12 channels

Table 1-3 *Aironet 1300 Properties*

Network Standard	Speed	Range	Security	Channels
802.11b and 802.11g	1, 2, 5.5, 6, 9, 11, 12, 18, 24, 36, 48, and 54 Mbps	**Aironet 1300 with integrated antenna:** 350 feet (105 meters) at 54 Mbps 1410 feet (430 meters) at 11 Mbps **Americas:** 865 feet (260 m) at 54 Mbps 3465 feet (1055 m) at 11 Mbps **ETSI:** 150 feet (45 m) at 54 Mbps 775 feet (235 m) at 11 Mbps **TELEC:** 485 feet (145 m) at 54 Mbps 1095 feet (330 m) at 11 Mbps **Aironet 1300 with optional, add-on antennas:** 865 feet (260 m) at 54 Mbps 3,465 feet (1055 m) at 11 Mbps **Americas:** 350 feet (105 m) at 54 Mbps 1410 feet (430 m) at 11 Mbps **ETSI:** 195 feet (60 m) at 54 Mbps 630 feet (190 m) at 11 Mbps **TELEC:** 195 feet (60 m) at 54 Mbps 445 feet (135 m) at 11 Mbps	Cisco Wireless Security Suite	**Americas (FCC):** 2.4-GHz Band: 11 channels 5-GHz Band: 12 channels **China:** 2.4-GHz Band: 13 channels 5-GHz Band: 4 channels **ETSI:** 2.4-GHz Band: 13 channels 5-GHz Band: 9 channels **Japan (TELEC):** 2.4-GHz Band (OFDM): 13 channels 2.4-GHz Band (CCK): 14 channels 5-GHz Band: 4 channels **North America:** 2.4-GHz Band: 11 channels 5-GHz Band: 12 channels

Table 1-4   *Cisco 1000 Series Lightweight AP Properties*

Network Standard	Speed	Range	Security	Channels
802.11a, 802.11b, and 802.11g	1, 2, 5.5, 6, 9, 11, 12, 18, 24, 36, 48, and 54 Mbps	**802.11a Indoor:** 45 ft (14 m) at 54 Mbps 110 ft (34 m) at 18 Mbps 165 ft (50 m) at 6 Mbps **802.11a Outdoor:** 100 ft (30 m) at 54 Mbps 600 ft (183 m) at 18 Mbps 1000 ft (305 m) at 6 Mbps **802.11b Indoor:** 160 ft (49 m) at 11 Mbps 410 ft (125 m) at 1 Mbps **802.11b Outdoor:** 1000 ft (305 m) at 11 Mbps 2000 ft (610 m) at 1 Mbps **802.11g Indoor:** 90 ft (27 m) at 54 Mbps 180 ft (55 m) at 18 Mbps 300 ft (91 m) at 6 Mbps **802.11g Outdoor:** 250 ft (76 m) at 54 Mbps 600 ft (183 m) at 18 Mbps 1300 ft (396 m) at 6 Mbps	Cisco Wireless Security Suite	**Americas (FCC)** 2.4-GHz Band: 11 channels 5-GHz Band: 12 channels **China** 2.4-GHz Band: 13 channels 5-GHz Band: 4 channels **ETSI** 2.4-GHz Band: 13 channels 5-GHz Band: 9 channels **Japan (TELEC)** 2.4-GHz Band (OFDM): 13 channels 2.4-GHz Band (CCK): 14 channels 5-GHz Band: 4 channels **North America** 2.4-GHz Band: 11 channels 5-GHz Band: 12 channels

Table 1-5 *Aironet 1130 AP Properties*

Network Standard	Speed	Range	Security	Channels
802.11a, 802.11b, and 802.11g	1, 2, 5.5, 6, 9, 11, 12, 18, 24, 36, 48, and 54 Mbps	**802.11a Indoor:** 80 ft (24 m) at 54 Mbps 150 ft (45 m) at 48 Mbps 200 ft (60 m) at 36 Mbps 225 ft (69 m) at 24 Mbps 250 ft (76 m) at 18 Mbps 275 ft (84 m) at 12 Mbps 300 ft (91 m) at 9 Mbps 325 ft (100 m) at 6 Mbps **802.11a Outdoor:** 100 ft (30 m) at 54 Mbps 300 ft (91 m) at 48 Mbps 425 ft (130 m) at 36 Mbps 500 ft (152 m) at 24 Mbps 550 ft (168 m) at 18 Mbps 600 ft (183 m) at 12 Mbps 625 ft (190 m) at 9 Mbps 650 ft (198 m) at 6 Mbps **802.11g Indoor:** 100 ft (30 m) at 54 Mbps 175 ft (53 m) at 48 Mbps 250 ft (76 m) at 36 Mbps 275 ft (84 m) at 24 Mbps 325 ft (100 m) at 18 Mbps 350 ft (107 m) at 12 Mbps 360 ft (110 m) at 11 Mbps 375 ft (114 m) at 9 Mbps 400 ft (122 m) at 6 Mbps 420 ft (128 m) at 5.5 Mbps 440 ft (134 m) at 2 Mbps 450 ft (137 m) at 1 Mbps **802.11g Outdoor:** 120 ft (37 m) at 54 Mbps 350 ft (107 m) at 48 Mbps 550 ft (168 m) at 36 Mbps 650 ft (198 m) at 24 Mbps 750 ft (229 m) at 18 Mbps 800 ft (244 m) at 12 Mbps 820 ft (250 m) at 11 Mbps 875 ft (267 m) at 9 Mbps 900 ft (274 m) at 6 Mbps 910 ft (277 m) at 5.5 Mbps 940 ft (287 m) at 2 Mbps 950 ft (290 m) at 1 Mbps	Cisco Wireless Security Suite	**Americas (FCC)** 2.4-GHz Band: 11 channels 5-GHz Band: 12 channels **China** 2.4-GHz Band: 13 channels 5-GHz Band: 4 channels **ETSI** 2.4-GHz Band: 13 channels 5-GHz Band: 9 channels **Japan (TELEC)** 2.4-GHz Band (OFDM): 13 channels 2.4-GHz Band (CCK): 14 channels 5-GHz Band: 4 channels **North America** 2.4-GHz Band: 11 channels 5-GHz Band: 12 channels

For more information on connecting your APs, flip ahead to Chapter 5.

NOTE: You might still see Cisco Aironet 350 APs in organizations that were early adopters of wireless networking technology. These devices operated using only the 802.11b protocol. Cisco has phased out this device and no longer supports it. However, because it employs the 802.11b protocol, it is still compatible with other 802.11g devices. The Aironet 350 bridge is still available. Bridge devices are discussed in the section, "Cisco Wireless Bridges."

Airespace

Cisco completed its acquisition of a company called Airespace in early 2005. Now, the new Cisco 1000 Series Lightweight AP and WLAN controllers are included in its Wi-Fi catalog. These components work in tandem to deliver easy setup and configuration and a robust radio frequency (RF) environment.

Cisco 1000 Series Lightweight AP

This device has its benefits. It can be installed and connected to the network, with no configuration or setup needed on the AP, because configuration data is downloaded to the thin AP from a WLAN controller. This device is shown in Figure 1-9.

Figure 1-9 *Cisco 1000 Series Lightweight AP*

Although its easy installation and setup are big selling points for this device, it does much more. Because the AP's functioning is somewhat centralized to the WLAN controller, the AP can feed information about the RF environment back to the WLAN controller and the Cisco Wireless Control System. This allows these applications to make real-time decisions.

The data is forwarded and the RF environment monitored, which eliminates the need for additional nodes dedicated to those management functions. In turn, the overall network design is much simpler and more cost efficient. Within the 1000 series are three models:

- **1010**—Offers two internal, sectorized antennas, used in places such as classrooms or office spaces.
- **1020**—Offers two internal, sectorized antennas and connectors for external antennas, used in places such as factories or for outdoor applications.
- **1030**—Offers two internal, sectorized antennas and connectors for external antennas. Also known as a Remote-Edge AP, this device is designed for use at branch offices to communicate with centrally located WLAN controllers using WAN technologies. This allows IT staff to centrally control service set identifiers (SSID), security settings, and configuration for a cohesive wireless environment.

The 1000 series allows power over Ethernet connections and over the air QoS.

The 1000 series also operates using 802.11a and 802.11g radios, affording compatibility with both standards and operation on up to 15 nonoverlapping channels.

Cisco WLAN Controllers

Earlier, we discussed the lines of the Cisco Lightweight APs. The APs and wireless control system are two legs of a three-legged stool; WLAN controllers comprise the other.

WLAN controllers are the hub of systemwide WLAN operation. They are the devices on which information is stored and disseminated to thin APs. In return, environmental data is sent back to the WLAN controller for analysis and action. The information stored on the WLAN controllers includes:

- Voice and data service
- Security policies
- Intrusion prevention
- RF management
- QoS
- Mobility
- Thin AP configuration

WLAN controllers communicate with the thin APs over Layer 2 or Layer 3 infrastructure using the Lightweight Access Point Protocol (LWAPP). This protocol ensures that communication between WLAN controllers and thin APs is secure.

Cisco offers three series of WLAN controllers: the 2000 Series, the 4100 Series, and the 4400 Series.

The Cisco 2000 Series WLAN controller is targeted at small- to medium-sized enterprise applications. Its 2006 model is capable of controlling up to 6 thin APs. The 2000 is shown in Figure 1-10.

Figure 1-10 *Cisco 2000 Series WLAN Controller*

The Cisco 4100 Series WLAN controller is targeted at medium- to large-sized enterprise applications. Its three models—the 4112, 4124, and 4136—offer support to 12, 24, or 26 thin APs, respectively. This series features dual Gigabit Ethernet uplinks for LAN connectivity. The 4100 Series is shown in Figure 1-11.

Figure 1-11 *Cisco 4100 Series WLAN Controller*

These WLAN controllers can detect and adapt to changes in the RF environment. This level of management affords the following functionality:

- Channels are dynamically assigned to optimize network coverage and lessen interference.
- The system detects interference and makes changes to the network to remedy the interference.
- Load balancing prevents a large number of users from overburdening a specific thin AP.
- The power outpoint of the thin APs is adjusted to detect and correct coverage holes.
- Power is automatically adjusted across the network to specific APs, based on changing network conditions.

WLAN controllers use up-to-date security features that include WPA2, WPA, WEP, multiple EAP types, and a VPN termination module for IPSec and Layer 2 Tunneling Protocol.

Other security features include:

- The capability to detect and avoid unwanted RF propagation.
- Intrusion prevention and location to ensure that rogue APs are not only found, but located.
- Network admission control that manages client access based on policies.

Because the WLAN controller operates at both Layer 2 and 3 levels, users can roam among APs, switches, and routed subnets without interruption in service. In addition, security and QoS information follows them, so the operation environment is consistent.

Cisco Wireless Bridges

In the past, connecting buildings on a campus or constructing a metropolitan-area network (MAN) required copper, fiber optic cabling, or expensive microwave equipment. Thanks to Wi-Fi technology, it is possible to unite geographically dispersed networks wirelessly. Cisco provides several options for wireless network connectivity.

The ranges for these devices depend on a number of factors, especially the antenna. Antennas are explained in greater detail in Chapter 2.

As you read through the product descriptions for APs and bridges (and later when client adapters are introduced), you might wonder why it is important to have an AP or bridge with a range of several thousand feet, or even a few miles, especially when client adapters can reach only a few hundred feet. It is important to understand that bridges and APs serve different functions. Although the job of an AP is to provide a point of connection to wireless clients, a bridge's main function is to connect with other bridges, and it serves as a link between two or more networks. APs, on the other hand, can also be added to enhance the range of a WLAN. Extending the network by adding APs can provide access to clients that are too far away from the WLAN to connect. As such, the greater ranges that APs and bridges afford are useful when bridges have to communicate with each other and when APs are placed to increase overall range. Enhancing your network's reach with additional APs is examined in Chapter 5.

Cisco Aironet 1300 Series as a Bridge

As noted in the previous section, the Cisco Aironet 1300 can be used as an outdoor AP or it can be used to connect several LANs in a MAN or campus environment—or even mobile networks. For optimal results in this capacity, the AP must be configured with the proper antenna.

The Aironet 1300 can serve as either a point-to-point or point-to-multipoint bridge. This is illustrated in Figure 1-12.

Figure 1-12 *Aironet Bridges Can Connect with One or Several Other Wireless Bridges*

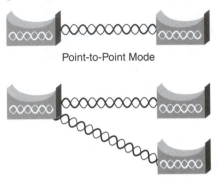

Point-to-Point Mode

Point-to-Multipoint Mode

The Aironet 1300 bridge can also perform double duty. While connecting with bridges at other sites, the Aironet 1300 can simultaneously perform the functions of a wireless AP, accepting wireless clients.

If operating as a *workgroup bridge*, the Aironet 1300 connects wired Ethernet-enabled devices (laptops, network printers, and so on) to your WLAN. When the bridge is connected to an Ethernet switch, up to 255 devices can be added. Figure 1-13 illustrates this.

Figure 1-13 *Workgroup Bridging Connects Ethernet Devices to the WLAN*

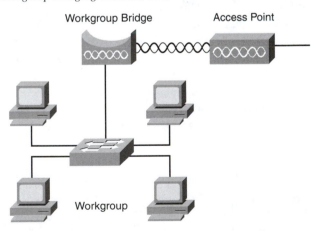

The Aironet 1300 comes with either integrated antennas or it can be purchased with connectors for external antennas.

As noted in the AP section, the Aironet 1300 bridge is capable of 802.11g. It offers a range up to 9 miles (in the United States) at 11 Mbps. For vehicle deployments, vehicles traveling over 60 mph (100 kph) with data rates at 12 Mbps and 24 Mbps and 128-byte packets experience a 1 percent packet error rate.

Cisco Aironet 1400 Series

Like the Aironet 1300, the 1400 series—shown in Figure 1-14—comes with either an integrated antenna or connectors for optional external antennas.

Figure 1-14   *Cisco Aironet 1400 Series Bridge*

Using the 802.11a protocol, the Aironet 1400 with a built-in antenna allows 54-Mbps data rates up to 8.5 miles for point-to-point links and up to 2.75 miles for point-to-multipoint links. Adding an upgradeable antenna, speeds of 9 Mbps can be achieved at a distance of 23 miles.

The Aironet 1400 can be deployed in several ways, depending on your network's need. For example, it can be configured to be the singular connection between two geographically disparate networks. Alternately, it can be used as either the primary or the backup connection, in tandem with a second type of connection, such as a T1 line.

The Cisco Wireless Security Suite manages security on both the Aironet 1300 and 1400 series. Centralized management is employed through a Remote Authentication Dial-In User Service (RADIUS) server.

Wireless Bridge Quick Comparison

Each model of Cisco Aironet device offers its own attributes including speeds, network standards, and protocols. Table 1-6 compares the two series.

Table 1-6   *Comparison of Cisco Aironet Bridges*

Feature	Cisco Aironet 1300	Cisco Aironet 1400
Network Standard	802.11b and 802.11g	802.11a
Point-to-Point Range	**Aironet 1300 with integrated antenna:** Americas: 1.3 miles (2 km) at 54 Mbps 9 miles (15 km) at 11 Mbps EMEA: 0.2 miles (0.36 km) at 54 Mbps 2.3 miles (3.5 km) at 11 Mbps TELEC: 0.7 miles (1.1 km) at 54 Mbps 3.2 miles (5 km) at 11 Mbps Note: 13-dBi integrated antenna at root and nonroot bridge **Aironet 1300 with upgradeable antennas:** Americas: 4.5 miles (7 km) at 54 Mbps 14 miles (23 km) at 11 Mbps EMEA: 5.5 miles (9 km) at 11 Mbps TELEC: 4.5 miles (7 km) at 54 Mbps 12 miles (20 km) at 11 Mbps Note: 21-dBi dish antenna at root and nonroot bridge	**Aironet 1400 with integrated antenna:** Americas: 8.5 miles (14 km) at 54 Mbps 16 miles (26 km) at 9 Mbps Korea: 5.5 miles (9 km) at 54 Mbps 11.25 miles (18.25 km) at 9 Mbps Australia and New Zealand: 3.5 miles (5.75 km) at 54 Mbps 9.5 miles (15.25 km) at 9 Mbps Ireland and China: 1.75 miles (2.75 km) at 54 Mbps 7.25 miles (11.5 km) at 9 Mbps **Aironet 1400 with upgradeable antennas:** 13 miles (21 km) at 54 Mbps 23 miles (37 km) at 9 Mbps

Table 1-6   *Comparison of Cisco Aironet Bridges (Continued)*

Feature	Cisco Aironet 1300	Cisco Aironet 1400
Point-to-Multipoint Range	**Aironet 1300 with integrated antenna:** Americas: 1.1 miles (1.8 km) at 54 Mbps 8 miles (13 km) at 11 Mbps EMEA: 0.25 miles (0.4 km) at 54 Mbps 1.1 miles (1.8 km) at 11 Mbps TELEC: 0.8 miles (1.3 km) at 54 Mbps 3.6 miles (5.8 km) at 11 Mbps Note: 14-dBi sector antenna at root and 13-dBi integrated antenna at nonroot **Aironet 1300 with upgradeable antennas:** Americas: 2.0 miles (3.3 km) at 54 Mbps 10 miles (16 km) at 11 Mbps EMEA: 2.5 miles (4 km) at 11 Mbps TELEC: 2.0 miles (3.3 km) at 54 Mbps 9.0 miles (14 km) at 11 Mbps Note: 14-dBi sector at root and 21 dBi dish at nonroot	**Aironet 1400 with integrated antenna:** Americas: 2.75 miles (4.5 km) at 54 Mbps 8.5 miles (14 km) at 9 Mbps Korea: 1 mile (1.75 km) at 54 Mbps 5 miles (8 km) at 9 Mbps Australia and New Zealand: 0.75 miles (1.2 km) at 54 Mbps 3.25 miles (5.25 km) at 9 Mbps Ireland and China: 0.4 miles (0.6 km) at 54 Mbps 1.75 miles (2.75 km) at 9 Mbps **Aironet 1400 with upgradeable antennas:** 4.25 miles (7 km) at 54 Mbps 11 miles (18 km) at 9 Mbps
Speeds	1, 2, 5.5, 6, 9, 11, 12, 18, 24, 36, 48, and 54 Mbps	6, 9, 12, 18, 24, 36, 48, and 54 Mbps
Security	Cisco Wireless Security Suite including: 802.1X supported authentication, using LEAP. Encryption includes support for static and dynamic 40- and 128-bit WEP keys. Encryption also uses prestandard TKIP WEP enhancements (key hashing and Message Integrity Check [MIC])	Cisco Wireless Security Suite

continues

Table 1-6   *Comparison of Cisco Aironet Bridges (Continued)*

Feature	Cisco Aironet 1300	Cisco Aironet 1400
Operations Band	2.5 GHz 802.11b: DSSS 802.11g: Orthogonal Frequency Division Multiplexing (OFDM)	5 GHz / Coded Orthogonal Frequency Division Multiplexing (COFDM)
Channels	11	4

Cisco Client Adapters

As we move down the wireless food chain, we come to the devices connecting users with the wireless network. Wireless adapters can be fitted to a multitude of devices—client PCs, personal digital assistants, network printers, and so forth. Cisco offers four client adapters for its Aironet line:

- Cisco Aironet 350
- Cisco Aironet 802.11a, 802.11b, and 802.11g CardBus Wireless Client LAN Adapter
- Cisco Aironet 802.11a, 802.11b, and 802.11g Peripheral Component Interconnect (PCI) Wireless Client LAN Adapter
- Cisco Aironet 5 GHz 802.11a Adapter

The type of client adapter you use depends on what type of computer you need to connect. Laptops and other devices with Personal Computer Memory Card International Association (PCMCIA) and CardBus combination slots use a CardBus device. Desktop and tower-style PCs use PCI adapters.

Cisco Aironet 350

The entry-level model of Cisco client adapters is its venerable Aironet 350 adapter, shown in Figure 1-15. These adapters are designed as PCMCIA or PCI devices, which allow them to work with both desktop and laptop PCs.

These adapters can be used in either ad hoc (meaning two or more computers connect among themselves) or infrastructure environments (meaning the clients connect to a WLAN) and use the 802.11b protocol, which allows them to work in the 2.4-GHz band with a range up to 800 feet at 11 Mbps. Although this product operates at just 11 Mbps, it is compatible with 802.11g APs (although speed is limited to the adapter's top speed of 11 Mbps).

Figure 1-15   *Cisco Aironet 350 Client Adapters in PCMCIA and PCI Forms*

Cisco Aironet 802.11a, 802.11b, and 802.11g CardBus and PCI Wireless Client LAN Adapters

The Aironet 802.11 a/b/g CardBus and PCI Wireless Client LAN Adapters allow for a variety of uses and applications. Although they provide the same functionality, the difference between the CardBus and PCI devices is their physical design and construction. The CardBus devices are suited for laptops and tablet PCs, but the PCI device is meant for desktop PCs.

The CardBus device (shown in Figure 1-16) plugs into an open CardBus or combo CardBus/PCMCIA slot and the end sticks out an inch or so, allowing its internal antenna to communicate with the WLAN. The PCI device (shown in Figure 1-17) is a card that plugs into an open PCI slot on the PC. The card is connected to a small antenna that can be adjusted for best connectivity to the WLAN.

Figure 1-16   *Cisco Aironet 802.11 a/b/g CardBus Wireless Client LAN Adapter*

Figure 1-17   *Cisco Aironet 802.11a, 802.11b, and 802.11g PCI Wireless Client LAN Adapter*

In spite of their physical differences, the devices offer the same functionality and are the most feature-rich and functional. They both offer:

- 802.11a coverage
- 802.11b coverage
- 802.11g coverage
- Dual mode 802.11a and 802.11g coverage
- Trimode 802.11a, 802.11b, and 802.11g coverage

These devices support Wi-Fi Protected Access (WPA) and WPA2. They also support 802.1X authentication, which includes LEAP, EAP-TLS, PEAP-GTC, EAP-FAST, and PEAP-MSCHAP V2. Wireless security is explored in Chapter 4.

In addition, RADIUS servers can be used for strong security and user management.

Cisco Aironet 5 GHz 802.11a Adapter

The Cisco Aironet 5 GHz 802.11a Adapter serves clients that need access to a WLAN using 802.11a technology, shown in Figure 1-18. This device uses a CardBus form and is designed for use with APs, such as the Cisco Aironet 1200 Series 802.11a AP or the Aironet 1130AG AP.

Figure 1-18   *Cisco Aironet 5 GHz 802.11a Adapter*

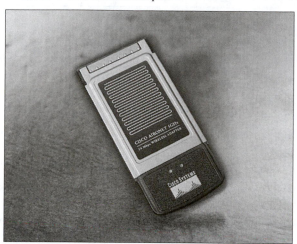

Because the device offers 802.11a functionality, it operates at speeds of up to 54 Mbps in the 5-GHz band. Data rates can be reduced to extend the device's range.

The adapter uses the Cisco Wireless Security Suite, which offers the EAP framework for user-based authentication. It also supports a number of 802.1X authentication modes that include Cisco LEAP, EAP-TLS, PEAP, and EAP-SIM. Authentication methods are explained in more detail in Chapter 4.

Client Adapter Quick Comparison

Cisco offers a number of options for client adapters. Choosing which adapter is ideal may come down to a number of variables or just one. Table 1-7 compares these devices and their attributes.

Table 1-7   *Comparison of Cisco Client Adapter Features*

Feature	Cisco Aironet 350	Cisco Aironet CardBus WLAN Adapter	Cisco Aironet PCI WLAN Adapter	Cisco Aironet 5-GHz 54-Mbps 802.11a WLAN Client Adapter
Network Standard	802.11b	802.11a, 802.11b, and 802.11g	802.11a, 802.11b, and 802.11g	802.11a
Form Factor	PCMCIA Type II	CardBus Type II	PCI	CardBus Type II

continues

Table 1-7   *Comparison of Cisco Client Adapter Features (Continued)*

Feature	Cisco Aironet 350	Cisco Aironet CardBus WLAN Adapter	Cisco Aironet PCI WLAN Adapter	Cisco Aironet 5-GHz 54-Mbps 802.11a WLAN Client Adapter
Range	**Indoor:** 130 ft (40 m) at 11 Mbps 350 ft (107 m) at 1 Mbps **Outdoor:** 800 ft (244 m) at 11 Mbps 2000 ft (610 m) at 1 Mbps	**802.11a Indoor:** 45 ft (13 m) at 54 Mbps 110 ft (33 m) at 18 Mbps 165 ft (50 m) at 6 Mbps **802.11a Outdoor:** 100 ft (30 m) at 54 Mbps 600 ft (183 m) at 18 Mbps 1000 ft (304 m) at 6 Mbps **802.11b and 802.11g Indoor:** 90 ft (27 m) at 54 Mbps 180 ft (54m) at 18 Mbps 160 ft (48 m) at 11 Mbps 300 ft (91 m) at 6 Mbps 410 ft (124 m) at 1 Mbps **802.11b and 802.11g Outdoor:** 250 ft (76 m) at 54 Mbps 600 ft (183 m) at 18 Mbps 1000 ft (304 m) at 11 Mbps 1300 ft (396 m) at 6 Mbps 2000 ft (610 m) at 1 Mbps	**802.11a Indoor:** 45 ft (13 m) at 54 Mbps 110 ft (33 m) at 18 Mbps 165 ft (50 m) at 6 Mbps **802.11a Outdoor:** 100 ft (30 m) at 54 Mbps 600 ft (183 m) at 18 Mbps 1000 ft (304 m) at 6 Mbps **802.11b and 802.11g Indoor:** 90 ft (27 m) at 54 Mbps 180 ft (54m) at 18 Mbps 160 ft (48 m) at 11 Mbps 300 ft (91 m) at 6 Mbps 410 ft (124 m) at 1 Mbps **802.11b and 802.11g Outdoor:** 250 ft (76 m) at 54 Mbps 600 ft (183 m) at 18 Mbps 1000 ft (304 m) at 11 Mbps 1300 ft (396 m) at 6 Mbps 2000 ft (610 m) at 1 Mbps	**Indoor:** 60 ft (18m) at 54 Mbps 130 ft (40m) at 18 Mbps 170 ft (52m) at 6 Mbps **Outdoor:** 100 ft (30m) at 54 Mbps 600 ft (183m) at 18 Mbps 1000 (304m) at 6 Mbps

Table 1-7   *Comparison of Cisco Client Adapter Features (Continued)*

Feature	Cisco Aironet 350	Cisco Aironet CardBus WLAN Adapter	Cisco Aironet PCI WLAN Adapter	Cisco Aironet 5-GHz 54-Mbps 802.11a WLAN Client Adapter
Speed	1, 2, 5.5, and 11 Mbps	1, 2, 5.5, 6, 9, 11, 12, 18, 24, 36, 48, and 54 Mbps	1, 2, 5.5, 6, 9, 11, 12, 18, 24, 36, 48, and 54 Mbps	6, 9, 12, 18, 24, 36, 48, and 54 Mbps
Security	Cisco Wireless Security Suite, which includes: Authentication: 802.1X (Cisco LEAP, PEAP, EAP-TLS, and EAP-SIM) MAC addresses and basic 802.11 authentication tools Encryption: 40- and 128-bit WEP keys TKIP WEP enhancements (key hashing, message integrity check, and broadcast key rotation)	Cisco Wireless Security Suite	Cisco Wireless Security Suite	Cisco Wireless Security Suite
Operations Band / Wireless Medium	2.4 GHz / DSSS	**802.11a:** 5 GHz / OFDM **802.11b and 802.11g:** 2.4 GHz / DSSS and OFDM	**802.11a:** 5 GHz / OFDM **802.11b and 802.11g:** 2.4 GHz / DSSS and OFDM	5 GHz / OFDM

Cisco Wireless Router and Switch Services

While the preceding devices are the most common that organizations use in constructing and maintaining a WLAN, Cisco offers other devices that can help your organization provide a robust, feature-rich wireless solution.

Cisco 3200 Series Wireless and Mobile Routers

To connect mobile networks to a wireless network, Cisco offers its Cisco 3200 Series wireless and mobile routers, shown in Figure 1-19. Contained in rugged enclosures and offering 802.11g functionality, these small devices (they are about as wide and long as a pen) can fit in vehicles or in outdoor locales. They offer the capability to transfer voice, data, and video across mobile wireless networks.

Figure 1-19 *Cisco 3200 Series Wireless and Mobile Routers*

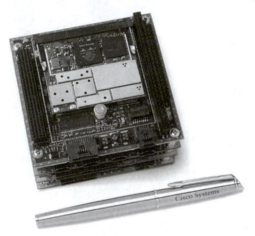

These routers are targeted at public safety, homeland security, defense agencies, and transportation agencies that need a durable router in a compact design that can be installed in vehicles.

Cisco Catalyst 6500 Series Switches

The Cisco Catalyst 6500 Series switches are a popular line of Cisco switches. In addition to serving wired clients, these switches can also be upgraded with a WLAN Services Module (WLSM). The WLSM is a key component of the Cisco SWAN architecture and enables fast, secure WLAN roaming within and across IP subnets. It also enhances WLAN security and smoothes out WLAN deployment and subsequent management.

Cisco Wireless 7920 IP Phone

Convergence is bandied about in the world of technology. Think of convergence as a techie's Swiss Army knife. We have cellular telephones that can play video games and MP3s players that can take pictures. Who knows what else they will be able to do in the coming years. Cisco is no stranger to the world of convergence. In the realm of wireless networks, one of the more compelling and useful devices is the Cisco Wireless 7920 IP phone. This telephone, shown in Figure 1-20, looks like a cellular telephone; however, it connects via the WLAN infrastructure (through an Aironet AP, for instance) then to the organization's gateway to allow VoIP telephone calls.

Figure 1-20   *Cisco Wireless 7920 IP Phone*

The phone uses the 802.11b protocol and Cisco CallManager. The product is ideally suited for environments in which users need telephony, but are constantly on the move and cannot be pinned down to a hardwired telephone. For example, hospitals, warehouses, universities, and retailers are ideally suited for these telephones.

NOTE: The 7920 IP phone works with a VoIP-enabled network with an AP, but it will not work with cellular telephone networks. If you get outside the range of the organization's APs, the phone does not work. Look for this to be enhanced in the future as Cisco works with cellular companies to make a product that works in both environments.

Cisco Compatible Extensions (CCX)

As wireless technology has exploded in popularity, Cisco has seen the necessity for providing a mechanism through which third-party vendors can ensure compatibility among products. As a result, Cisco developed the CCX program.

Through the CCX program, WLAN vendors license—free of charge—WLAN technology from Cisco. After that technology is implemented into the vendor's product, it is tested at an independent, third-party lab. If the product passes the testing procedures, the vendor is allowed to add a Cisco-compatible logo with the product, indicating that it not only works with Cisco equipment, but also takes advantage of advanced features. Intel is an example of this program in action. The company earned Cisco-compatible status with its Centrino mobile technology. This has been integrated in a number of laptop computers, such as Dell, Hewlett Packard, and Toshiba, among others.

The CCX program has been rolled out in three iterations. The requirements of CCX Version 2 build on the requirements of Version 1. For example, Version 1 of CCX security demands:

- WEP
- IEEE 802.11 and 802.1X
- Wi-Fi compliance
- Windows Hardware Quality Labs (WHQL)

Version 2 also requires WPA compliance.

From connection for two wireless clients working in ad hoc mode to a hospital nurse connected via a wireless IP phone; from an enterprise connecting its clients and office buildings in a MAN to police cars equipped with wireless routers, Cisco has a number of devices that enable a plethora of wireless networking functionality.

Version 3 includes EAP-FAST, wireless multi-media, CCKM for EAP-FAST, and single sign on.

Other Resources

For more information on these devices and services, Cisco provides more information at its website:

- **Cisco Aironet 1100 APs**

  http://www.cisco.com/en/US/products/hw/wireless/ps4570/index.html

- **Cisco Aironet 1200 APs**

  http://www.cisco.com/en/US/products/hw/wireless/ps430/index.html

- **Cisco Aironet 1300 APs and bridges**

  http://www.cisco.com/en/US/products/ps5861/index.html

- **Cisco Aironet 1400 bridges**

  http://www.cisco.com/en/US/products/hw/wireless/ps5279/index.html

- **Cisco Aironet client adapters**

  http://www.cisco.com/en/US/products/hw/wireless/ps4555/index.html

- **Cisco Wireless IP Phone 7920**

  http://www.cisco.com/en/US/products/hw/phones/ps379/ps5056 index.html

- **Cisco Compatible Extensions Program**

  http://www.cisco.com/en/US/partners/pr46/pr147 partners_pgm_concept_home.html

- **Cisco 3200 Series wireless router**

  http://www.cisco.com/en/US/products/hw/routers/ps272/index.html

- **WLAN Services Module**

  http://www.cisco.com/en/US/products/hw/switches/ps708/products_data_sheet09186a00802252b7.html

Chapter 2 Contents

Cisco Antennas

Bodybuilders say, "You can't fire a cannon from a canoe." This aphorism is used to illustrate the need to develop all muscle groups, rather than focus just on beach muscles, such as your arms or chest. It's also necessary to focus on stabilizer muscles, such as the core and lower body to fully realize your upper body development.

Don't worry—you haven't wandered off into a bodybuilding handbook. However, this illustrates an important point in the world of wireless networking: It's critical to recognize that Cisco access points (APs) and client adapters cannot do the job all by themselves. They rely on another component to get the job done: antennas.

Models

Cisco offers a number of antennas, and each caters to a different need, a different function, and a different range. The following models are basic types of antennas that you are likely to encounter in your Wi-Fi adventures:

- **Omnidirectional antennas**—The signal radiates out in a circle from the antenna. That is, a client to the left of the antenna can receive the same signal as a client the same distance away on the right.

- **Directional antennas**—The signal is focused into a tighter beam and projected a greater distance than the omnidirectional antenna. Although range is increased, the antenna serves only clients in a given direction. Examples of directional antennas include the Yagi antenna, patch antenna, and parabolic dish.

- **Diversity antennas**—Two antennas reduce multipath distortion. The radio receives a signal on both antennas; however, it transmits on the one with the best signal reception.

NOTE: Multipath distortion is covered in greater depth later in this chapter.

Antenna Tech Primer

Before looking at the models of antennas Cisco offers, it is helpful to understand what the statistics next to each device mean.

Beam Width

This describes how the signal radiates from an antenna and is expressed in degrees horizontally and vertically. For example, an omnidirectional antenna radiates its signal 360 degrees horizontally. It depends on the model; it might have as much coverage area as 75 degrees vertically. As such, it doesn't radiate its signal in a complete sphere around the antenna. Rather, it's more of a donut shape. This is illustrated in Figure 2-1.

Figure 2-1   *An Antenna's Beam Width Measures the Horizontal and Vertical Angles at Which a Signal Emanates from the Antenna*

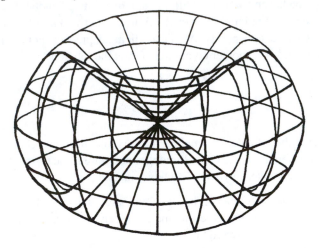

Gain

Gain is a measurement of increase in power, measured in decibels (dB). The decibel scale is logarithmic, and it is used to demonstrate the ratio of one power value to another.

The decibel communicates the amount of signal loss or gain within a system. The decibel is somewhat confusing because it is not a concrete measurement, such as meters, kilometers, or kilograms. The decibel is not a measure of signal strength; rather, it's a ratio between two power levels.

When power is lost or gained in a system, it does not occur in regular, fixed amounts. Instead, power is lost by varying increments, such as one half, one quarter, and so on. To determine how much loss has occurred, you cannot just add $\int$ and π. These amounts must be multiplied. Decibels make this process simpler to understand. Loss and gain are easier to calculate in a system in which you simply add the decibels. Following is the equation for how decibels are calculated:

$dB = 10 \log (P_0/P_1)$

Where P_0 is the antenna used for comparison and P_1 is the antenna that's evaluated.

For example, if your signal gains 3dB, then it has doubled in power. If it gains 6dB, then the power has quadrupled. If it has lost 3dB, then the power is cut in half.

Although the decibel is not a measure of signal strength, the *decibel milliwatt* (dBm) is. It's easy to confuse dB and dBm. A *dBm* is the signal power in relation to 1 milliwatt. For example, a signal power of 0dBm is 1 milliwatt. Because of logarithms, a signal power of 3dBm is 2 milliwatts.

Because the decibel is a ratio of two signal powers, you need a reference point to talk about antenna gain. When you look at antenna statistics, note the *dBi* abbreviation. In this case, an antenna rating is to the gain of an *isotropic* antenna. An isotropic antenna does not really exist. It's a theoretical antenna that radiates its signal in a perfect sphere around itself.

dBi is a comparison of the antenna against this theoretical antenna. The isotropic antenna has a power rating of 0dB (that is, there is no gain and no loss when the antenna is compared against itself).

Standard dipole antennas (which are common on Cisco gear) are typically omnidirectional. Because the omnidirectional antenna "concentrates" its signal in the donut shape around itself, it has an increase in gain over the isotropic antenna. As such, an antenna such as the AIR-ANT4941 has a 2dBi gain in comparison to our theoretical antenna.

NOTE: If you see the notation dBd, the antenna is compared to a dipole antenna. For example, our AIR-ANT4941 antenna would have a 0dBd gain.

To determine the dBi rating of an antenna with a dBd rating, simply add 2.14. For instance, in the case of a 3dBd omnidirectional antenna, such as the AIR-ANT-2506, you simply add 2.14 to arrive at the correct dBi rating of 5.14. This is sometimes rounded up to 5.2dBi.

NOTE: A dipole antenna is an antenna that contains two different elements. An example of a dipole antenna is the rabbit ear antenna on a television set, although a dipole does not necessarily have to be in a v shape.

Cisco 2.4-GHz Antennas

Although APs typically come with their own antennas, you can easily upgrade, depending on your particular organization and its needs. To serve 802.11b and 802.11g devices, Cisco offers a number of different antennas. Table 2-1 compares these antennas, stacking their type, beam width, gain, and ranges up against each other.

Table 2-1   *Cisco 2.4-GHz Antennas*

Part Number	Type	Description	Beam Width	Gain	Range
AIR-ANT5959	Diversity Omnidirectional	Ceiling-mounted, indoor, diversity antenna. Low profile design makes it inconspicuous.	360 degrees horizontal 80 degrees vertical	2dBi	350 ft. at 1 Mbps 295 ft. at 6 Mbps 130 ft. at 11 Mbps 88 ft. at 54 Mbps
AIR-ANT4941	Omnidirectional	Single dipole antenna providing indoor, omnidirectional coverage.	360 degrees horizontal 65 degrees vertical	2.2dBi	350 ft. at 1 Mbps 300 ft. at 6 Mbps 130 ft. at 11 Mbps 90 ft. at 54 Mbps
AIR-ANT1728	Omnidirectional	Ceiling-mounted, indoor antenna. Unobtrusive, medium-range.	360 degrees horizontal 38 degrees vertical	5.2dBi	497 ft. at 1 Mbps 142 ft. at 11 Mbps
AIR-ANT3213	Diversity Omnidirectional	Pillar-mounted (mounting equipment includes two, six-inch poles that keep the antenna away from the mounting surface), diversity, indoor, medium-range.	360 degrees horizontal 30 degrees vertical	5.2dBi	497 ft. at 1 Mbps 379 ft. at 6 Mbps 142 ft. at 11 Mbps 114 ft. at 54 Mbps

Table 2-1   *Cisco 2.4-GHz Antennas (Continued)*

Part Number	Type	Description	Beam Width	Gain	Range
AIR-ANT1729	Patch	Wall-mounted, indoor and outdoor directional patch antenna. Can also be used as a medium-range bridge antenna.	75 degrees horizontal 65 degrees vertical	6dBi	Connected to an AP at 1 Mbps: 542 ft. Connected to an AP at 6 Mbps: 403 ft. Connected to an AP at 11 Mbps: 155 ft. Connected to an AP at 54 Mbps: 121 ft. Connected to a bridge at 11 Mbps: 1900 ft.
AIR-ANT2012	Diversity Patch	Wall-mounted, indoor or outdoor diversity antenna.	80 degrees horizontal 55 degrees vertical	6dBi	547 ft. at 1 Mbps 167 ft. at 11 Mbps
AIR-ANT3549	Patch	Wall-mounted, indoor antenna. Small, unobtrusive design. Can also be used as a medium-range bridge antenna.	60 degrees horizontal 60 degrees vertical	9dBi	Connected to an AP at 1 Mbps: 1700 ft. Connected to an AP at 6 Mbps: 507 ft. Connected to an AP at 11 Mbps: 200 ft. Connected to an AP at 54 Mbps: 153 ft. Connected to a bridge at 11 Mbps: 3390 ft.
AIR-ANT2410Y-R	Yagi	Outdoor directional antenna. Designed as a bridge or for point-to-point communications.	47 degrees horizontal 55 degrees vertical	10dBi	800 ft. at 1 Mbps 548 ft. at 6 Mbps 230 ft. at 11 Mbps 165 ft. at 54 Mbps

Cisco 5-GHz Bridge Antennas

The 5-GHz, 802.11a devices operate at a higher frequency than 802.11b and 802.11g devices. As with the 2.4-GHz devices, Cisco offers a broad range of antennas for unique needs. Table 2-2 compares these models.

Table 2-2 *Cisco 5-GHz Bridge Antennas*

Part Number	Type	Description	Beam Width	Gain	Range
AIR-ANT58G9VOA-N	Omni-directional	Used with the Cisco 1400 Wireless Bridge. Nondiversity antenna for outdoor applications.	360 degrees horizontal 6 degrees vertical	9dBi	8 miles at 9 Mbps 2 miles at 54 Mbps
AIR-ANT58G10SSA-N	Sector	Used with the Cisco 1400 Wireless Bridge. Nondiversity antenna for outdoor applications.	60 degrees horizontal 60 degrees vertical	9.5dBi	8 miles at 9 Mbps 2 miles at 54 Mbps
AIR-ANT58G28SDA-N	Dish	Used with the Cisco 1400 Wireless Bridge. Nondiversity antenna for outdoor applications. Designed for use at the client sites of a point-to-point or point-to-multipoint deployment.	5.7 degrees horizontal 6 degrees vertical	28dBi	23 miles at 9 Mbps 12 miles at 54 Mbps

Cisco 2.4-GHz Bridge Antennas

The bridges that work in the 2.4-GHz bands (like the Cisco 1300) have their own line of antennas. Table 2-3 compares these antennas.

Table 2-3 *Cisco 2.4-GHz Bridge Antennas*

Part Number	Type	Description	Beam Width	Gain	Range
AIR-ANT2506	Omni-directional mast mount	Outdoor, short-range, point-to-multipoint connections.	360 degrees horizontal 38 degrees vertical	5.2dBi	3.3 miles at 2 Mbps 1.66 miles ft. at 11 Mbps .21 miles at 54 Mbps

Table 2-3   *Cisco 2.4-GHz Bridge Antennas (Continued)*

Part Number	Type	Description	Beam Width	Gain	Range
AIR-ANT24120	High-gain omnidirectional mast mount	Outdoor, medium-range, point-to-multipoint connections.	360 degrees horizontal 7 degrees vertical	12dBi	15.83 miles at 2 Mbps 7.92 miles at 11 Mbps 1 mile at 54 Mbps
AIR-ANT2414S-R	Vertically polarized sector	Outdoor, long-range, point-to-multipoint connections.	90 degrees horizontal 8.5 degrees vertical	14dBi	16.71 miles at 2 Mbps 8.89 miles at 11 Mbps 1.26 miles at 54 Mbps
AIR-ANT1949	Yagi mast mount	Outdoor, medium-range, directional connections.	30 degrees horizontal 25 degrees vertical	13.5dBi	18.33 miles at 2 Mbps 11.19 miles at 11 Mbps 1.41 miles at 54 Mbps
AIR-ANT3338	Solid dish	Outdoor, long-range, directional connections.	12.4 degrees horizontal 12.4 degrees vertical	21dBi	26.49 miles at 2 Mbps 20.1 miles at 11 Mbps 4.46 miles at 54 Mbps

Diversity

There are many issues involved to get the best signal range and quality in a WLAN deployment. One concern comes from *multipath distortion*. Consider the wireless connection shown in Figure 2-2.

Figure 2-2 *Multipath Distortion Occurs When Obstacles and Other Environmental Obstructions Cause Radio Frequency Signals to Arrive Out of Synch*

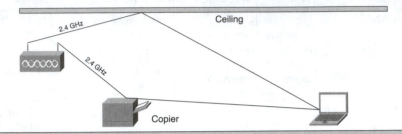

When a radio frequency broadcast is transmitted from the antenna, part of the signal can travel directly to its destination, although other parts bounce off of obstructions.

As 802.11 signals are broadcast, the signal bounces around the room, creating multiple copies of the signal. Because the signals that bounce around travel a longer path than a signal that is received directly from the antenna, the multiple signals are no longer in phase with each other. Instead, they are in a random phase. Multiple signals that are in-phase are ideal; they create better reception. However, out-of-phase signals can cancel each other out or cause packet retries to occur.

Multipath distortion occurs most often in places with highly RF-reflective surfaces, such as metal, coated glass, or furniture. Unfortunately, places where multipath distortion is prevalent are also those places where wireless networking is so useful, such as:

- Manufacturing centers
- Distribution centers
- Office environments
- Homes
- Places where the signal is exposed to metallic surfaces

The solution to the problem of multipath distortion is *diversity*.

Configuring Multiple Antennas for Diversity

To mitigate multipath distortion, two antennas are used in tandem. Diversity uses these antennas, placed a short distance apart, for each radio. Figure 2-3 shows this.

Figure 2-3 *Diversity Antennas Use Two Antennas Located a Short Distance Apart*

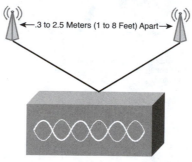

The idea behind this solution is that with two antennas deployed, the odds of the radio that receives an acceptable signal from one of the two antennas is increased. Multipath distortion is localized to a specific location (either antenna A or antenna B). Because of this, if the distortion vexes antenna A, then antenna B does not suffer the same distortion problems. The radio simply switches to whichever antenna receives the strongest signal. Either antenna can be repositioned to a better location to ensure good reception and reduced multipath distortion.

To get a better understanding of how diversity works, it's important to realize that the receiver does not simultaneously listen to both antennas. Instead, it listens to only one antenna at a time. When it encounters multipath distortion, it checks the other antenna to see if it gets a better reception. If so, it switches to that antenna.

NOTE: As you might surmise, if the receiver listened to both antennas, then a multipath environment would occur because the device would receive the radio signals at slightly different times.

Optimal Antenna Placement for Diversity

Because each antenna is used independently from the other, to select and locate antennas for decreasing multipath distortion, you must follow two important guidelines:

- The antennas must have the same radiation characteristics (beam width, gain, and so on). This is shown in Figure 2-4.
- The antennas must be located to cover the same cell area. This is shown in Figure 2-5.

Figure 2-4 *Diversity Antennas Must Have the Same Radiation Characteristics*

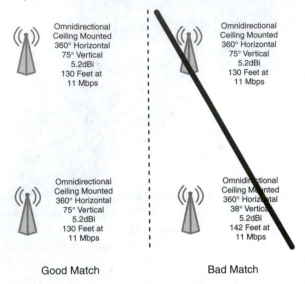

Omnidirectional
Ceiling Mounted
360° Horizontal
75° Vertical
5.2dBi
130 Feet at
11 Mbps

Omnidirectional
Ceiling Mounted
360° Horizontal
75° Vertical
5.2dBi
130 Feet at
11 Mbps

Omnidirectional
Ceiling Mounted
360° Horizontal
75° Vertical
5.2dBi
130 Feet at
11 Mbps

Omnidirectional
Ceiling Mounted
360° Horizontal
38° Vertical
5.2dBi
142 Feet at
11 Mbps

Good Match   Bad Match

Figure 2-5 *Diversity Antennas Must Be Located to Cover the Same Physical Area*

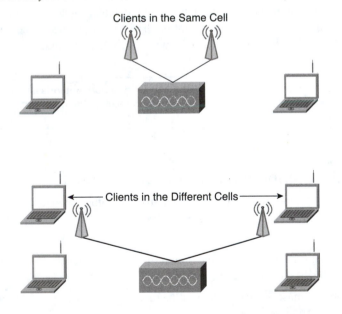

Clients in the Same Cell

Clients in the Different Cells

Because it is necessary for the antennas to be physically separated from each other, it's easy to assume that they should be located on opposite ends of the building. Not so. In fact, most often the antennas should be located between .3 and 2.5 meters (1 to 8 feet) apart. On the other hand, antennas placed closer than .15 meters (6 inches) do not experience the diversity needed to quash multipath distortion.

The farther apart you locate the antennas, the more disparate the areas the antennas cover. If they are too far apart, the antennas cover different clients. Whenever the AP decides to switch to the other antenna, the group of clients covered is cut off, and vice versa. Diversity relies on the antennas to cover the same radio cell.

Upgrading Antennas

There will likely come a time when you need an additional antenna for your WLAN. Perhaps you want to extend the range of your network, or maybe you want to move to a diversity antenna arrangement. As a result, there are several considerations to bear in mind when you select a new antenna.

Adding a New Antenna

Before you decide on a new antenna, you should consider what needs you have that your current antenna or antennas do not serve.

For example, at a manufacturing center that uses an omnidirectional antenna to service its wireless clients, employees notice that the range of handheld computers falls off after 100 feet. Rather than add additional APs (also a viable solution), the center's networking staff has decided to upgrade to a different antenna. They decide to replace the stock antenna with a wall-mounted, diversity patch AIR-ANT2012 antenna, which provides an additional 60 feet of range.

The center might also consider where they need wireless capabilities. Consider the diagram of our center in Figure 2-6. Although the antenna is located in the center of the facility, the fact of the matter is that no one in the office needs wireless capabilities—they're all on a wired LAN. As such, a diversity patch antenna (shown in the center of the figure) is a good solution that provides more coverage on the manufacturing floor.

Figure 2-6 *Consider Where Your Organization Needs Wi-Fi Coverage*

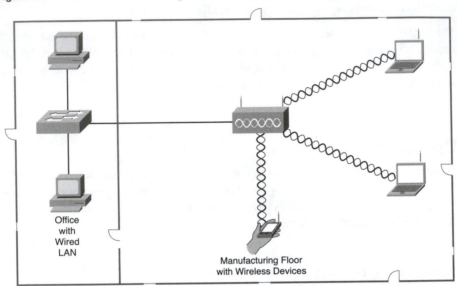

In addition, the manufacturing center might run into trouble with a single antenna and multipath distortion. Because of the exposed I-Beams, metallic surfaces, and other obstacles, to employ a diversity antenna system resolves these issues.

Placement Considerations with a New Type of Antenna

There are two issues involved with antenna placement that you should manage and balance:

- Range
- Interference

Range

Range is impacted largely by the type of antenna you use. For instance, if you've purchased an AP that comes with an omnidirectional antenna, you might want to install a patch antenna. Omnidirectional antennas provide a signal in a circle around the AP. However, if the AP is located near a wall, the patch antenna can focus the signal into a beam that radiates in a given direction, and for a greater range.

In addition, range can be enhanced if you ensure there are few obstacles between your clients and your antennas. This naturally leads to a discussion on interference.

Interference

When you deal with interference, it is best handled if you start with a site survey. The mechanics of site surveys are covered in Chapter 5, "Installing and Configuring Access Points," but, in essence, a site survey involves checking your environment for sources of interference and the best placement of Wi-Fi equipment.

If you connect outdoors, don't forget to factor in weather conditions and trees. A wireless bridge that works well on a clear, beautiful day might encounter retries and other performance issues when it rains, snows, or is foggy. As such, a higher gain antenna might be needed.

You might experience more interference when you use the 802.11b and 802.11g protocols. This is because many consumer appliances use this band (such as cordless telephones). If you opt to use 802.11a equipment, you might encounter less interference because it uses the 5.4-GHz band.

NOTE: The omnipresent microwave oven can also be a source of interference. Even though it's encased in metal boxes, it still radiates some microwaves, especially older microwaves with door that were slammed shut too many times. Some companies even use specialized microwave ovens to dry paint. These are more powerful than standard microwave ovens and can cause interference.

Try to keep your antennas as far away from microwave ovens as possible. This is an issue not only for SoHo networking, but also for organizations that place antennas near the employee break room.

In a corporate setting, you should keep your antennas away from the following sources of interference:

- Microwave lighting
- Microwave paint dryers
- Magnetic resonance imaging (MRI) devices
- Radar (in military installations)
- I-beams

If there are too many sources of interference, your best bet can be to place an additional AP, so that mobile clients are closer to an AP and better able to access the WLAN. Ceiling placement is usually a good bet because it is elevated above the clients and has a clearer line of transmission than an AP on a bookshelf.

Alignment

Placing an omnidirectional antenna is reasonably straightforward: Simply position it in the middle of the area you wish to serve.

NOTE: Naturally, "the middle of the area" depends on more than the physical middle of the room. Other considerations can include obstacles, such as walls and RF sources.

When you align two directional antennas to communicate (most commonly in a bridging environment) you must take into consideration the radiation angle for each antenna. For example, Yagi antennas have 25- to 30-degree radiation patterns, whereas parabolic dish antennas are much tighter—and with a greater range—at 12.5 degrees.

Antenna radiation patterns must match as closely as possible. If just the edges of their radiation patterns connect, communication can be spotty. Problems include lost packets, high retry counts, and low signal strength.

Use a bridge link test to align your bridge antennas. The link test is covered in more detail in Chapter 5.

The Best Antenna for the Best Scenario

Looking at a laundry list of antennas and their capabilities might overwhelm you. Now that the raw data has been presented, we show you a few examples of how these antennas can be used.

Warehouses

Because warehouses and manufacturing facilities are large installations, an omnidirectional antenna, mounted at 25 feet up, provides good coverage. You want to place the antenna high enough so that it clears racks of equipment. However, you don't want to place it so high that you lose range. Remember that although omnidirectional antennas radiate in a 360-degree horizontal plane, they don't often exceed 75 degrees vertically.

Optimally, you can locate the antenna in the center of the facility. However, in cases where an antenna must be placed against a wall, a directional antenna is best.

Offices

It should come as no surprise that different sized offices will require different antennas:

- Small offices are well suited with an omnidirectional antenna. However, if the antenna is located in the back of the office, a directional antenna can improve performance. The antenna should be wall mounted, above as many obstructions as possible.

- Large offices are best served with omnidirectional antennas, mounted just under the ceiling girders or the drop ceiling. Ideally, the antenna is placed in the center of the coverage cell and in as open an area as possible. Again, if it must be placed against a wall, a directional antenna is ideal.

Bridging

Antennas for wireless bridging vary, and they depend on the type of bridging you employ:

- Point-to-point deployments must take into consideration distance, obstructions, and the antenna's location. If connecting indoors, a dipole or mast mount omnidirectional antenna can be used. When used outdoors, a directional high-gain antenna should be used. Locate these antennas as high as possible and avoid obstacles.

NOTE: You can even increase outdoor ranges if you use a parabolic dish antenna—25 miles with 2.4-GHz systems and 12 miles with 5-GHz systems.

- Point-to-multipoint bridges generally use two different types of antennas. At the main communications point, an omnidirectional antenna should be used. Remote sites use directional antennas that are aimed at the main site's antenna. This is shown in Figure 2-7.

Figure 2-7 *The Main Communications Point in a Point-to-Multipoint Solution Should Employ an Omnidirectional Antenna, Whereas Remote Sites Should Use Directional Antennas*

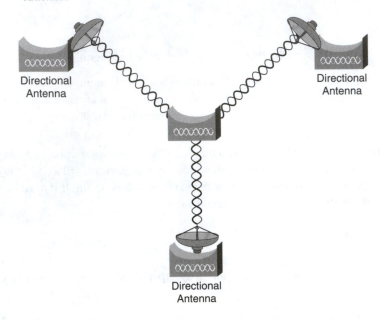

Directional
Antenna

Directional
Antenna

Directional
Antenna

Rules, Regulations, and Legalities of Antenna Usage and Placement

The Federal Communications Commission (FCC) has been generous with its governance over the world of Wi-Fi communications. Because Wi-Fi operates in the unlicensed area of the broadcast spectrum, anyone can set up a wireless network. However, you should know some important regulations that concern your wireless network.

The Right Antenna for the Right Device

On July 12, 2004, the FCC issued rule 04-165, which has important implications for devices that operate in the 2.4-GHz and 5-GHz bands. As you recall, those are the bands in which 802.11a, 802.11b, and 802.11g reside.

The important part of this rule talks about "Replacement Antennas for Unlicensed Devices." Until this point, the FCC required any antenna used with a wireless device to be tested and certified as part of a system. That is, you could not mix and match equipment and antennas.

NOTE: Further, the FCC required unique connectors for each manufacturer and also required the development of new connectors as existing ones became prevalent.

Although you can go to a vendor and purchase antennas to connect with your wireless devices, there's a lawyer ball going on here. It's akin to buying a switchblade kit. The kit can be sold (and it's perfectly legal); however, assembling the kit is illegal.

The new FCC rule does not wave a magic hand across all antennas, providing broad and unrestricted legality. There are still some provisos.

When you use a replacement antenna (and the antenna is different than what was originally provided by the manufacturer) then such an antenna can be used, provided it is of the same family of antennas. That is, if it is a patch, omni, Yagi, and so on. Also, an antenna's gain must be equal to or less than the gain for which the manufacturer has attained approval. For example, if Cisco has certified a 13.5-dBi Yagi, a 13.5-dBi Yagi or lower gain antenna from another antenna vendor can be used.

Power Regulation

The FCC has not given *carte blanche* to wireless networks simply because they operate in the unlicensed bands of the spectrum. It still regulates how much power an antenna can output and gain.

In the 5.725-GHz to 5.825-GHz band (also known as the Unlicensed National Information Infrastructure 3 [UNII3] band), antennas are limited to a power of 1 watt or 30dBm. Antenna gain for omnidirectional antennas is limited to 6dBi. Antennas with a gain higher than 23dBi must have power reduced 1 dB for every 1dB above 23dBi. The Cisco 1400 Bridge operates in the UNII3 band.

Antennas transmitting in the 2.4-GHz band are also limited to 1 watt with a maximum antenna gain of 6dBi. That said, there are also maximum values that depend on the type of system employed—namely, point-to-point versus point-to-multipoint deployments:

- In point-to-point systems that use a directional antenna, for every decibel the transmitter is below 30dBm, the antenna can increase by 3dBi. For example, a 29dB transmitter can have a 9-dBi antenna; a 28-dB transmitter can have a 12-dBi antenna.

- In point-to-multipoint systems, the FCC has limited the maximum effective isotropic radiated power (EIRP) to 36dBm. For every dB that the transmitter is reduced, the antenna increases by 1dB.

Amplification

Simply put, unless an amplifier came as part of your wireless system, the FCC does not want you to use one. You are allowed to use only an amplifier that comes certified with your wireless system. Unless an amplifier was submitted for testing along with the radio and antenna, it cannot be sold in the United States and it cannot be sold separately.

NOTE: Bear in mind, if a system incorporates an amplifier, it must still adhere to the aforementioned regulations about power output and gain.

Other Resources

- **Complete text of FCC rules about certified antennas and equipment:**

  http://gullfoss2.fcc.gov/prod/ecfs/
  retrieve.cgi?native_or_pdf=pdf&id_document=6516285598

- **Radiolabs.com article on antennas and different types:**

  http://www.radiolabs.com/Articles/wifi-antenna.html

- **The Cisco website contains detailed information about its complete line of antennas:**

  — **2.4-GHz antennas**:

    http://www.cisco.com/en/US/products/hw/wireless/ps469/products_data_
    sheet09186a008022b11b.html

  — **5-GHz antennas**:

    http://www.cisco.com/en/US/products/hw/wireless/ps469/products_data_
    sheet09186a008022fb7f.html

Chapter 3 Contents

Cisco Wireless Technologies

In the past, the functional extent of wireless networking was simply a means to remove clients from network cabling. This allowed users to roam freely and provided network access from remote locations.

Wireless networking has evolved. The enormous popularity and utility of wireless networks has increased the importance and difficulty of managing them. To help manage wireless networks, Cisco has developed two useful technologies:

- Cisco Structured Wireless Aware Network (SWAN)
- Cisco Mobile Wireless Center (MWC)

This chapter examines these two technologies and explains how you can use them in your own organization.

Finally, as a network professional, you might consider a wireless networking certification to prove your skill with Cisco wireless technologies. The last part of this chapter examines current wireless certifications and what those certifications encompass.

Cisco SWAN

With so many organizations wanting to adopt wireless networking technology, Cisco realized it was difficult—if not impossible—for many organizations to quickly and effectively deploy their own wireless solutions. When users decide they need wireless capabilities, problems often occur. For example, users take it upon themselves to install wireless components. This initiative poses performance and security issues for the network. To help address this problem, Cisco developed its SWAN solution.

For any size network, SWAN makes it possible to quickly add wireless infrastructure and then configure the WLAN in a manner consistent with the rest of the network.

SWAN Highlights

SWAN is not an off-the-shelf product; rather, SWAN is an architecture built from many Cisco components. To build your own SWAN, you need the following components, as illustrated in Figure 3-1:

- Wireless network adapters
- Aironet access points (AP)
- Airespace APs
- Switches (such as the Catalyst 6500 with the WLAN Services Module [WLSM])
- Routers

NOTE: Switches and routers are not required equipment for a SWAN infrastructure, but compatible devices can be included in your SWAN solution.

- AAA server (such as the Cisco Access Control Server [ACS]) for authentication

Figure 3-1 *Cisco SWAN Components*

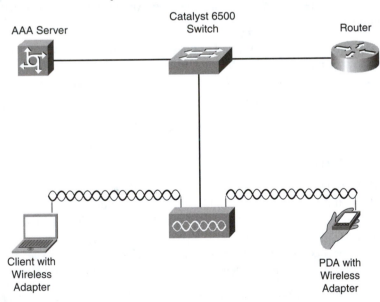

You must also include the CiscoWorks LAN Management Solution software and the Wireless Solutions Engine (WLSE) appliance for management.

NOTE: WLSE is covered in more depth in Chapter 10, "CiscoWorks Wireless LAN Solution Engine (WLSE)."

Alhough this sounds like a lot of equipment, chances are you already have most of it because of your support for wired LANs. Additionally, routers and switches are not mandatory for a SWAN solution.

Overall, SWAN focuses on two main areas:

- **Secure mobility** —Encompasses fast, secure, seamless roaming (at Layers 2 and 3)
- **Radio frequency (RF) management**—Involved with such issues as rogue AP detection, site surveys, RF monitoring, and performance

Roaming

SWAN introduces the Cisco Wireless Domain Services (WDS) technology. In essence, WDS is a set of Cisco IOS Software features that run on one of the WLAN's APs. The device, in addition to its own AP duties, also acts as a controller for other APs on the same subnet. To speed up Layer 2 roaming (roaming in the same subnet) and Layer 3 roaming (roaming between subnets), all APs register with the WDS AP using 802.1X. As clients power up, they are initially authenticated with the AAA server. This information is sent through the WDS, which transfers it to the AP.

NOTE: Layer 3 roaming is supported if WDS runs on a router or a WLSM module in a Catalyst 6500 series switch.

As the client roams from cell to cell, WDS sends the client key to the new AP. As such, the client does not need to re-authenticate with the AAA server, which makes roaming much more efficient and speedy. Figure 3-2 illustrates the roaming process as facilitated by WDS.

Figure 3-2 *WDS Transmits a Client's Key to APs the Client Has Roamed into, Making Roaming Faster*

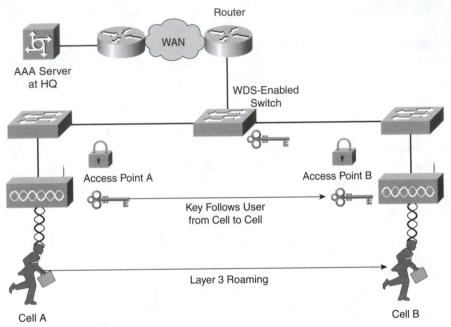

Further, the WDS acts as a backup local authenticator for remote offices if the WAN connected to an AAA server in a head office fails.

NOTE: When an AP is used as an authenticator, the WDS can handle only 50 accounts, and it is not synchronized to the central Remote Authentication Dial-In User Service (RADIUS) server. For that functionality, you need to use WLSE, which is used for the management of hundreds of APs. More accounts can be handled if an external RADIUS server is used.

RF Management

SWAN adds the following ease-of-use features that make WLAN management much simpler and smoother for both setup and ongoing use:

- **Rogue AP detection**—APs with WDS can aggregate RF statistics from other APs, and then pass along the data to the WLSE. This shows rogue APs on the WLAN. After it is identified, a rogue AP can be isolated from the rest of the network.

- **Site surveys**—To effectively deploy any WLAN, a site survey is necessary. (Site surveys are covered in more detail in Chapter 5, "Installing and Configuring Access Points.") Most often, a consultant or IT staff member who is knowledgeable about site surveys conducts them. Unfortunately, this can be costly and time-intensive.

  With SWAN, however, site surveys can be assisted without required extensive RF knowledge. Site surveys are assisted using site survey tools that are integrated into the WLSE. Although SWAN can help conduct a survey, it is not a replacement for conventional site surveys.

  The stream of RF statistics (used for rogue AP detection) can also help the WLSE create a map of wireless coverage and use existing APs to conduct site surveys. You can identify areas in your WLAN where there is no coverage. To do this, import floor plans into the software, and then you can see where extra APs are needed. If performance falls under a specified threshold, a site survey can be automatically initiated, which can sometimes help track down the problem.

- **Interference detection**—SWAN's site surveys are equally important to its capability to detect RF interference. Interference that affects network performance can come from a number of sources, which include rogue APs and even microwave ovens. When interference is detected, SWAN can be used to locate the source. This WLAN controller can also readjust channels to avoid interference.

- **Self-healing features**—Because SWAN can manage thousands of APs, if an AP fails, the network can detect the outage and compensate with other APs. Adjustments can automatically be made to the power and cell coverage of neighboring APs.

Cisco Mobile Wireless Center

The Cisco MWC is an automated operational support system (OSS) for mobile wireless domain management, and it is targeted at mobile operators and service providers. Specifically, MWC provides management capabilities to Cisco Mobile Exchange, a framework that links radio access networks (RAN) to IP networks.

The Mobile Exchange framework can be managed as if it were a single device, saving time and money when deploying new services, by reducing errors, and when implementing user training.

MWC performs device configuration, provisioning, fault mediation, and performance mediation for the following services:

- **Mobile services**—Mobile services are means to provide content to users on the go. In addition, the services are used for organizations to track usage data:

— **Service Selection Gateways (SSG)**—SSGs allow service providers to offer differentiated services, such as video conferencing, streaming video, and gaming.

— **Content Services Gateways (CSG)**—The CSG examines HTTP requests, gathering URL data and other header information for accounting purposes.

- **Packet services**—Packet services provide a bridge between wired networks and wireless devices:

  — **Packet Data Service Nodes (PDSN) and Home Agent (HA)**—The PDSN is the gateway between the RAN and the packet data network.

  — **Gateway GPRS Support Nodes (GGSN)**—GGSNs provide access from a wireless device to the Internet or a customer's LAN using a virtual private network (VPN).

There are three components at work in an MWC:

- Provisioning Manager
- Fault Mediator
- Performance Mediator

Figure 3-3 shows how these components fit into the larger MWC picture.

Figure 3-3 *Provisioning Manager, Fault Mediator, and Performance Mediator Are at the Heart of the Cisco Mobile Wireless Center*

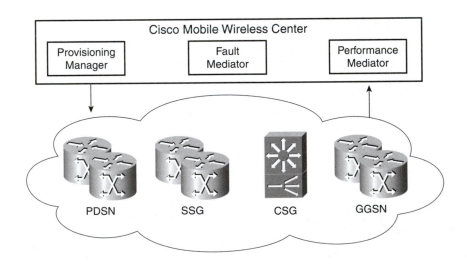

The sections that follow cover the three MWC components in greater detail.

Provisioning Manager

The Provisioning Manager performs all network configurations and user-level security. This is the component that configures devices on an exchange network.

The Provisioning Manager keeps a list of configured devices and provides a simplified way to update configuration information to those devices.

Devices are managed via a web-based user interface, which allows the user to manage devices through the Internet.

Troubleshooting is aided by an activity log, which tracks all user activity. In addition, the Provisioning Manager uses a template-based tool to make setup and provisioning simple. For example, this template-based tool might be used by a wireless service provider that needs to perform load balancing with its servers or configure its servers based on their geographic locations.

Fault Mediator

The Cisco MWC Fault Mediator keeps an eye on the network, and it looks for changes. This is the component used to alert you when network behavior deviates from specified metrics.

If a fault is detected, it can be forwarded to management applications, such as Cisco Information Center. Fault Mediator provides broad thresholding capabilities in addition to those that Cisco IOS Software provide.

Part of the Fault Mediator is a discovery engine that locates all Cisco Mobile Exchange nodes, Catalyst switches, and service components attached to the IP network. This discovery engine monitors the presence of these devices and the connectivity among them. This information is useful when new devices are added or the network topology changes.

Performance Mediator

Performance Mediator supplies performance management functionality that is used to compile information about a network's performance.

Performance Mediator provides a single AP to the managed devices for performance data. The use of a centralized approach eliminates the need for additional types of data retrieval.

As Performance Mediator collects network performance and usage data, it combines and forwards this information to the network management applications. The data collection mechanisms are dynamic and can be modified as the network administrator sees fit.

Configuration is accomplished via either a web browser interface or through a data bus. Data can be delivered via File Transfer Protocol (FTP). Using the Cisco CNS Integration Bus, performance data can be converted into extensible markup language (XML) files for easy integration with the service provider OSSs and other third-party applications.

Cisco Wireless Certifications

A number of certification programs can prove your knowledge in various Cisco technologies. WLANs are no different. Cisco offers three certification tracks for WLANs:

- WLAN Design Specialist
- WLAN Sales Specialist
- WLAN Support Specialist

WLAN-certified specialists must understand 802.11 radio technologies and be able to configure WLAN products, specifically the Cisco Aironet line of APs, bridges, and client adapters.

NOTE: Cisco acquired Airespace in 2005. Look for Airespace content to be added to its wireless certification programs.

NOTE: Training courses are available through Cisco learning partners. For more information on training courses or training in your area, go to: http://www.cisco.com/go/learningpartners.

WLAN Design Specialist

The Cisco WLAN Design Specialist certification is targeted at individuals who want to demonstrate their knowledge and skill at designing WLANs. The prerequisite for this exam is to have completed Cisco Certified Design Associate (CCDA) certification. Passing the WLAN for System Engineers (WLANSE 642-577) exam is required for this certification.

The recommended classroom training for this exam includes either one of the following:

- Aironet WLAN Fundamentals and Cisco Aironet Wireless Site Survey (4 days, classroom)
- Aironet WLAN Fundamentals v4.0 (3 days, classroom) and Cisco Aironet Wireless Site Survey v4.0 (1 day, classroom)

The WLAN for System Engineers (WLANSE 642-577) exam covers the following topics:

- Radio technology (including specifics for 802.11's different standards, as well as regulatory issues)
- Antenna concepts (including decibel calculations, multipath distortion, and antenna types)
- WLAN topologies (including components of a WLAN and nonoverlapping channels)
- Wireless bridges (including deployment and configuration)
- Wireless APs (including configuration and filtering)
- Aironet Client Utility and drivers
- Security
- WLAN management
- Metropolitan mobile wireless solutions

WLAN Sales Specialist

The WLAN Sales Specialist certification is meant for Cisco channel partners and resellers. This certification allows a specialist to show knowledge of Cisco WLAN concepts, systems, and applications, especially as they relate to sales. A prerequisite certification as a Cisco Sales Expert as well as successfully passing the WLAN for Account Managers (WLANAM 646-102) exam are required for this certification.

The recommended classroom training for this exam includes both of the following:

- Account Manager Learning Environment (AMLE)—WLAN 3.0
- Cisco Products Solutions Essentials (CPSE) 8.0 for AMs—Wireless for AMs

The WLAN for Account Managers (WLANAM 646-102) exam focuses on explaining Cisco WLAN offerings, with an emphasis on how they can help various organizations. The test evaluates an applicant's knowledge of the following topics:

- WLANs
- Building-to-building wireless products

- WLAN security
- WLANs functionality in vertical markets (education, retail, healthcare, and hospitality)
- WLAN functionality in horizontal markets (enterprise and financial industries)
- WLAN uses
- WLAN security features

WLAN Support Specialist

After a WLAN has been designed and deployed, specialists are needed to maintain and support the network. The WLAN Support Specialist certification is used to prove a specialist's skill in support and maintenance. CCNA certification is a prerequisite for this exam.

Passing the WLAN for Field Engineers (WLANFE 642-582) exam is required for this certification.

The recommended classroom training for this exam includes either one of the following:

- Aironet WLAN Fundamentals and Cisco Aironet Wireless Site Survey (4 days, classroom)
- Aironet WLAN Fundamentals v4.0 (3 days, classroom) and Cisco Aironet Wireless Site Survey v4.0 (1 day, classroom)

The WLAN for Field Engineers (WLANFE 642-582) exam covers the following topics:

- Radio technology (including specifics for 802.11's different standards, as well as regulatory issues)
- Antenna concepts (including decibel calculations, multipath distortion, and antenna types)
- WLAN topologies (including components of a WLAN and nonoverlapping channels)
- Wireless bridges (including deployment and configuration)
- Wireless APs (including configuration and filtering)
- Aironet Client Utility and drivers
- Security
- WLAN management
- Site survey (including the components used in a site survey, antenna and AP mounting issues, and using the WLSE Assisted Site Survey Tool)

Wireless networking technology is constantly evolving. As wireless networks add more functionality, it will be important to understand and effectively deploy and maintain these systems.

Other Resources

- **Cisco SWAN site**

  http://www.cisco.com/go/swan

- **Cisco Mobile Wireless Center Information**

  http://www.cisco.com/go/mwc

- **Cisco wireless certifications**

  http://www.cisco.com/go/certification

- **Cisco training programs and learning partners**

  http://www.cisco.com/go/learningpartners

- **The following resources provide additional sources of training for Cisco certifications:**

  — **CCPrep**

    http://www.ccprep.com

  — **Certification Zone**

    http://www.certificationzone.com/cisco

  — **Learn Key**

    http://www.learnkey.com

  — **Clickx3**

    http://www.clickx3.com

  — **Boson**

    http://www.boson.com

  — **Group Study**

    http://www.groupstudy.com

Chapter 4 Contents

Wireless Security

Network security is extremely important. Security becomes even more complicated and critical when wireless devices are added to the network. Because data floats around in the ether, anyone can pick it up. This chapter addresses the issues of security in a wireless network and shows how to bolster your network's security mechanisms.

Security Overview

Applying strong wireless security mechanisms is the key to ensure that a wireless network is protected against unauthorized access and eavesdropping. Unfortunately, wireless security is vulnerable if implemented improperly. The following sections examine some of the issues surrounding wireless security and how you can avoid trouble.

WEP Overview

The first, most basic level of securing a wireless LAN (WLAN) is to set up a wired equivalent privacy (WEP) key. This is a means of encryption that encodes transmissions between an access point (AP) and client. This is a basic means of security, but it is not thorough. When wireless devices were first introduced, this was a quick and easy way to provide security. Unfortunately, WEP is inherently flawed; however, it might be your only option if you work with older equipment or client software.

If enough traffic is passed back and forth between client and AP, the packets can be intercepted and the encryption key deduced. This is not a likely issue for homes and small offices that have light wireless activity and uninteresting data. However, in an organization with high volumes of wireless traffic and critical data, it is easy for an intruder to crack the code. It is perhaps worth the effort of the intruder.

NOTE: The Aironet 1100 Series, 1200 Series, 1300 Series APs, and the 1400 Series bridges that run Cisco IOS Software are especially vulnerable because they send any WEP key in cleartext to the simple network management protocol (SNMP) server if the **snmp-server enable traps wlan-wep** command is enabled. If you use WEP, make sure this command is disabled.

WEP Weaknesses

WEP is vulnerable to attack for several reasons:

- Distributing WEP keys manually is a time-intensive, laborious task. Because it is tedious to manually rekey the WEP code, the keys are not likely to change frequently. Therefore, an attacker probably has enough time to decipher the key.

- When keys are not changed often, attackers can compile so-called *decryption dictionaries*. These are huge collections of frames, encrypted with the same key. These frames can then be analyzed and used for attack.

- Standardized WEP implementations use 64- or 128-bit shared keys. Although the 128-bit key sounds excessively durable, it is still possible to crack a key this size within a short interval with sustained traffic.

- WEP uses RC4 for encryption. Of all the possible RC4 keys, the statistics for the first few bytes of output are nonrandom, which can provide information about the key.

NOTE: RC4 is the most widely used software stream cipher. In addition to WEP, it is also used in secure sockets layer (SSL), the encryption medium used for web pages. Although widely deployed and adequate for web use, it is generally not considered a good means of encryption for WLANs.

IEEE 802.1X Authentication

The Institute of Electrical and Electronics Engineers (IEEE) 802.1X standard is an improvement over the capabilities of the WEP. Although WEP provides encryption services, 802.1X provides authentication services. WEP offers a certain measure of encryption between AP and client; however, the data still floats in the ether, exposing it to analysis and examination. In a wired network, unauthorized devices can be blocked from the network if you disable unused RJ-45 jacks and associating Media Access Control (MAC) addresses to Ethernet switch ports.

Manage Port Access

WLANs can include or exclude devices based on MAC addresses using access control lists (ACLs). For more on MAC filtering, skip ahead to Chapter 8, "Wireless Security: Next Steps." Although this type of ACL is easy to implement and manage on small networks, they are tough to manage in large and dynamic networks because individual MAC addresses have to be entered manually for each authorized device. Obviously, this is laborious.

Attacking with MAC

Because ACLs use MAC addresses, they are also prone to attack. An intruder can sit nearby and pick up traffic between the AP and authorized clients. Although the contents of a WEP conversation are encrypted, the MAC address is not. As a result, an attacker can do one of two things:

- The patient attacker can wait until the monitored station disassociates from the network, and then simply reconfigure the network interface card (NIC) to broadcast the intercepted MAC address.

- The impatient attacker can simply send a disassociate request to the AP, bumping the legitimate station off the WLAN. Before the legitimate station can re-associate, the attacker can associate with the spoofed MAC address.

The LAN Port Access Control framework, outlined by the 802.1X standard, helps control access to one's WLAN.

802.1X Protocols

802.1X can be thought of as a control inside your Ethernet switches and APs. The control starts in the OFF position. It considers 802.1X requests and if it decides to grant access, the control moves to the ON position. After a period of time, the station times out or disconnects, moving the control back to the OFF position.

Although the credibility of WEP has taken a beating, it's not totally out of the WLAN security game. WEP is a necessary part of an 802.1X deployment. WEP, used in conjunction with 802.1X, is far more secure than when it is used in static deployments. An even more robust security mechanism, Wi-Fi Protected Access (WPA), is discussed later in this chapter.

There are several protocols used with the 802.1X standard for LAN Port Access Control. Within the 802.1X framework, a LAN station is not allowed to pass traffic through an Ethernet device or WLAN AP until it has successfully authenticated itself. After it has been authenticated, the client can pass traffic on the LAN.

There are 43 protocols that work within the framework of 802.1X authentication. Some of the popular protocols you are likely to see in Cisco wireless networking include a variety of Extensible Authentication Protocol (EAP) authentication frameworks. These are covered in the sections that follow.

Extensible Authentication Protocol

The EAP is a framework that supports multiple methods of authentication. In essence, EAP manages the authentication, but the variant of EAP used dictates how clients are authenticated. Some authentication methods include:

- Token cards
- Kerberos
- Public key authentication
- Certificates
- Smart cards
- One-time passwords (OTP)

Several variations on EAP are possible. Depending on your organization's need, it allows different types of authentication.

As Figure 4-1 shows, EAP authentication is a multistep process:

1. The client associates with the AP.

2. The AP blocks the client from accessing the network.

3. The client provides login information.

4. A Remote Authentication Dial-In User Service (RADIUS) server and client authenticate each other.

5. A RADIUS server and client agree on a WEP key.

6. Authentication is completed.

Figure 4-1 *The EAP Authentication Process*

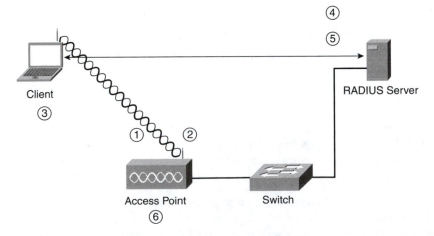

This is the basic framework of how EAP works. However, individual authentication methods can make the process slightly different.

EAP-TLS

EAP with Transport Layer Security (EAP-TLS) requires that both the station and RADIUS server authenticate themselves using public key cryptography, such as smart cards or digital certificates.

This conversation is secured with an encrypted TLS tunnel. That is, only the authentication is encrypted. After that is complete, then WEP, WPA, or WPA2 provide user data encryption. Although this makes EAP-TLS resistant to decryption dictionary and man-in-the-middle (MitM) attacks, the station's identity (and the name bound to the certificate) can still be culled by attackers.

Because EAP-TLS is standard on Microsoft Windows XP, Windows 2000, and Windows Server 2003, it is popular in Windows-based environments. Figure 4-2 shows EAP-TLS in action.

Figure 4-2 *The EAP-TLS Authentication Process*

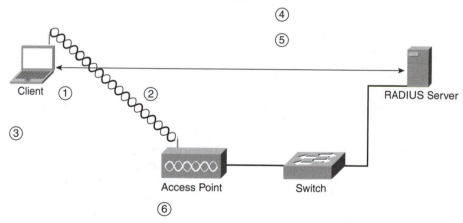

The EAP-TLS authentication process is as follows:

1. The client associates with the AP.

2. The AP blocks the client from accessing the network.

3. The client authenticates the server with a certificate.

4. The RADIUS server authenticates the client with a certificate.

5. The RADIUS server and the client agree on a WEP key.

6. A secure tunnel is established between the client and the server.

The downside to this method is that issuing digital certificates to each station is time consuming, and most organizations prefer to use usernames and passwords for wireless authentication. Protected EAP (PEAP), which is discussed later in this chapter, is a good substitute for EAP-TLS.

Cisco Wireless EAP

The Cisco proprietary take on EAP is known as Cisco Wireless EAP.

NOTE: Cisco Wireless EAP is also known as Lightweight EAP (LEAP). However, some users interpreted "lightweight" with a negative connotation, so Cisco opted to call it Cisco Wireless EAP instead.

Cisco Wireless EAP provides username and password-based authentication between a wireless client and AP, via an authentication server.

Cisco Wireless EAP server and client derive a session key, so that future frames can be encrypted with a key different than keys used by other sessions, thus providing stronger security. In addition, new keys are generated each time the client roams to a new AP.

Dynamic keys, a feature in all EAP implementations, address an enormous vulnerability inherent with static encryption keys. Static keys are shared among all stations on the WLAN. If an attacker can crack the static shared key, he can eavesdrop on all WLAN traffic. Dynamic session keys make it more difficult for the attacker because there is less traffic to analyze, and consequently, it reduces the potential for finding a flaw. In addition, if the attacker is able to crack the key, the session might already be over.

When using Cisco Wireless EAP, dynamic per-user, per-session WEP keys are generated each time the user authenticates to the WLAN. You can strengthen security even further by requiring WEP key timeouts, which forces re-authentication. This generates a new WEP key, even for existing sessions. Figure 4-3 shows the Cisco Wireless EAP process.

The Cisco Wireless EAP authentication process is as follows:

1. The client associates with the AP.

2. The AP blocks the client from accessing the network.

3. The client provides login credentials to the RADIUS server.

4. The RADIUS server and the client authenticate each other.

5. The RADIUS server and the client derive a session key.

6. Secure communications are established between the client and the server.

Figure 4-3 *The Cisco Wireless EAP Authentication Process*

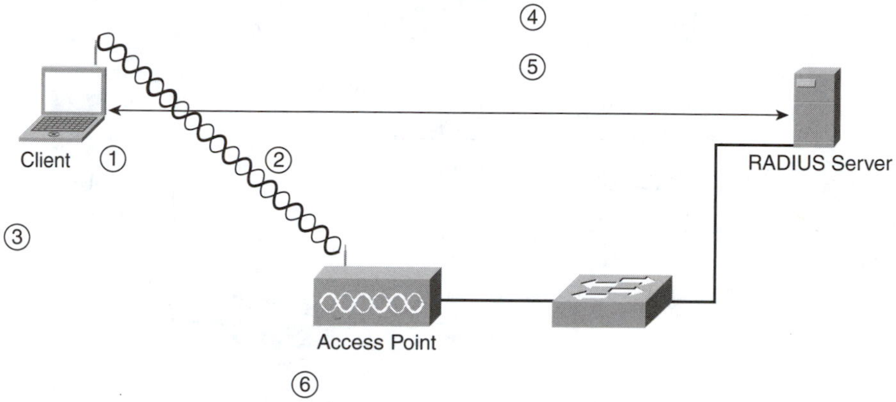

PEAP

PEAP was developed by Cisco, Microsoft, and RSA Security. PEAP allows authentication of WLAN clients without requiring certificates. This protocol simplifies the architecture of WLAN security.

PEAP Overview

PEAP, like the competing tunneled transport layer security (TTLS), uses transport layer security (TLS). Think of it as a stronger version of SSL, the protocol used to secure HTTP sessions. TLS establishes an end-to-end tunnel to transmit the client's credentials. A certificate is required on the server.

There are two phases to PEAP functionality:

- **Phase 1**—Server-side TLS authentication starts, and an encrypted tunnel is created. This creates a server-side authentication system, such as the kind used to authenticate using SSL. When this phase is completed, all authentication data is encrypted.

- **Phase 2**—The client is authenticated using either MS-CHAP Version 2 or other authentication schemes (which are explained in the next section, "PEAP Version 0 and Version 1").

Figure 4-4 shows how PEAP works.

Figure 4-4 *The PEAP Authentication Process*

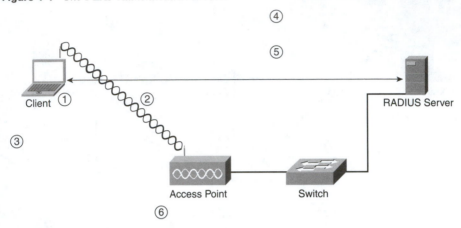

The PEAP authentication process is as follows:

1. The client associates with the AP.

2. The AP blocks the client from accessing the network.

3. The client verifies the RADIUS server's certificate.

4. The RADIUS server authenticates the client using MS-CHAP or other means, such as an OTP.

5. The RADIUS server and the client agree on the WEP key.

6. A secure tunnel is established between the client and the server.

An organization can use Windows logins and passwords if it has not issued certificates to every station. RADIUS servers that support EAP-TTLS and PEAP can check LAN access requests with Windows domain controllers, Active Directories, and other existing user databases.

PEAP Version 0 and Version 1

There are two versions of PEAP:

- PEAP Version 0 (also known as Microsoft PEAP)

- PEAP Version 1 (also known as Cisco PEAP)

Each version supports a different method of client authentication through its TLS tunnel. Version 0 authenticates clients using MS-CHAP Version 2. This limits user databases to those supporting MS-CHAP Version 2, such as Active Directory.

Version 1 (Cisco PEAP) authenticates clients using OTPs and logon passwords, which allow OTP support from vendors and logon password databases in addition to Microsoft databases.

In addition, Version 1 enables users to hide name identities until the TLS tunnel is created. This ensures that usernames are not broadcast during the authentication phase.

EAP-FAST

EAP-FAST is like EAP-TLS in that it uses a certificate-like Protected Access Credential (PAC) file for authentication, and it is like PEAP in that it authenticates the station using a username and password via an encrypted TLS tunnel. EAP-FAST is unique in that it is designed to speed re-authentication as stations roam among APs. EAP-TLS and PEAP require lengthy message exchanges between the station and the server, taking several seconds to re-authenticate. Applications that are not latency sensitive do not need to worry much about this; however, applications that are sensitive to latency (such as voice over IP) suffer if re-authentication takes more than a few milliseconds.

EAP-FAST uses shared secret keys to accelerate the re-authentication process. Public keys are convenient because the station and AP can authenticate each other without having to know each other in advance. (Public keys are used when connecting to a secure website, for instance.) Secret keys are faster, but require that both the station and the AP already have the secret key. Figure 4-5 shows how EAP-FAST works.

Figure 4-5 *The EAP-FAST Authentication Process*

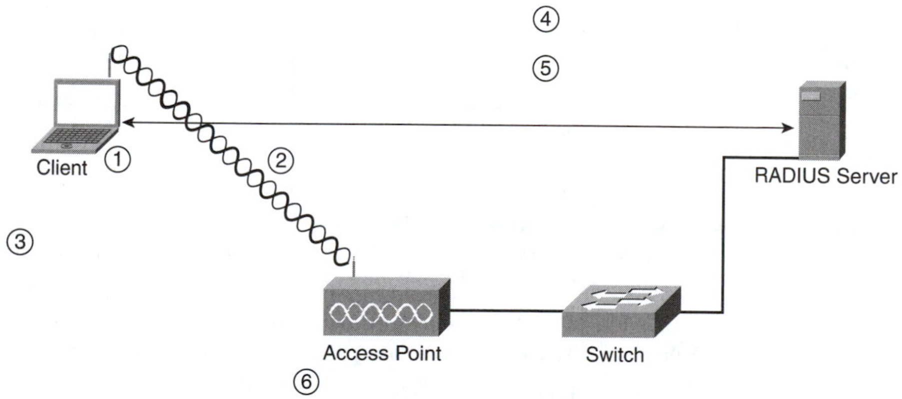

The EAP-FAST authentication process is as follows:

1. The client associates with the AP.

2. The AP blocks the client from accessing the network.

3. The client verifies the RADIUS server's credentials with the shared secret key.

4. The RADIUS server authenticates the client with the shared secret key.

5. The RADIUS server and the client agree on the WEP key.

6. A secure connection is established.

Comparison of 802.1X Authentication Methods

There are a lot of differences among PEAP, Cisco Wireless EAP, EAP-TLS, and EAP-FAST. To help sort the attributes of these protocols, Table 4-1 compares the various features of these different authentication methods.

Table 4-1 *Comparing 802.1X Authentication Methods*

Characteristics	EAP-TLS	Cisco Wireless EAP	PEAP Version 1 (with Generic Token Card)	PEAP Version 0 (with MS-CHAP Version 2)	EAP-FAST
User Authentication Database and Server	OTP LDAP Novell NDS Windows NT Domains Active Directory	Windows NT Domains Active Directory	OTP LDAP Novell NDS Windows NT Domains Active Directory	Windows NT Domains Active Directory	Windows NT Domains Active Directory LDAP
Server Certificates Required?	Yes	No	Yes	Yes	No
Client Certificates Required?	Yes	No	No	No	No
Operating Systems	Windows XP/2000/CE Other OSes supported with third-party utility.	Windows 98/2000/NT/ME/XP/CE Mac OS Linux DOS	Windows XP/2000/CE Other OSes supported with third-party utility.	Windows XP/2000/CE Other OSes supported with third-party utility.	Windows XP/2000/CE Other OSes supported with third-party utility.
Characteristics	EAP-TLS	Cisco Wireless EAP	PEAP Version 1 (with Generic Token Card)	PEAP Version 0 (with MS-CHAP Version 2)	EAP-FAST

Table 4-1   *Comparing 802.1X Authentication Methods (Continued)*

Credentials Used	Digital certificate	Windows password	Clients: Windows, Novell NDS, LDAP password, and OTP or token. Server: Digital certificate	Windows password Server: Digital certificate	Windows password, LDAP user ID and password PAC
Single Sign-On Using Windows Login?	Yes	Yes	No	Yes	Yes
Password Expiration and Change?	–	No	No	Yes	Yes
Fast Secure Roaming Compatible?	No	Yes	No	No	Yes
WPA Compatible?	Yes	Yes	Yes	Yes	Yes

Wi-Fi Protected Access (WPA)

Another means of WLAN security comes in the form of Wi-Fi Protected Access (WPA). WPA was introduced in 2003 by the Wi-Fi Alliance, a nonprofit association that certifies WLAN product interoperability based on IEEE 802.11 specifications. Two versions of WPA exist: WPA and WPA2. They are described in the sections that follow.

WPA

WPA was designed as a replacement for WEP. The Temporal Key Integrity Protocol (TKIP) is an improvement over WEP. It causes keys to automatically change, and when used in conjunction with a larger initialization vector (IV), it makes discovering keys highly unlikely.

NOTE: An IV is a block of bits added to the first block of data of a block cipher. This block is added—or hashed—with the base key and is used with other types of ciphers. This block strengthens security because the same transmissions with the same key yield the same output. As a result, attackers can notice the similarities and derive both the messages and the keys being used.

On top of authentication and encryption improvements, WPA secures the payload better than in WEP. With WEP, cyclic redundancy checks (CRC) are used to ensure packet integrity. However, it is possible to alter the payload and update the message CRC without knowing the WEP key because the CRC is not encrypted. WPA uses message integrity checks (MIC) to ensure packet integrity. The MICs also employ a frame counter, which prevents replay attacks.

NOTE: Replay attacks occur when an attacker intercepts a transmission, and then rebroadcasts that transmission at a later time. For example, if a password is intercepted, the attacker does not need to know how to read the message; he can simply rebroadcast it later, and then gain access using the victim's credentials.

NOTE: MICs are often called Michael in Wi-Fi parlance.

Breaking into a WLAN using WPA is more difficult than WEP because the IVs are larger, there are more keys in use, and there is a sturdier message verification system.

WPA2

As you might deduce from its name, WPA2 is the second and latest version of WPA.

The most important difference between the two is the method of encryption. WPA uses RC4, whereas WPA2 uses AES. Not only is the AES encryption method much stronger, it is also a requirement for some government and industry users.

WPA2 is backward compatible with WPA, and many WPA-certified products can be upgraded with software to WPA2. However, some products might require hardware upgrades. WPA was designed to be a software upgrade to WEP. However, WPA2 didn't have such a design goal. As such, in many cases a hardware upgrade will be necessary to update to WPA2.

Encryption

Scrambling a WLAN's data as it leaves the AP, and then unscrambling it when it arrives at the client, requires an encryption method. The popular RC4 has already been discussed, but sturdier, stronger encryption methods are out there and in use in WLAN systems, as described next.

Data Encryption Standard (DES)

Data Encryption Standard (DES) is an encryption method that uses a secret key. It is so hard to break (it provides 72 quadrillion possible keys) that the U.S. government forbids its exportation to other countries. It is tough to break because the key is randomly chosen from an enormous pool.

DES applies a 56-bit key to each 64-bit block of data. This is considered *strong* encryption. Of course *strong* is a relative term, and if someone is really determined and has the resources, it is possible to crack DES. Many organizations employ triple DES, which applies three keys in succession.

Advanced Encryption Standard (AES)

Advanced Encryption Standard (AES) is poised to become the *de facto* encryption standard. AES applies 128-, 192-, or 256-bit keys to 128-, 192-, or 256-bit blocks of data.

As of 2004, there had been no reported cracks of AES, and it is the first time that the U.S. Government's National Security Agency (NSA) authorized an encryption tool for transmission of top-secret, classified information.

Other Resources

- **University of California, Berkeley Internet Security, Applications, Authentication and Cryptography (ISAAC) Report on WEP insecurity**
  http://www.isaac.cs.berkeley.edu/isaac/wep-faq.html
- **Wi-Fi Alliance**
  http://www.wi-fi.org/
- **National Institute of Standards and Technology**
  http://www.nist.gov

Chapter 5 Contents

Installing and Configuring Access Points

The largest hurdle toward getting your wireless LAN (WLAN) up and running is the configuration of your access points (APs) and wireless clients. The next two chapters examine how you can install and configure both devices. First, let's consider the AP.

Site Survey

Before you install or configure an AP, you should first conduct a site survey. This exercise shows you where the best—and worst—places are in your organization for Wi-Fi reception.

You use an AP and a client to conduct a site survey. Both the AP and client move around to various, temporary locations in an effort to find ideal placement.

Once completed, a thorough site survey tells you:

- Coverage of APs and the ideal location of APs in your WLAN.
- Bit rates and error rates in different locations.
- Whether the number of APs you plan to deploy is enough.
- The performance of applications on the WLAN.

AP Location for Site Survey

When you perform a site survey, try to situate the AP as close to its ultimate location as possible. This helps resolve any problems that might creep up after you mount the AP.

In most cases, you should mount APs at ceiling height. In warehouses and other sites with high ceilings, it's best to mount them between 15 and 25 feet. If you mount them at this height, power delivered to the devices must be addressed. Power over Ethernet (PoE) is discussed in greater detail later, but this is an excellent scenario where you should deliver power in via a power injector, line-power enabled devices (such as Catalyst switches), or line-power patch panels (sometimes referred to as a *mid-span* device). PoE can save a lot of headache and expense.

In some environments it might be desirable to keep the AP out of sight. If you opt to place the AP above ceiling panels, you should place antennas below the ceiling for optimal reception. If this is the case, you should purchase an AP that fits for remote antenna capability.

NOTE: Check your local fire codes. You might need plenum-rated APs and cabling if they are placed above the ceiling tiles.

Performing the Survey

There are two ways you can perform a site survey: manually or assisted. You typically use the manual method when you first install a WLAN.

If you already have a WLAN in place and just want to tweak it, an assisted site survey saves you a lot of shoe leather.

Manual Site Survey

The first way to conduct a site survey is called a *manual* site survey. This means you pick up a Wi-Fi-enabled laptop, palmtop, or specialized wireless survey device and walk around your site and record data from the temporarily located AP as you go.

You should place the AP and antennas where you decide to mount them. However, before you actually mount them, perform the survey, and take your Wi-Fi-enabled device to various client locations within its coverage area.

Cisco wireless client adapters (which are examined in greater detail in Chapter 6, "Configuring Clients") include the Cisco Aironet Desktop Utility, which includes a site survey tool component. This tool allows you to view the strength of your AP's signal, the quality of the signal, packet retries, and a host of other data. This tool is shown in Figure 5-1.

Figure 5-1 *Aironet Desktop Utility Site Survey Tool*

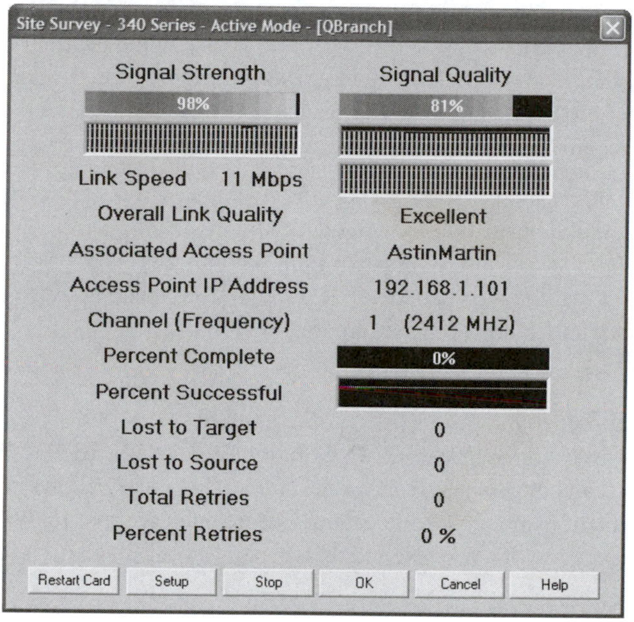

When you conduct a site survey, be aware of these issues:

- Wood floors can cause floor-to-floor interaction between APs. Think three dimensionally. Make sure channel selections are appropriate for APs located on adjacent floors.

- Office and room doors should be closed before beginning the survey. This shows how the WLAN performs in real, day-to-day functioning.

- Metal blinds should be closed because, in this position, they are major disruptors of signal quality.

Follow these steps when you perform a manual site survey:

Step 1. Start with a building map or layout that shows all the coverage areas.

Step 2. Identify and record possible sources of interference, including elevators, microwave ovens, HVAC units, power distribution closets, and so forth. Metal bookshelves and cabinets can also disrupt your AP's signal.

Step 3. Move around your facility, and make note of signal strength, signal-to-noise ratio (SNR), and packet retry counts.

Step 4. Move the AP to a different location and with a fresh copy of the facility schematic, repeat step 3.

It's easy to look at the signal strength meter on your site survey tool and make assumptions based on the strength of the signal you receive. However, you should also be cognizant of the signal-to-noise ratio (SNR). If noise in the band is too high, it can cause reception problems—even if you have a strong signal from the AP. Use the SNR and *packet retry count* (the number of times packets were retransmitted for successful reception) to get an accurate view of your signal quality.

Packet retry count should be below 10 percent in all areas. You should use packet retry in tandem with the SNR reading for a good picture of signal quality. The signal might be strong enough, but because of noise or multipath interference, packets are resent. Without an SNR reading, you cannot tell if packet retries spike because you are out of range, there's too much noise, or the signal is too low.

Assisted Site Survey

If you use the CiscoWorks Wireless LAN Solution Engine (WLSE) or a Wireless LAN Controller, you can perform an *assisted* site survey. This survey allows you to simulate the optimal radio transmit power and channel selection in an existing WLAN. You can select specific APs in your WLAN, and then generate your results. The assisted site survey allows you to:

- Select specific APs to test
- Perform a radio scan
- Perform a client walkabout (not performed on the WLAN Controller)
- Generate radio parameters

The benefit of this test is that it allows you to conduct the site survey without the need to walk all over your office (unless you chose the client walkabout test, of course). It also allows you a certain level of granularity, to pick and choose which devices to test. Although this tool is great for WLANs with existing APs, it's not ideal for pre-installation work.

We discuss CiscoWorks WLSE in greater detail in Chapter 10, "CiscoWorks Wireless LAN Solution Engine (WLSE)."

Analyzing Your Site

After you conduct your site survey, it's time to analyze the data. If you conduct a manual site survey, bring a map along with you and record site data for each location. After you complete the survey, sit down and examine the map. Do you notice poor signal reception in certain areas? What characteristics are at play in that area that might affect signal quality?

You should also experiment with different AP and antenna locations to find the best site. Use different maps for different AP placement options, as this helps you keep your data clear and easy to understand.

If you encounter interference you simply cannot locate, you might need to use a spectrum analyzer. These devices scan a wide frequency band to locate transmissions. Unfortunately, they are also expensive. You can expect to pay thousands of dollars for one (or you can rent one). On top of the expense, there's a steep learning curve in their configuration, setup, and use. If the purchase of a spectrum analyzer is not in your budget, you might hire a consultant with specialized tools to conduct the site survey.

Cabling

There are four options to power your AP. The options depend on whether or not your AP receives power from a power supply or if it receives inline power. The four connection options are:

- A switch with inline power (such as a Catalyst switch).
- An inline power patch panel between the switch and the AP.
- A power injector between the switch and the AP. A power injector is a device that plugs into a wall socket, and then connects into the Ethernet line to provide power to one port (in this case, the AP).
- A local power supply.

Of these power methods, the first three use PoE to supply power to the AP.

NOTE: If you use the AP's 5-GHz radio, make sure your switch and patch panel provide enough power to the device. The 2.4-GHz radios are widely covered, but there might not be enough support for the 5-GHz radio.

PoE is a technology that eliminates the need for a separate power supply to plug into the AP. That is, power is delivered—as the name suggests—over the same Ethernet cable used to deliver data. This is ideal for places where it might be difficult, if not impossible, to provide a separate power source.

NOTE: You should not use PoE in conjunction with a separate power supply. This can cause the powered Ethernet switch port to shut down.

You must also consider the distance between the AP and the switch. The maximum range for 100BaseT Ethernet is 100 meters.

Encryption and Authentication

Wired Equivalent Privacy (WEP) keys protect your data and keep your WLAN secure at the most basic level. WEP is easy to beat, so a better option is 802.1X authentication. This section explains how you can set up either of these mechanisms on your AP.

40/64-Bit Versus 104/128-Bit Encryption

Although WEP keys are not the best option for WLAN security, they are better than nothing. If you find yourself in a situation in which 802.1X authentication is not possible, you should at least use WEP keys. WEP keys come in two "strengths": 64- and 128-bit.

NOTE: WEP keys are often referred to as 40- and 104-bit, or 64- and 128-bit. The terms are interchangeable. 40-bit and 64-bit keys offer the same level of protection.

So what's happening to the other 24 bits?

Those "missing" 24 bits are the key's initialization vector. So, in a 64-bit WEP environment, only 40 bits are considered part of the actual key.

Ideally, you use 128-bit encryption whenever possible, because it is more difficult to break than 64-bit encryption. So why include 64-bit encryption at all? It's largely a matter of backwards compatibility with early wireless clients that supported only 64-bit encryption. In almost every case, if you have to use WEP, opt for 128-bit over 64-bit encryption.

To establish a WEP setting is straightforward and you can perform it quickly with the **Express Security** selection on the AP configuration screen (the first screen that appears when you log onto your AP). Simply open the screen and enter your WEP key.

You can perform more detailed WEP key tasks if you follow these steps:

Step 1. On the Cisco 1130AG AP, use a web browser and navigate to the device's home page.

Step 2. On the menu located to the left side of the window, click **Security**.

Step 3. When the Security section expands, click **Encryption Manager**. This spawns the screen shown in Figure 5-2.

Figure 5-2   *Managing WEP Keys on the Cisco AP*

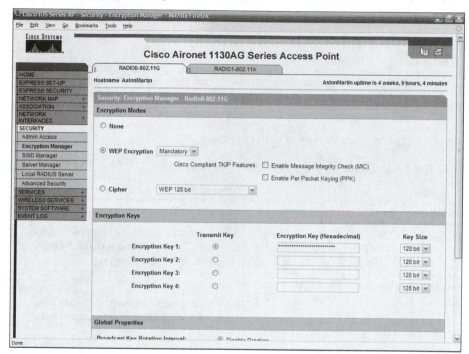

Step 4. This screen allows you to manage your WEP key settings:

- The Encryption Modes area contains settings to disable WEP, enable WEP, or establish cipher settings.

- The Encryption Keys area is the section in which up to four WEP keys and their lengths are entered. For security, the WEP keys are not shown as you enter them. Because of this, it is somewhat difficult to determine if you mistype the key. Enter a key on each line if you plan on rotating through WEP keys.

- The Global Properties area is used to manage the behavior of your WEP keys. Here, you can select whether to rotate between keys, how long the interval is between each rotation, and how to manage keys within your group.

Step 5. Because the Cisco 1130 AP has both 2.4-GHz and 5-GHz radios, you can apply these settings to one radio or both radios. In this case, click **Apply-Radio0** to establish these settings for the 2.4-GHz radio. **Apply-All** sends the settings to both radios.

Setting WEP Keys Using the CLI

If you prefer to use the command-line interface to configure WEP keys on your Aironet AP, follow these settings:

```
ap1130# configure terminal
ap1130(config)# configure interface dot11radio 0
ap1130(config-if)# encryption vlan 07 key 1 size 128 abc123abc123abc123abc123cc
    transmit-key
ap1130(config-ssid)# end
ap1130# copy running-config startup-config
```

Table 5-1 explains the meaning of each command.

Table 5-1   *Configuration Commands for WEP Key Configuration.*

Command	Description
configure terminal	Enters global configuration mode.
**configure interface dot11radio {0	1}**	Enters interface configuration mode for the radio. The 2.4-GHz radio is **0**; the 5-GHz radio is **1**.
encryption [vlan *vlan-id*] **key** *key-number* *size* {**40	128**} [**transmit-key**]	Establishes the settings for your WEP key. **vlan** is optional. It allows you to select the VLAN for which you wish to use the WEP key. Sets which key number you want to use. You can set up to four WEP keys. Enters the size of the WEP key. Settings are either 40- or 128-bit and contain 26 hexadecimal digits. **transmit-key** is optional. By default, the key in slot 1 is the default transmit key, but you can use this setting to specify which key (1 through 4) to use.
End	Returns to privileged EXEC mode.
copy running-config startup-config	An optional step that allows you to save your entries to the configuration file.

In this example, a 128-bit WEP key was configured on the AP's 2.4-GHz radio. The key—specified as the first key—was established as a transmit key in the 07 VLAN.

802.1X Configuration

A stronger means of security is 802.1X authentication. Like most other aspects of Aironet configuration, Cisco gives you the option to set it up quickly, or really dig down into the configuration details.

NOTE: To set up 802.1X authentication, you must have a RADIUS server on your network. Without it, you cannot set up 802.1X authentication. The AP itself, or routers, can also act as RADIUS servers.

To configure 802.1X authentication, follow these steps:

Step 1.   Navigate to the AP's home page.

Step 2.   Click **Express Security** from the menu on the left. This calls up the screen shown in Figure 5-3.

Figure 5-3   *802.1X Input Information on the Express Security Screen.*

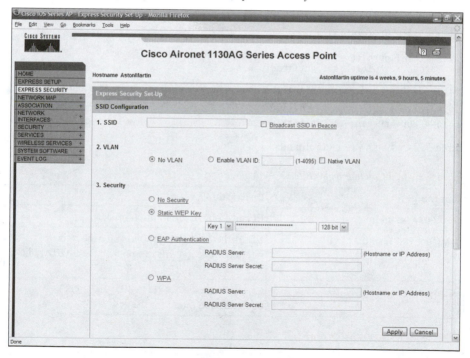

Step 3.   In the Security area, you establish whether you want no security, a static WEP key (along with a place to enter the key), Extensible Authentication Protocol (EAP) authentication, or Wi-Fi Protected Access (WPA) authentication.

Step 4. To set up LEAP, Protected EAP (PEAP), EAP-Transport Layer Security (EAP-TLS), EAP-Tunneled TLS (EAP-TTLS), EAP- Generic Token Card (EAP-GTC), EAP-Subscriber Identity Module (EAP-SIM), and other 802.1X/EAP-based protocols, click the **EAP Authentication** radio button. To use WPA, click the **WPA** radio button.

Step 5. In the boxes next to the **EAP Authentication** radio button or **WPA** radio button, enter the name of the RADIUS server and the secret that will be shared between the AP and the RADIUS server.

Step 6. Click **Apply**.

These settings allow for a quick configuration of 802.1X authentication. For more control over your AP's handling of 802.1X, click **Security** from the menu on the left. This allows you to do such things as specify backup RADIUS servers, enable accounting, manage the authentication port, and manage several other details.

802.1X CLI Configuration

If you prefer to use the command-line interface to configure authentication on your Aironet AP, follow these settings:

```
ap1130# configure terminal
ap1130(config)# interface dot11radio 0
ap1130(config-if)# ssid qbranch
ap1130(config-ssid)# authentication open mac moneypenny alternate eap moneypenny
ap1130(config-ssid)# authentication key-management wpa optional
ap1130(config-ssid)# end
ap1130# copy running-config startup-config
```

Table 5-2 explains these commands.

Table 5-2 *CLI Commands for 802.1X Authentication*

Command	Description
configure terminal	Enters global configuration mode.
interface dot11radio {1 | 0}	Enters the configuration mode for the radio interface. The 2.4-GHz radio is **0**; the 5-GHz radio is **1**.
ssid *ssid-string*	Create a Service Set ID (SSID) and enter configuration mode for the new SSID.

Table 5-2   *CLI Commands for 802.1X Authentication (Continued)*

Command	Description
authentication open [**mac-address** *list-name* [**alternate**]] [**eap** *list-name*]	This step is optional. It sets the authentication type to open for this SSID.
	mac-address sets the SSID's authentication type to open with MAC address authentication. This requires all clients to perform MAC address authentication before joining the network.
	The keyword **alternate** is used to allow clients to join using either EAP or MAC authentication.
	eap sets the SSID's authentication type to open with EAP authentication. The AP requires all clients to perform EAP authentication before joining the network.
	For *list-name*, specify the authentication method list.
authentication shared [**mac-address** *list-name*] [**eap** *list-name*]	This is an optional step and is used to set the authentication type for the SSID to shared key.
	mac-address sets the SSID's authentication type to shared key with MAC address authentication. For *list-name*, enter the authentication method list.
	eap sets the SSID's authentication type to shared key with EAP address authentication. For *list-name*, enter the authentication method list.
authentication network-eap *list-name* [**mac-address** *list-name*]	This step is optional. It is used to set the authentication type for the SSID to Network-EAP. It is used to authenticate an EAP client with an EAP-compatible RADIUS server.
	The SSID's authentication type can be altered so that it also requires MAC address authentication. For *list-name*, enter the authentication method list.

continues

Table 5-2 *CLI Commands for 802.1X Authentication (Continued)*

Command	Description
authentication key-management {[**wpa**] [**cckm**]} [**optional**]	This is an optional step and is used to set the authentication type for the SSID to WPA, Cisco Centralized Key Management (CCKM), or both. If you use the keyword **optional**, clients that do not use WPA or CCKM are allowed to use the SSID. However, if **optional** is not used, clients must use WPA or CCKM to connect.
	If you choose to enable CCKM for an SSID, you must also enable Network-EAP authentication. To enable WPA for an SSID, you must also enable Open authentication, Network-EAP, or both.
end	Return to privileged EXEC mode.
copy running-config startup-config	This step is optional and saves your entries in the configuration file.

In this example, the authentication type for the SSID qbranch on the 2.4-GHz radio has been set to Network-EAP with WPA key management. Clients that use qbranch are authenticated with the moneypenny server list.

Antenna Placement

APs that require external antennas need special care. You need to configure the antennas properly, consider what role the AP serves (AP or bridge), and consider where the antennas are placed.

For more information on Wi-Fi antennas, flip back to Chapter 2, "Cisco Antennas."

Ideally, you locate the AP as close as possible to the antennas. The farther the signal has to travel across the cabling between the AP and the antenna, the more signal reduction (also known as *RF attenuation*) you experience. For instance, if you are locating an antenna in a courtyard to service clients roaming outside, don't place the AP in a closet, dozens of feet away from the antenna. Instead, place the AP outside in a weatherproof enclosure, so it's closer to the antenna. An even better idea is to use a 1300 series, which is weatherproof.

Signal loss depends on what type of cable you use. Cisco offers two types of cable. One is similar to LMR400 and has a loss of 6.7dB per 100 feet, whereas the other is similar to LMR600 with 4.4dB per 100 feet. For every 3dB, you lose about half the signal's power. This loss occurs on both transmission and reception. You can use higher-quality cable to reduce signal loss over longer cables, but keep in mind that higher-quality cable is more expensive.

In addition, if you use an 802.11a product, cable loss is an even more significant issue. Loss increases with frequency, and coaxial cable has even more attenuation with 5-GHz signals than 2.4-GHz signals.

Initial Settings

Cisco APs contain pages and pages of configuration settings. These settings are good when you need to fine tune your AP's performance and role in the network; however, if you want to get started right away, the AP contains two *express* pages:

- Express Set-Up
- Express Security Set-Up

Express Security Set-Up was covered earlier in this chapter. Express Set-Up is the page you want to use when you first configure your Cisco AP.

Express Set-Up

Express Set-Up is shown in Figure 5-4. This page allows you to manage such details as:

- Host name
- How an IP address is acquired (dynamic host configuration protocol [DHCP], or statically)
- IP address
- IP subnet mask
- Default gateway
- SNMP community
- The radio's role in the network (AP or repeater)
- Options for general AP performance optimization
- Whether Aironet extensions are enabled or disabled

Figure 5-4 *Express Set-Up Allows You to Quickly Enter AP Information in One Place*

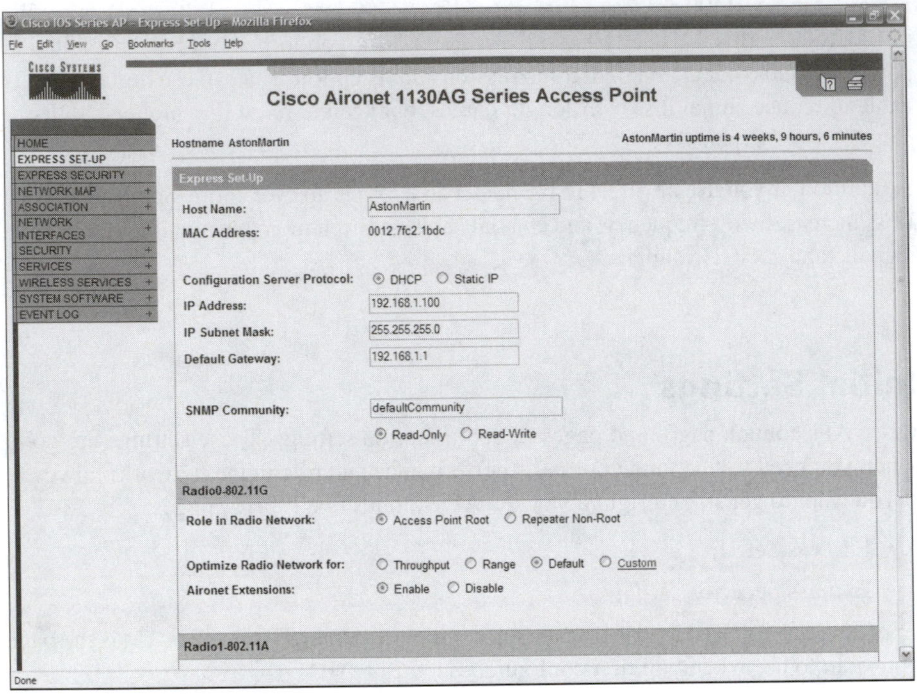

Express Security Set-Up

Express Security Set-Up is used to quickly manage your AP's security features. Similar to Express Set-Up, this screen is used to manage the broad strokes of your device's security functions. The details are managed from elsewhere on the device. Figure 5-3 shows the Express Security Set-Up screen.

This page allows you to:

- Establish your AP's SSIDs
- Enable and specify VLANs
- Set up security protocols
  - WEP (including specifying WEP keys)
  - WPA
  - 802.1X
- View a table that shows your AP's SSIDs

APs as Repeaters

Most of this chapter deals with the issue of how to connect an AP to your WLAN. However, to extend the range of your WLAN, you can add a repeater AP to the network. This AP is not physically connected to the WLAN, but is instead added to augment range and the clients that access the WLAN.

NOTE: Because APs have two radios, only one can be used as a repeater. You must configure the other as a root radio.

Repeater Overview

The repeater forwards traffic between wireless clients and the AP connected to the wired LAN (or other repeaters). APs configured as repeaters do not forward traffic from the Ethernet port (although this might change in future versions of the software).

NOTE: After your AP is configured as a repeater, it shuts down its Ethernet connection. Any devices connected to the Ethernet port are disconnected from the AP.

You can configure multiple APs as a chain of repeaters. However, throughput suffers as additional APs are added to the chain, because each repeater must receive and then retransmit the packet on the same channel. Because of this, throughput is cut in half for each repeater added.

Following are some guidelines to bear in mind when you place an AP in repeater mode:

- It's best to use repeaters to serve clients that do not demand high throughput.
- Cisco AP repeaters work best when clients are Cisco devices. Problems occur when third-party devices try to associate with repeater APs.
- Ensure the data rates configured on the repeater AP match the data rates of the parent AP.

Configuring Repeater APs

Follow these steps to configure your Cisco AP as a repeater AP:

Step 1.   The first step to configure a repeater AP is to enable Aironet extensions on both the parent and repeater APs. By default, these extensions are enabled. Aironet extensions are useful for the AP to communicate with other Cisco wireless devices. However, if you have problems getting non-Cisco equipment to talk to the AP, a first step is to disable Aironet extensions.

Step 2.   Next, open the Security page from the menu at the left of the AP's main page.

Step 3.   Select **SSID Manager** from the submenu.

Step 4.   Click the tab at the top of the screen to indicate which radio you want to set up as a repeater.

Step 5.   Scroll to the bottom of the screen to the section named Global Radio0-802.11G SSID Properties. Of course, if you had selected to manage the 802.11a radio, you would have to scroll to the section indicating that radio. This is shown in Figure 5-5.

Figure 5-5   *Selecting the Radio's SSID Properties*

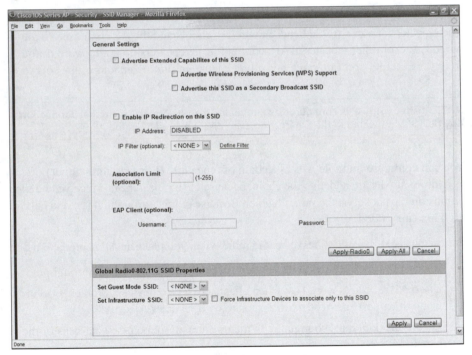

Step 6.   In the **Set Infrastructure SSID** drop-down menu, select the name of the SSID the repeater uses to associate to a root AP.

Step 7.   Clicking the checkbox next to the drop-down menu forces infrastructure devices to associate to the repeater AP that uses this SSID.

Step 8.   Click **Apply**.

Step 9.   Click the **Express Setup** selection from the menu at the left.

Step 10.   For the radio you want to establish as a repeater, click the radio button next to **Repeater Non-Root**.

Step 11. In the Aironet Extensions section, click the radio button next to **Enable**.

Step 12. Click **Apply** at the bottom of the screen.

Most WLAN problems stem from improperly configured APs or clients. If you properly install and configure your APs, you are on the right track to an effective WLAN.

Configuring a Repeater Using the CLI

If you want to configure your AP as a repeater and use the command-line interface, the following is an example configuration setting. This example configures the AP with two parents:

```
ap1130# configure terminal
ap1130(config)# interface dot11radio 0
ap1130(config-if)# ssid qbranch
ap1130(config-ssid)# infrastructure-ssid
ap1130(config-ssid)# exit
ap1130(config-if)# station-role repeater
ap1130(config-if)# dot11 extensions aironet
ap1130(config-if)# parent 1 0012.7fc2.1bdc 1000
ap1130(config-if)# parent 2 0012.44b4.b250 1000
ap1130(config-if)# end
ao1130# copy running-config startup-config
```

Table 5-3 explains each command in this list.

Table 5-3   *CLI Commands for Configuring an AP as a Repeater*

Command	Description
configure terminal	Enters global configuration mode.
interface dot11radio {1 | 0}	Enters the configuration mode for the radio interface. The 2.4-GHz radio is 0; the 5-GHz radio is 1.
ssid *ssid-string*	Creates the SSID the repeater uses to associate to a root AP. The next step is used to designate this SSID as an infrastructure SSID. If an infrastructure SSID was created on the root AP, create the same SSID on the repeater.
infrastructure-ssid [optional]	Assigns the SSID as an infrastructure SSID. This is the SSID the repeater uses to associate to the root AP. Infrastructure devices must associate to the repeater AP and use this SSID unless the **optional** keyword is entered.

continues

Table 5-3 *CLI Commands for Configuring an AP as a Repeater (Continued)*

Command	Description
exit	Exits SSID configuration mode and returns to radio interface configuration.
station-role repeater	Establishes this AP's role as a repeater.
dot11 extensions aironet	Enables Aironet extensions.
parent {*parent-number*} *mac-address* [*timeout*]	This step is optional and is used to enter the MAC address for each AP to which the repeater should associate. MAC addresses for up to four parents can be entered. If the repeater fails to associate to the first parent, it moves to the next on the list. You can enter a timeout value (numerous seconds between 0 and 65535), which establishes how long the repeater tries to associate to a parent before it moves to the next.
end	Returns to privileged EXEC mode.
copy running-config startup-config	This step is optional and saves your entries in the configuration file.

In this example, the SSID qbranch is configured as a repeater and attempts to associate to one of two parent APs. qbranch attempts to associate to each parent for 1000 seconds before it moves on to the next.

Other Resources

The complete reference guides for Cisco APs are found online; just follow these steps:

Step 1. Go to www.cisco.com.

Step 2. In the Quick Links section, click **Products & Solutions**.

Step 3. Click **Wireless**. A window appears that contains a partial list of Cisco products.

Step 4. Click **All Wireless Products**.

Step 5. Scroll down to the Product Portfolio section to locate the Wireless LAN subsection.

Step 6. Select the desired Cisco AP.

- **Cisco 1000 deployment guide that includes site survey guide**:

  http://www.cisco.com/univercd/cc/td/doc/product/wireless/airo1000/a1kinit/1dep.pdf

Chapter 6 Contents

Configuring Clients

In Chapter 5, "Installing and Configuring Access Points," you learned how to configure and install access points (AP). This chapter continues the discussion of configuring wireless LANs (WLAN) and explains how to configure your clients. In this chapter, you see many of the same characters (service set identifiers [SSIDs], 802.1X authentication methods, and wireless equivalent protocol [WEP] keys, for example), but their implementation on a wireless client is different than on the AP.

Client Utilities

You can configure a Cisco wireless client adapter either through the computer's operating system or with Cisco-supplied utilities. This chapter explains how to configure your wireless adapters with the Cisco utilities.

Cisco wireless clients come with the following four useful applications and tools to help configure, manage, and troubleshoot wireless connections:

- Aironet Client Utility (ACU)
- Aironet Client Monitor (ACM)
- Client Encryption Manager (CEM)
- Link Status Meter (LSM)

When you install your client adapter driver, these tools are also installed.

ACU and Aironet Desktop Utility (ADU)

The application you will use most often is the Aironet Client Utility (ACU) or the Aironet Desktop Utility (ADU). ACU has been around for a while, and the ADU is becoming more prevalent in Cisco wireless clients. This chapter focuses on the ACU; however, you might come across the ADU. Although the two applications are not identical, they carry much of the same functionality and many of the same features.

The ACU, which is explained in greater depth as this chapter progresses, is used to configure your client adapter, monitor your connection, assess connection quality, and manage security features.

ACM, CEM, and LSM are activated in the ACU.

ACM

You can get a quick and easy overview of your client's connection and association to an AP by looking at the ACM. The ACM provides a few of the features available through ACU and allows you to perform basic tasks.

Figure 6-1 shows the ACM icon. It is accessible through the Windows system tray, and it gives you an instant overview of your system's connection.

Figure 6-1 *The Aironet Client Monitor Is Accessed Through an Icon in the Taskbar*

Aironet Client Monitor

NOTE: If more than one client adapter is installed, an ACM icon appears for each adapter.

ACM gives you information and configuration options in three ways:

- The color of the icon.
- A tool tip window that appears when you move your mouse over the icon.
- A pop-up menu when you right-click the icon.

Table 6-1 explains the icon colors and what they represent.

Table 6-1 *ACM Icon Colors and Meaning*

Icon Colors	Description
White	The client adapter is turned off.
Dark grey	The client adapter is not associated to an AP.
Light grey	The client adapter is associated to an AP, but the user is not authenticated.
Green	The client adapter is associated to an AP, and the link quality is excellent.
Yellow	The client adapter is associated to an AP, but the link quality is fair.
Red	The client adapter is associated to an AP, but the link quality is poor.

When you move your mouse over the icon, a tool tip window appears and describes your association status and other details. Table 6-2 explains the components of the tool tip window.

Table 6-2 *Tool Tip Window Components*

Component	Description
Active profile	The profile that the client adapter uses. If auto profile selection is used, the profile name is preceded by *Auto*.
SSID	The name of the network to which you are currently associated.
Connection status	Describes the current operation of your client adapter, including: • Radio Off • Not Associated • Associated • Authenticating • Authenticated • Authentication Failure

continues

Table 6-2   *Tool Tip Window Components (Continued)*

Component	Description
Link quality	A description of the client adapter's signal strength and signal quality, expressed as: • Excellent • Good • Fair • Poor
Link speed	Your client adapter's connection rate with the AP.
Client adapter	Description of the client adapter.
Client adapter IP address	The client adapter's IP address.

Right-clicking the ACM calls a pop-up menu. From it, you can perform the following tasks:

- Launch ACU.
- Troubleshoot a connection.
- Manage preferences; add or remove features to the pop-up menu.
- Turn radio on or off.
- Reauthenticate with the AP.
- Select a profile.
- Show connection status.

CEM

The CEM is launched from the ADU and is used to manage your WEP keys. This tool is explained in more detail later in this chapter.

LSM

The LSM is an extremely useful tool that graphically depicts your client's connection quality to the AP. This tool, although not specifically meant for site surveys, can be used to perform some basic site survey functions. It is explained in greater detail in Chapter 13, "Diagnosing Client Connection Problems."

Network Discovery

Connecting to a wired LAN is easy. Just plug the Cat 5 cabling poking out of the wall into the back of the computer, and you are pretty much in business. However, if you connect to a wired LAN in this way, you cannot tell which networks are available—let alone which ones you can connect to—in a WLAN.

As the network professional, of course, you can tell users to which network they should connect. However, if users find themselves in new territory—a different office, a public hot spot, and so forth—it is helpful to have a tool that allows them to discover which networks are available.

A quick and easy way to check for available networks is through Windows XP. Follow these steps to check for, and connect to, available WLANs:

Step 1. Right-click the network connection icon in your taskbar, and then click **View Available Wireless Networks**. This calls up the Wireless Network Connection screen shown in Figure 6-2.

Figure 6-2 *Using Windows XP to View Available Wireless Networks*

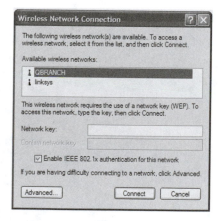

Step 2. Under Available Wireless Networks, click the wireless network to which you want to connect.

Step 3. If a network key is required for WEP, do one of the following:

- If the network key is automatically provided (that is, it is derived using 802.1X), leave the Network Key field blank.

- If the network key is not provided, in the Network Key field, type the key.

Step 4. Click **Connect**.

Client Configuration

When you locate the network to which you want to connect, the following sections walk you through the process of configuring your client. However, different versions of your software will vary slightly. Because of this, what you have on your client might differ from what's presented here, but the steps should be similar.

Profiles

Profiles allow you to establish settings for different WLAN configurations without a need to reconfigure the client adapter with each change. ACU can manage up to 16 profiles. The benefit to establish different profiles is that you can have a profile for the home, one for the office, and 14 more for different environments, so you do not have to change client adapter settings each time you move to a new environment.

To start the ACU's profile manager, double-click the ACU icon on your desktop (or in your Start menu), then click **Profile Manager** from the command drop-down menu. The Profile Manager screen appears, such as the one shown in Figure 6-3.

Figure 6-3 *Profile Manager*

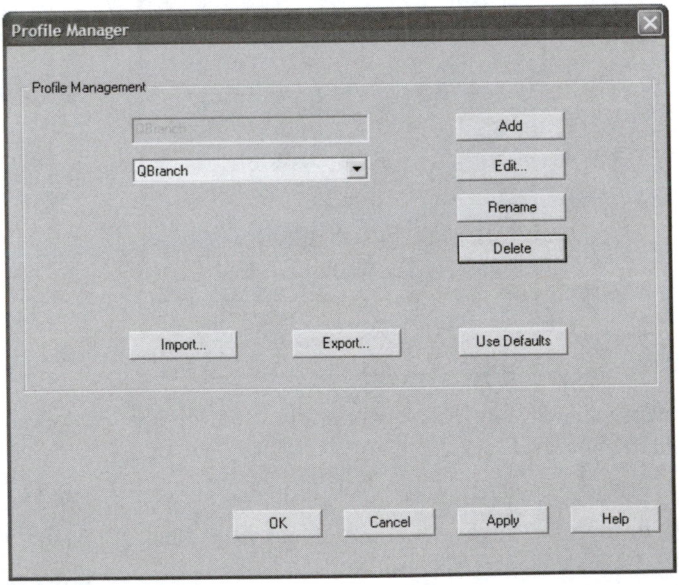

Profile Manager is used to handle many tasks as they relate to profile management, including:

- Creating a profile
- Editing a profile
- Setting default profile values

- Deleting a profile
- Importing a profile
- Exporting a profile

Creating a Profile

The following steps are used to create a new profile:

Step 1. Click **Add**.

Step 2. Enter a name for your new profile and press **Enter**.

Step 3. When the Properties screen appears, do one of the following:

- To use the default values for this profile, click **OK**.

- To change any of these settings, go to the "Setting System Parameters" section for steps that explain how to make changes.

Step 4. Click **OK**.

Selecting an Active Profile

After your profiles have been created, you must select which profile to use. To do this, follow these steps:

Step 1. Open the ACU and then choose **Select Profile** from the command drop-down menu. Figure 6-4 shows the Select Profile screen.

Figure 6-4 *Selecting a Profile*

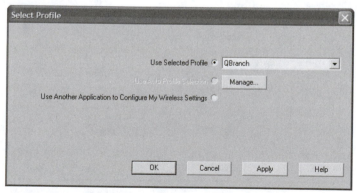

Step 2. Choose one of the following options:

- **Use Selected Profile**—Allows you to select the profile you wish to use for the adapter. If you select this option, it requires the selection of a profile from the drop-down box. If the adapter is unable to associate to an AP or loses its association, it does not automatically select another profile to attempt a connection.

- **Use Auto Profile Selection**—The adapter driver automatically selects a profile from the list. The profile used appears in the box to the right of the Use Auto Profile Selection option. In this case, if the association is not made or is lost after 10 seconds (or—if Lightweight EAP LEAP is enabled—a time longer than that specified by the LEAP authentication timeout value in the LEAP Settings screen), the driver switches to another profile and attempts reassociation.

- **Use Another Application To Configure My Wireless Settings**—Allows other applications, such as Windows XP, to configure the client adapter.

Step 3. Click **OK**.

Setting System Parameters

System parameters are managed to prepare a client adapter for use in a wireless network. This screen is shown in Figure 6-5 and appears when you create a new profile, or edit an existing profile.

Figure 6-5 *Setting System Parameters*

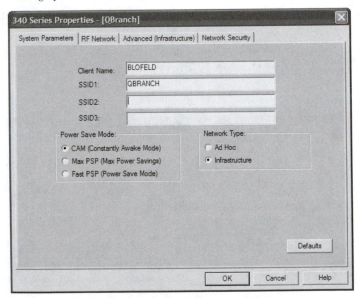

Table 6-3 describes the various parameters you can manage on this screen.

Table 6-3   *System Parameter Settings*

Parameter	Description
Client Name	Name your client here. It allows the identification of your client on the network. It also appears on the AP's list of connected clients.
SSID1	The service set identifier (SSID) indicates which wireless network you want to access. If this parameter is left blank, the client can associate to any AP that is configured to allow broadcast SSIDs.
SSID2	An optional SSID that allows the client to roam to another network without the need to reconfigure the client adapter.
SSID3	A second optional SSID that allows the client to roam to another network without the need to reconfigure the client adapter.
Power Save Mode	The power saving settings are: • **Constantly Awake Mode (CAM)**—The client is constantly powered for maximum response. This option consumes the most power. • **Maximum Power Savings (Max PSP)**—Using Max Power Save Protocol (PSP), the AP buffers incoming messages for the client. The client "wakes" up periodically and checks with the AP, which then sends for any buffered messages. This mode conserves the most power, but offers the least amount of throughput. • **Fast PSP (power save mode)**—Alternates between PSP and CAM modes, depending on network traffic. When the client receives buffered traffic, the client switches to CAM mode. When the packets are received, it switches back to PSP mode.
Network Type	Used to specify to which type of network your adapter can connect. The options are: • **Ad Hoc**—Use this when the wireless network is comprised of a few wireless devices that are not connected to a wired LAN. • **Infrastructure**—Use this setting when you connect to a wired network through an AP. Setting this radio button impacts the next tab, which differs based on the network type you select. You learn more about these options in the next section.

After you choose your settings, click **OK** to return to the Profile Manager screen.

Choosing Between Infrastructure and Ad Hoc

Wireless clients can connect to a network in two ways:

- *Infrastructure* mode allows a client to connect to the wired network via an AP.
- *Ad hoc* mode is used when two or more clients access one another without the benefit of an AP.

This section describes the two tabs on the ACU that allow you to configure your client for either infrastructure or ad hoc connections.

NOTE: The RF Network tab is not explained in this chapter because it has advanced features that will likely not change.

Advanced Infrastructure Parameters

The Advanced (Infrastructure) tab is shown in Figure 6-6. This screen allows you to set parameters to control how the client operates within an infrastructure network.

Figure 6-6   *Advanced Infrastructure Settings*

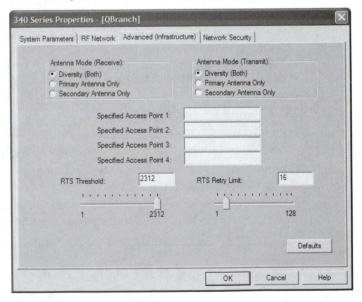

Table 6-4 describes the various parameters.

Table 6-4   *Advanced (Infrastructure) Parameters*

Parameter	Description
Antenna Mode (Receive)	Selects which antenna the client uses to receive data. The default setting uses "Diversity," which employs both antennas and is most effective, especially in environments where multipath distortion is an issue. Alternately, you can choose between the primary or secondary antennas. PCI card adapters must use only the Primary Antenna Only setting.
Antenna Mode (Transmit)	Selects which antenna the client uses to transmit data. You can select the primary, secondary, or both with the antenna's receive mode.
Specified Access Point 1-4	Identifies the MAC addresses of up to four preferred APs. If those APs are not available, the client can associate to another AP. It's best to use these settings for APs in repeater mode. For clients operating normally, these fields should be left blank because if you specify an AP, it slows the roaming process.
RTS Threshold	Sets the size of the data packet that the RF protocol issues to a request-to-send (RTS) packet. The lower this setting, the more RTS packets are sent and the more bandwidth is consumed. However, smaller values allow the system to recover faster from interference and collisions caused by multipath distortion or obstructions.
RTS Retry Limit	Specifies the number of times the client adapter resends the RTS packet if it does not receive a clear-to-send packet from previously sent RTS packets.

Advanced Ad Hoc Parameters

If you operate in Ad Hoc mode, the Advanced (Ad Hoc) tab looks similar to the one shown in Figure 6-7. However, there are two additional settings when you connect to an ad hoc network. Table 6-5 describes these settings.

Figure 6-7 *Advanced Ad Hoc Settings*

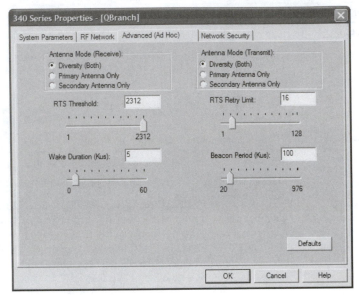

Table 6-5 *Advanced (Ad Hoc) Settings*

Parameter	Description
Wake Duration (Kµs)	Indicates the amount of time following a beacon that the client stays awake to receive announcement traffic indication messages (ATIM). ATIMs are used by the adapter to keep it awake until the next beacon. This parameter works in conjunction with the Power Save Mode parameter in Table 6-3. When the client adapter is in CAM mode, this setting is limited to 0 Kµs. In Max PSP or Fast PSP, this setting is between 5–60 Kµs.*
Beacon Period (Kµs)	Sets the duration of time between beacon packets.

*Kµs is a unit of time measurement. Where $K=1024$, $\mu=10^{-6}$, and s=seconds. Therefore, Kµs is short for 1.024 milliseconds.

Configuring Security

To configure encryption and security on your client, you use the Network Security screen, which is the fourth tab at the top of the ACU. The Network Security screen is shown in Figure 6-8; it allows you to manage the client adapter's security settings for connection with the AP, encryption, and authentication on the WLAN.

Figure 6-8   *The Network Security Screen Is Used to Configure Client Security Settings*

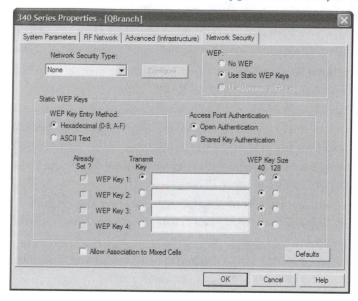

Unlike the preceding tabs, the Network Security tab contains many complicated steps. Before you make any changes to the client adapter's security settings, you must first decide how to set the Allow Association to Mixed Cells parameter, located at the bottom of the screen.

The Allow Association to Mixed Cells parameter is used to specify whether the client can associate to an AP, which allows both WEP and non-WEP association. Check the **Allow Association to Mixed Cells** box if the AP to which the client associates has WEP set to Optional and WEP is enabled on the client adapter. Clear the check box if the AP does not have WEP set to Optional.

Configuring WEP Keys

To configure WEP keys for a given profile, follow these steps:

Step 1.   Select **None** from the Network Security Type drop-down box in the Network Security screen.

Step 2.   Select **Use Static WEP Keys**.

Step 3.   Select one of the following WEP key formats:

- **Hexadecimal (0-9, A-F)**—WEP keys are entered in the hexadecimal format; that is, it is comprised of numbers 0–9 and letters A–F (upper- or lowercase).

- **ASCII Text**—WEP keys are entered in ASCII text, which includes characters, numbers, and punctuation marks.

Step 4.   Select an AP authentication option. This establishes how your client authenticates with the AP:

- **Open Authentication**—The client adapter is allowed to authenticate and communicate with the AP, regardless of WEP settings.

- **Shared Key Authentication**—The client adapter can communicate only with APs having the same WEP key.

Step 5.   Select a key size from the right side of the screen. Choices are 40 or 128 bits. Clients with 128-bit adapters can use either size key, but clients with 40-bit adapters can use only 40-bit keys.

Step 6.   Enter the WEP key in the field. You must adhere to key size and format. You can choose between two WEP key sizes:

- 40-bit keys contain 10 hexadecimal characters (for example, 1b2D3f1B2d) or 5 ASCII text characters (for example, JB0ND).

- 128-bit keys contain 26 hexadecimal characters (for example, 123abc456dEF123Abc321Cba78) or 13 ASCII text characters (for example, St@vR0bL0f31d).

NOTE: The client adapter's WEP key must match—exactly—the WEP key used by your AP or other clients when in ad hoc mode. Be mindful of capitalization and whether "0" or "o" are used.

Step 7.   Click the **Transmit Key** radio button to the left of the key you wish to use to transmit packets.

Step 8.   Click **OK** to return to the Profile Manager screen.

Step 9.   Click **OK** to save your settings.

Configuring 802.1X Authentication

Configuring 802.1X authentication is more complicated than the process to enable WEP keys. Not only are there configuration steps using the ACU, but Extensible Authentication Protocol-Transport Layer Security (EAP-TLS), Extensible Authentication Protocol-Message Digest algorithm 5 (EAP-MD5), Protected Extensible Authentication Protocol (PEAP), and Extensible Authentication Protocol-Subscriber Identity Module (EAP-SIM) authentication require configuration on your operating system. In addition, you cannot switch between these authentication modes if you change profiles. If you must change authentication methods, you have to enable the authentication type in Windows. Because Windows can be set up for one type of authentication at a time only, multiple authentication methods must be switched within

Windows after switching profiles in the ACU. You can use two 802.1x authentication methods with ACU:

- LEAP
- Host-based EAP

LEAP

To configure LEAP (also known as Cisco EAP) authentication on the client, follow these steps:

Step 1.   Select **LEAP** from the Network Security Type drop-down box located at the bottom of the Network Security screen.

Step 2.   Click **Configure**. Figure 6-9 shows the resulting LEAP Settings screen.

Figure 6-9   *Configuring LEAP Settings*

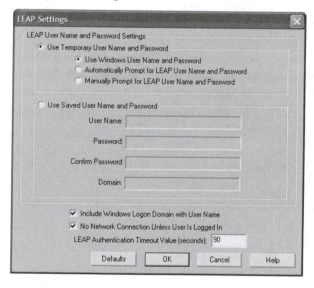

Step 3.   You are asked for a LEAP username and password settings option:

- **Use Temporary User Name and Password**—A username and password is required each time the computer reboots to authenticate to the network.

- **Use Saved User Name and Password**—A username and password are not required at each reboot. Instead, authentication occurs because it uses a saved username and password.

Step 4.   If you chose **Use Temporary User Name and Password** in Step 3, select one of these options (otherwise skip ahead to Step 5):

- **Use Windows User Name and Password**—The client's Windows username and password are also used as LEAP username and password. This is the default setting.

- **Automatically Prompt for LEAP User Name and Password**—A username and password distinct from the client's Windows username and password is used for authentication. This information is asked during the Windows login process.

- **Manually Prompt for LEAP User Name and Password**—The client must ask for LEAP authentication.

Step 5.   If you chose **Use Saved User Name and Password** in Step 3, follow these steps:

      a. Enter a username and password.

      b. Enter the password, again, in the Confirm Password field.

      c. If necessary, enter a domain name that is passed to the RADIUS server, along with the client's username in the Domain field.

Step 6.   If you are in an environment with multiple domains and you want your Windows login domain and username passed to the RADIUS server, check the **Include Windows Logon Domain with User Name** check box.

Step 7.   To force a disassociation after the client logs off, select the **No Network Connection Unless User Is Logged In** check box.

Step 8.   In the LEAP Authentication Timeout Value field, enter the amount of time (in seconds) the client waits before authentication is considered failed. This value is between 45 and 300 seconds.

Step 9.   Click **OK** to save changes and take you to the previous window.

Step 10.   Click **OK** to save changes and take you to the previous window.

Step 11.   Click **OK** to save changes and take you to the previous window.

Host-based EAP

To enable host-based EAP, follow these steps:

Step 1.   Select **Host Based EAP** from the Network Security Type drop-down box on the Network Security screen.

Step 2.   Depending on what type of EAP you plan to use, select one of the following from the radio buttons in the upper-right corner of the window shown in Figure 6-10:

- If you authenticate with EAP-TLS, PEAP, or EAP-SIM, select **Use Dynamic WEP Keys** under WEP.

- If you use EAP-MD5 with static WEP to authenticate, select **Use Static WEP Keys**. Next, enter a static WEP key as explained in the "Configuring WEP Keys" section of this chapter.

- If you use EAP-MD5 without WEP, select **No WEP** under WEP.

Figure 6-10 *Selecting WEP Options*

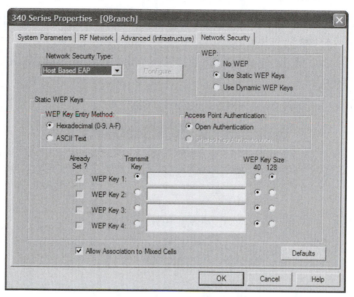

Step 3. Click **OK** to save changes and return to the previous window.

Step 4. Click **OK** to save changes and return to the previous window.

Configuring EAP in Windows

At this point, ACU cannot configure authentication on your client. You can mitigate this and configure authentication settings on the client's operating system.

Step 1. Do one of the following (make sure you know whether the client's operating system is Windows 2000 or Windows XP):

- Use the following process for Windows 2000 clients (the client must have Service Pack 3 and the Windows 2000 Wireless 802.1X hotfix):

  a. Follow **My Computer > Control Panel > Network > Dial-up Connections**.

  b. Right-click **Local Area Connection**.

    c. Click **Properties**, which brings up the Local Area Connection Properties screen.

- Use the following process for Windows XP clients:

    a. Follow **My Computer > Control Panel > Network Connections**.

    b. Right-click **Wireless Network Connection**.

    c. Click **Properties**, calling up the **Wireless Network Connection Properties** screen.

Step 4. Click the **Authentication** tab. The screen that appears is shown in Figure 6-11.

Figure 6-11   *Configuring Authentication Using Windows XP*

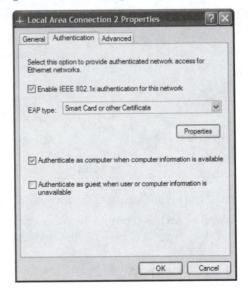

Step 5. Select the **Enable IEEE 802.1X Authentication for This Network** check box.

At this point, configuration branches off for each type of EAP authentication. EAP authentication methods include the following:

- EAP-TLS
- PEAP
- EAP-SIM

Perform the steps outlined in the following sections based on which EAP authentication method you use.

EAP-TLS

Follow these steps to select EAP-TLS as your authentication method:

Step 1. Under EAP type, select **Smart Card or Other Certificate**.

Step 2. Click **Properties**.

Step 3. From the Smart Card or Other Certificate Properties screen, select **Use a certificate on This Computer**.

Step 4. Check the **Validate server certificate** check box.

Step 5. Ensure that the name of the certificate authority (CA) from which the EAP-TLS certificate was downloaded is listed in the Trusted root certificate authority field.

Step 6. The check box next to the CA must be selected and the user or computer's certificate must be on the machine.

Step 7. Click **OK**.

PEAP

Follow these steps to select PEAP as your authentication method:

Step 1. Under EAP type, select **PEAP.**

Step 2. Click **Properties**.

Step 3. On the PEAP Properties screen, select the **Validate Server Certificate** check box if server certificate validation is required.

Step 4. Select the **Connect only if server name ends with** check box and enter the server name suffix in the text box.

Step 5. Ensure that the CA name from which you downloaded the server certificate is listed in the Trusted Root Certificate Authority field.

Step 6. Click **Properties**.

Step 7. On the Generic Token Card Properties screen, select either the **Static Password (Windows NT/2000, LDAP)** or the **One Time Password** option.

Step 8. If you chose One Time Password in Step 7, select one or both of the following check boxes:

- **Support Hardware Token**—The hardware token device obtains the one-time password.

- **Support Software Token**—The PEAP supplicant retrieves the one-time password.

Step 9. Click **OK**.

EAP-SIM

Follow these steps to select EAP-SIM as your authentication method:

Step 1. Under EAP type, select **SIM Authentication**.

Step 2. Click **Properties**.

Step 3. For access to resources on the SIM, the EAP-SIM supplicant must provide a valid PIN to the SIM card. To indicate how the EAP-SIM supplicant should handle the SIM card's PIN, select one of the following on the SIM Authentication Properties screen:

- Ask for my PIN once after I turn my computer on (recommended).

- Ask for my PIN every time the network asks for authentication.

- Let me give my PIN to the computer now and never ask me again; PIN will be encrypted and stored on computer (not recommended).

Step 4. Click **OK**.

Client configuration can seem like a lengthy process. However, if you understand the requirements of the client adapter and how you can configure by both the operating system and the ACU, it can be a straightforward process.

Chapter 7 Contents

Wireless and Wired LAN Integration Overview

Your wireless LAN (WLAN) becomes a component of your organization's existing wired LAN. Happily, integrating the WLAN into your wired LAN is straightforward. However, there are some issues to know when you bring the two together.

This chapter examines how to design and plan for your WLAN—topological considerations, integration tips, and how to configure roaming.

Wireless Network Design Considerations

To add a WLAN to your wired LAN requires you to think and plan before you affix access points (AP) to the ceiling and pass out wireless interfaces.

This section gives some guidelines when you consider the variables involved in your WLAN design and integration.

Establish Your Network's Size

The first step is to establish the size of your WLAN. There are three elements you must consider when you plan for the size of your network:

- The physical dimensions you plan to cover.
- The amount of stations that access the WLAN.
- The amount of bandwidth you need.

You must strike a balance between the amount of APs you deploy and their place-ment in relation to the amount of stations that access them. In general, about 25 stations can access a single AP. Consider the WLAN shown in Figure 7-1.

Figure 7-1 *Plan for the Physical Size of Your Network and the Amount of Stations that Access the WLAN*

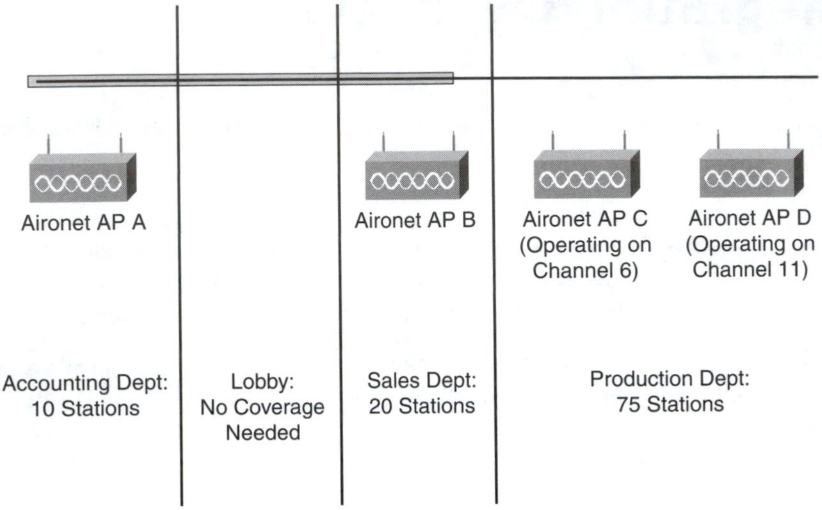

In this example, the organization is geographically dispersed and needs four APs to effectively cover its building. On the right side of the figure in the production area, 75 stations access the WLAN. Because of this, it is advisable to add a second AP. The sales and accounting departments are both served with one AP each.

A lobby area is in the middle section of the building; however, it's not an area where WLAN coverage is needed. Therefore, no AP is located in that area.

NOTE: If stations in the accounting department shown in Figure 7-1 were difficult to reach with Category 5 cabling, you could locate an AP in the lobby area simply to serve as a repeater.

Determining Bandwidth

You must also determine how much bandwidth your network requires. Pay special attention to the density of users, along with normal per-user bandwidth needs. For instance, if you locate an AP in a conference room, expect many users to try to access the AP on the same channel, so you want a smaller cell size. If you locate APs in a warehouse where there are fewer users and a large space, larger cells are best served with high-gain antennas.

Although it is necessary to know the number of users that use the AP, it's not the whole story. You must also factor in the bandwidth usage of your applications and how intense its use is. This is a hard number to quantify at the outset, and it's even more difficult to estimate for future applications. A good general rule of thumb: A single 802.11 channel can support up to 25 stations.

NOTE: Because there are so many factors at play with AP usage, WLANs are similar to wired LANs, and you must constantly keep on top of performance monitoring to find out if the WLAN is overburdened. Performance monitoring is covered in more depth in Chapter 12, "Network Tuning Tools and Resources."

You should also consider the number of IP addresses needed for wireless devices, and how to dole them out. If you don't have enough IP addresses to go around, you can take some away from your wired LAN.

Designing for Special Needs

When you design your WLAN, you must also take special needs and circumstances into consideration. There are numerous issues to balance, including your organization's needs, physical constraints, and antennas.

Organizational Needs

First, you must take into account your organization's needs. That is, if there is a department or a section of the building that does not need WLAN coverage, don't worry about whether a signal propagates in that area. By the same token, if there are areas where you do not *want* coverage (for instance, maybe you don't want your WLAN signal to radiate outside the building), you need to think about that, too. The signal might still radiate outside the building, but to minimize that propagation is helpful. Of course, this isn't a foolproof means of security, but it is one more weapon in your security arsenal.

For example, Figure 7-2 shows a campus set up. In this example, coverage is needed in both buildings. Although it would be nice for the employees to access the WLAN from the courtyard, it poses a point of access for potential attackers. Because of this, you do not want coverage in that area.

Figure 7-2 *Think About Where You Want Coverage and Where You Don't Want It*

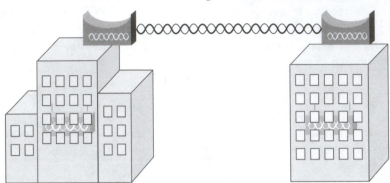

Physical Constraints

Next, consider the physical demands of your area. Perform a site survey to know what sort of range you can get from your equipment and where you need extra APs or antennas.

If you determine exactly where to place APs for your respective cells, you can save a lot of time. First start with a copy of your building plans to make some preliminary estimates about coverage, based on distances and the office layout. (The presence of cubicles versus closed offices has an impact on range.) Whenever possible, locate your APs as close to your users as possible. Don't just draw coffee coaster circles on your map; think about where you need coverage.

After you determine on paper where to place the APs, put your site survey skills to work. As you perform the site survey (flip back to Chapter 5, "Installing and Configuring Access Points," for more information on site surveys), you might also consider where you can run Ethernet cabling. Although APs can communicate with each other to extend the range of your WLAN, you still need to supply power to those devices. As such, you might consider APs that support power over Ethernet (PoE). Not only can you supply power to your APs, but you can also have a hardwired connection to the backbone to have a more reliable connection.

Antennas

It is necessary to plan for antennas (which are discussed in Chapter 2, "Cisco Antennas"). Because most APs come equipped with omnidirectional antennas, the antenna broadcasts in a complete circle (three dimensionally, resembling a donut shape) around the antenna. This is great for cells in the middle of your office, but if the antenna is located in the corner of the room, the signal radiates into the wall, neighboring offices, or the parking lot.

NOTE: Also consider the alignment of your antenna and the three-dimensional world. If your antenna is positioned in such a way, it might radiate the signal through the ceiling or floor.

If you locate an antenna against a wall or in a corner, consider a directional antenna — it not only reduces the signal's radiation into the neighboring lawyer's office, but it gets better range.

Design Checklist

When you design your WLAN, use the following checklists to consider the special needs described in this section.

Organizational Needs:

❑ Where do you need coverage?

❑ Where don't you want coverage?

❑ Where are the most stations located?

❑ Are there any areas that have more stations than a single AP can handle?

❑ How many IP addresses will your wireless solution need?

Physical Considerations:

❑ Have you performed a site survey?

❑ Are there sources of RF interference, such as the following:

— Microwave ovens

— Other radios broadcasting on your channel(s)

— Photocopiers

— Bluetooth devices

— Cordless phones

— Wireless surveillance cameras

❑ Which types of antennas are best for your organization?

❑ Do you have enough Category 5 cabling already in place to service new APs?

Antennas:

❑ Will you place the antenna(s) in the middle of your clients? If so, omnidirectional antennas are needed.

❑ Will you place the antennas next to a wall? If so, consider directional antennas.

❑ Will you locate APs on adjacent floors? If so, consider how APs on a neighboring floor would interfere with each other. That is, position the antennas so interference is minimized.

Topologies

If you had occasion to design a wired LAN, you know the issues involved when you design the topology of that network. You need to strike a balance to provide both the services and the throughput users need. With a WLAN, not only must you take the issues involved in a wireless network to heart, but you must also add the considerations of an 802.11 deployment.

After you design the physical topology, you must decide which wireless channels to use, along with their placement throughout your organization.

WLAN Topologies

There are two basic topology designs involved in a WLAN: ad hoc and infrastructure. You are more apt to see and use an infrastructure topology in your WLAN deployments, but it's useful to understand ad hoc and how it could be used in your own organization.

Ad Hoc

The most elementary topology is known as an ad-hoc topology. In this design, two or more devices link together, without the need for an AP. This sort of topology is useful not only when coworkers meet in a remote location and want to share files, but also in environments in which networking is desired, but in which you cannot run cabling. For example, disaster workers don't have time to set up network infrastructure when they show up on scene. The downside to an ad-hoc topology is that users do not have access to the network and its resources.

Ad-hoc networks are also difficult to troubleshoot. You cannot check the association status of all clients as you can with an AP.

Infrastructure

The more common type of topology that allows access to wired network resources is the infrastructure topology. In this topology, APs are added to a switch, which provides connectivity to wireless stations.

Figure 7-3 shows an example of an infrastructure topology.

Figure 7-3 *Infrastructure Topology*

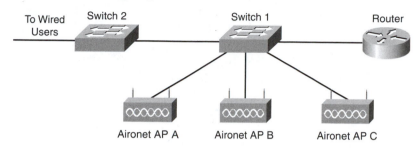

In this example, an AP backbone is added to the rest of the wired network.

Bridge Topologies

Typically, you can connect two devices to link bridges or you can link one bridge to multiple bridges. However, there's another topology you might consider when you deploy your own bridging solution.

The spanning-tree topology provides path redundancy and prevents network loops. When you use the spanning-tree algorithm, a loop-free path is computed within a layer 2 network. Bridges and switches send and receive regular bridge protocol data units (BPDU). These messages are used to construct a loop-free path. A loop in a network can cause duplicate messages and network instability.

Spanning-tree blocks redundant paths. If a network segment in the spanning-tree fails, the spanning-tree algorithm calculates the spanning-tree topology and activates the next path.

Figure 7-4 shows an example of the spanning-tree topology. In this example, Bridge D is elected as the spanning-tree root, which is the central bridge in the spanning-tree topology. This is because it was given a higher priority than the other bridges.

Figure 7-4 *Spanning-Tree Topology*

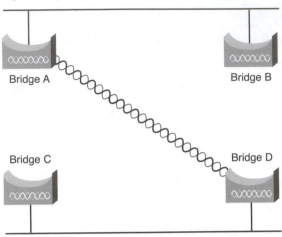

NOTE: If all the bridges have the same priority, the bridge with the lowest MAC address is elected as the spanning-tree root.

Channel Setup

When you think about an AP's range, you might think that "farther is better." That's not necessarily true. In some cases you might want a shorter range so that you can reuse channels. Also, a smaller cell size allows fewer users per AP, so you wind up with greater throughput. In a station-dense part of your organization, you can have three APs, each operating on a nonoverlapping channel.

In the United States, the 802.11b and 802.11g spectrum is divided into 11 channels. Ideally, when you place cells next to one another, you want neighboring cells at least five channels apart. Figure 7-5 shows a cellular layout that uses channels 1, 6, and 11.

Figure 7-5 *Channel Layout for Multiple Cells*

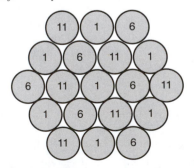

Channel layout is easy enough to do on paper, but reality is harder. You have to factor in the real range afforded by your environment, as well as the realities of a three-dimensional world. An AP on channel 6 on the third floor might interfere with an AP on channel 6 on the second floor.

NOTE: One way to avoid channel overlapping with 802.11b and 802.11g is to use an 802.11a solution. 802.11a offers 23 nonoverlapping channels. If you add 802.11a cells it's a little easier, because you can choose from more channels, and they don't overlap as much as 802.11b and 802.11g cells.

Integration Issues

When you design your WLAN, you must determine how it will fit in with your existing, wired LAN. This is an issue both of technology and your organization's policies.

Security Planning

First, you must establish a security plan, and then determine how to connect the APs into your existing LAN switches, with special attention paid to IP address management and application roaming.

Security plans must address:

- Authentication
- Privacy
- Access control
- Accounting

Your LAN's construction and its capabilities largely determine how you connect your WLAN to the existing LAN.

Virtual LANs

If your switches are powerful enough and have the bandwidth to spare, you might establish a virtual LAN (VLAN) for wireless users. You can establish a VLAN to handle address assignment and establish security policies for wireless users. For example, at a school, you might assign students to a VLAN with restricted access to the network, although faculty and staff would be on a VLAN with more privileges and access.

The best part of a VLAN solution, however, is that it improves one of the toughest parts of WLAN design: how to manage roaming users.

For the most part, clients should be able to move between subnets with little or no interruption. However, if disconnects are encountered, the problem can be fixed if clients restart their machines (if they've turned them off to move from one building to the next, for example) or renew their DHCP leases.

Using Cisco Equipment with Third-Party Vendors

If you use a pure Cisco environment, problems with connectivity and interoperability are rare, if ever. However, the risk increases as you consider working in a mixed environment. That is, if you use different equipment from different vendors.

If you use equipment from different vendors, standards come into play. Always check equipment before you buy it to ensure that it is compatible with your other gear. Even though a piece of equipment advertises itself as being a wireless device, with the huge popularity in wireless networking in recent years, companies have been eager to produce their products ahead of standardized protocols. Rather than wait for the protocols to develop, many vendors create their own proprietary protocols that simply don't work with other vendors' equipment.

One way you can avoid this problem and ensure equipment is compatible with your Cisco equipment is to buy third-party products that have been approved as part of the Cisco Compatible Extensions (CCX) program. As mentioned in Chapter 1, "Cisco Wireless Equipment," this program allows vendors to develop their own equipment, ensure compatibility with Cisco equipment, and be certified as such. Testing is performed by an independent party to ensure that it's impartial.

Integration Checklist

When you design your WLAN, consider the following points:

- ❏ How will the WLAN fit in with your existing security plan?
- ❏ Will the WLAN use a VLAN? Are existing switches VLAN-capable?
- ❏ Will your wireless equipment work together? Does the equipment comply with current industry standards?
- ❏ Is non Cisco equipment CCX-compatible?

Connecting Your Network

Happily, to connect an AP or AP backbone to your existing network, you need some infrastructure that you might already have in place. You can tap this to help with your wireless endeavors.

This section explains how you can use existing equipment, such as Dynamic Host Configuration Protocol (DHCP) and Remote Authentication Dial-In User Service (RADIUS) servers, to augment your AP's functionality.

Address Management

IP address management for your integrated network should be straightforward, but can be a chore if you do not have a DHCP server.

If you have a DHCP server already connected to your wired network, simply connect your APs, and they automatically assign IP addresses, as does any stations that connect to the AP.

During initial configuration of your Cisco AP, there is a screen that allows you to choose whether to use your network's DHCP server, or assign IP addresses automatically. You don't need a DHCP server; however, it will make your life a whole lot easier, especially if you have a big network that's getting even bigger.

If you select to have a DHCP server manage IP addresses, the server automatically assigns an IP address to the AP. If you opt to manually manage your own IP addresses, you are asked to enter the following, as shown in Figure 7-6:

- IP address
- IP subnet mask
- Default gateway

Figure 7-6 *IP Address Information on a Cisco 1130AG AP*

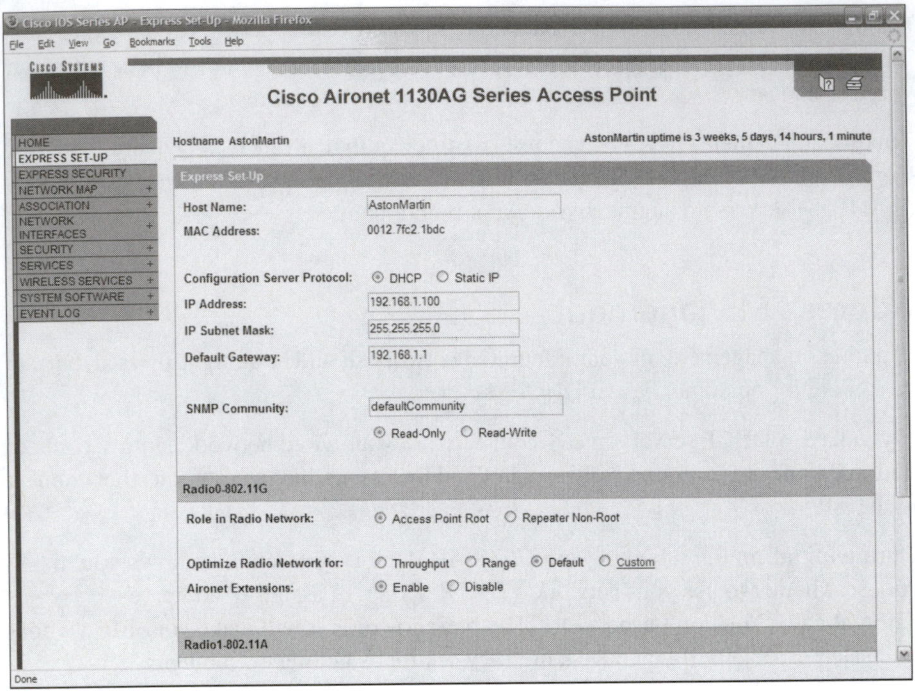

NOTE: Many APs include a built-in DHCP server. As such, DHCP features are managed on the AP, itself.

A word of caution—If you use multiple APs, all with DHCP servers, it's a bad idea to use the feature on all them. Unless you are meticulous about giving IP address ranges, it is likely that the APs will assign the same addresses to different stations on your WLAN, wreaking havoc. If you have multiple APs that are DHCP-capable, it's a better idea to shut off the APs' DHCP feature and use a centralized DHCP server.

Refer to Figure 7-7, which shows a sample WLAN integrated with a wired LAN. There are two places best to locate a DHCP server:

- On the AP backbone subnet. This server is responsible for wireless stations on the wireless subnet.

- Routers usually include DHCP relay. You can configure the router shown in Figure 7-7 with DHCP relay, and then IP address requests can forward through the network to the main DHCP server.

Figure 7-7   *Integrating a WLAN into a Wired LAN*

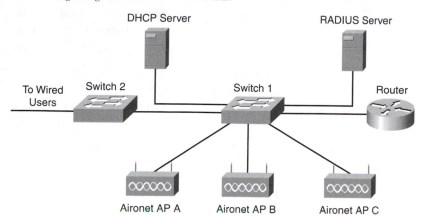

Access Control

To manage access to your WLAN, you need a strong way to authenticate users. As you remember from the discussion about 802.1X and EAP authentication in Chapter 4, "Wireless Security," if you connect your AP to a network with a RADIUS server, you provide excellent security for your wireless network.

You might already have a RADIUS server at the core of your network. If so, to configure your APs and the RADIUS server to work together is a straightforward task. The process of connecting to a RADIUS server is explained in more depth in Chapter 8, "Wireless Security: Next Steps." However, here's a brief overview of the process:

1. On the AP, identify the authentication server, and then establish a relationship with it.

2. The AP must be defined on the RADIUS as a AAA client.

3. Specify the type of authentication performed (Network EAP and OPEN with EAP or other versions of EAP).

Roaming

The ability to wirelessly connect to the network provides a wonderful freedom for mobile users. Users can move to different locations in a building or different locations on a campus and still access the network. This freedom comes in two forms: portability and mobility.

Portability is the act of being able to access the network from anyplace in the organization. That is, if he opens his laptop in the break room and is able to connect, he has portability. The important element here is that the user has moved from one cell to another and isn't concerned with constant coverage.

Mobility, on the other hand, is concerned with constant coverage. Consider the nurse who is using a wireless IP phone at a hospital. As she moves between cells, she cannot restart the phone to get access to the new cell. She needs to roam freely.

Cisco enables roaming via its fast, secure roaming technology. This section describes fast, secure roaming and configuring APs for roaming clients.

Fast, Secure Roaming

When stations move between APs, it is necessary to reauthenticate the devices to the AP. Obviously, if someone is using latency-sensitive applications (such as a nurse, for example), the time it takes to reauthenticate becomes troublesome.

Fast, secure roaming allows LEAP-enabled clients to roam between APs without the need to bother the server. Rather, Cisco Centralized Key Management (CCKM) is used on an AP, which is set up to provide Wireless Domain Services (WDS).

NOTE: WDS is a collection of IOS software features for such tasks as enhancing WLAN mobility as well as radio management and client tracking.

CCKM allows the authentication to occur quickly, and bypasses the authentication server. Figure 7-8 shows this process.

The WDS device keeps a list of credentials for CCKM clients that are part of the WLAN. When a station roams into the AP's service area, the station sends a reassociation request to the AP, which is then forwarded to the WDS device. After authenticated by the WDS, the WDS forwards the information to the AP, which then allows the connection. This seems like a lengthy process, but only two packets are sent between the station and the AP.

Figure 7-8   *Roaming Is Seamless with WDS*

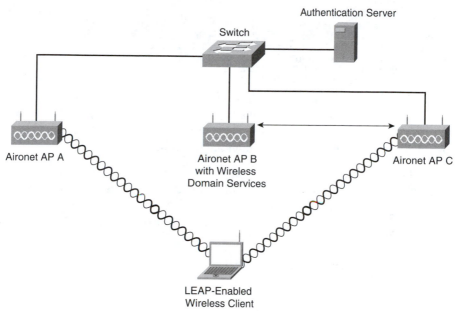

LEAP-Enabled
Wireless Client

Configuring WDS

The following steps show the command-line interface (CLI) instructions that you can issue to your AP to configure it as a WDS AP:

Step 1.   Configure your APs or switches as WDS devices.

Step 2.   Configure your APs to use the WDS device.

Step 3.   Enable Layer 3 Mobility to an SSID.

Step 4.   Configure the authentication server to support fast, secure roaming.

You must begin in Privileged Exec mode on the AP that you wish to configure.

Step 1: Configure Your APs or Switches as WDS Devices

You can enable WDS on either the WLSM-enabled switch or the AP. When you set up WDS on an AP, here are some tips to keep in mind:

- If you use an AP as the WDS device, disable the radio or use an AP that serves a small volume of clients. Client devices that associate to the WDS AP when it starts might take several minutes to authenticate.

- If the WDS AP serves client devices, it can serve 30 other APs. However, if the radio is disabled, it can serve up to 60 APs.

- APs that serve as repeaters cannot be used as WDS devices.

Use the following command-line instructions to configure APs as WDS devices.

```
AP# configure terminal
AP(config)# aaa new-model
AP(config)# wlccp wds priority 200 interface bvi1
AP(config)# wlccp authentication-server infrastructure MI5
AP(config)# wlccp authentication-server client any fieldops
AP(config-wlccp-auth)# ssid FelixLeiter
AP(config-wlccp-auth)# ssid Quarrel
AP(config)# end
```

This series of instructions specifies that infrastructure devices are authenticated from server group MI5. CCKM-enabled clients that use the SSIDs of FelixLeiter and Quarrel are authenticated with the server group fieldops.

The third line of code requires some explanation. Priority 200 is used to set the priority of this WDS candidate. You can configure multiple APs as WDS candidates, and when the candidate with the highest priority is taken out of service, the candidate with the next highest priority is elected. This number is a value between 1 and 255.

The fifth line allows you to specify what type of authentication to use. In this case, **any** has been specified. However, you could also put in EAP or LEAP, or specify your own list of authentication methods.

Step 2: Configure Your APs to Use the WDS Device

Next, you must configure the APs to use the WDS device. To do this, see the following instructions:

```
AP# configure terminal
AP(config)# wlccp ap wds ip address 10.10.10.1
AP(config)# wlccp ap username JamesBond password 7 a$t1nm@rt1n
AP(config)# end
```

Here, the AP is configured to authenticate with a specific WDS-enabled device, and it uses the username JamesBond and the password a$t1nm@rt1n. The 7 before the password means that the AP's password is encrypted. This value could be set to 0, and means the password is unencrypted.

You must use the same username and password on the AP as a client to the authentication server.

Step 3: Enable Layer 3 Mobility to an SSID

The next step is to map an SSID to a specific mobility network ID. Follow these commands:

```
AP# configure terminal
AP(config)# interface dot11radio 0
AP(config-if)# ssid MobileNet
AP(config-if-ssid)# mobility network-id 7
AP(config-if-ssid)# end
```

Here, the SSID MobileNet is mapped to mobility network ID 7.

Step 4: Configure the Authentication Server to Support Fast, Secure Roaming

Though the action seems to take place between the clients and the APs, don't forget that your WDS device and APs must also authenticate to the authentication server. Set up the server with usernames and passwords for the APs, along with username and password for the WDS device.

Your authentication server is similar to Access Control Server (ACS) (though the AP can also act as an authentication server for up to 50 clients), and it requires you to log into ACS, and then add the name, password, and IP address of each WDS device candidate.

You would also create user entries and passwords for the APs that use the WDS candidates.

Other Resources

- **Tech Republic article and tool to assess future bandwidth needs (a free membership is required to access this article):**

  http://techrepublic.com.com/5100-6313_11-5206594.html

- **More about power over Ethernet:**

  http://www.poweroverethernet.com

- **How users share 802.11 channels:**

  http://www.nwfusion.com/newsletters/wireless/2003/0929wireless2.html

- **Cisco Aironet AP EAP Authentication with a RADIUS Server:**

  http://www.cisco.com/en/US/products/hw/wireless/ps4570/
  products_configuration_example09186a00801bd035.shtml

Chapter 8 Contents

Wireless Security: Next Steps

Although a lot of attention is given to security on a wired network, the issue is somewhat different in a wireless LAN (WLAN) because of the nature of the network medium. These issues can be addressed using a handful of tools and techniques available to you through your access point (AP), clients, and RADIUS server.

This chapter covers security measures that you might implement beyond Wired Equivalent Privacy (WEP) keys and strong passwords.

Filtering

Managing access to a WLAN through WEP keys or authentication is one viable security measure. You can also configure access to be restricted according to device; to do this, you use the Media Access Control (MAC) address or Internet Protocol (IP) address. For example, you can employ filtering on your APs to keep out clients who do not have an authorized client adapter. Without an explicitly approved MAC address on the network adapter, it doesn't matter if the correct username and password are presented because the AP does not allow access.

Simply put, filtering checks a wireless client's MAC or IP address against a list of authorized MAC or IP addresses maintained on the AP. When a client tries to connect to the AP, it must be on the list. If it is not, the client cannot connect.

Filtering should not be the only security measure, however. Both MAC and IP addresses can be spoofed, thus circumventing this layer of security.

MAC Filtering

You can set up a MAC filter two ways:

- To pass traffic to and from all MAC addresses except those you specify.
- To block traffic to and from all MAC addresses except those you specify.

Furthermore, you can apply these filters to either or both the Ethernet and radio ports and to incoming or outgoing traffic.

NOTE: Be careful when setting MAC filters. If you incorrectly apply the setting, you can easily lock yourself out of the AP. If this does occur, use the command-line interface (CLI) to disable filters, and then go in and correct your mistake.

MAC filters are managed on the MAC Address Filters page (see Figure 8-1); simply follow these steps:

Step 1. On the AP's web page, click **Services** on the menu to the left of the page.

Step 2. Click **Filters** in the list of services.

Step 3. Click the **Mac Address Filters** tab on the Apply Filters page.

Figure 8-1 *MAC Address Filters Page*

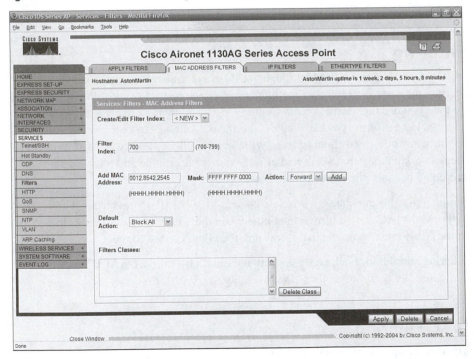

After you reach the Apply Filters page, you can enable MAC address filters.

NOTE: Be aware that software often changes. The version of the AP firmware you use might differ from what is shown here, but the steps are similar.

Setting MAC Filters

To configure a MAC filter, follow these steps:

Step 1.   To create a new MAC address filter, click **Create > Edit Filter Index > <NEW>**. To edit a filter, select the filter number from the menu.

Step 2.   In the Filter Index field, identify the filter with a number between 700 and 799. This number is used to assign an access control list (ACL) for the filter.

Step 3.   Enter a MAC address in the Add MAC Address field. The address is entered as three groups of four characters, separated by periods (for example, 0125.4275.7879).

Step 4.   Use of the Mask entry field enables the filter to check against certain bits, but not others. For example, if you have several clients whose MAC addresses all end in the same four bits, you can use the mask to allow any clients whose MAC address matches those four bits. If you want to force an exact match of the MAC address, in the Mask entry field, enter **FFFF.FFFF.FFFF**. If you just want to check the last four bits, enter **FFFF.FFFF.0000**.

Step 5.   Choose **Action > Forward** or choose **Action > Block**.

Step 6.   Click **Add**. The MAC address you entered has been added to the Filters Classes field. You can remove this address by selecting it and clicking **Delete Class**.

Step 7.   Choose **Default Action > Forward All** or **Default Action > Block All**. You must establish the default action for this filter, and it must be the opposite of the action for at least one of the MAC addresses in the filter. For example, if you chose **Forward** for several MAC addresses, you should select **Block All** as the filter's default action.

Step 8.   Click **Apply**.

Step 9.   Click the **Apply Filters** tab. This is shown in Figure 8-2.

Figure 8-2 *Apply Filters Tab*

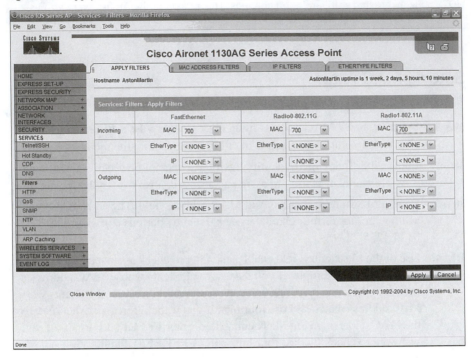

Step 10. Select the filter number from one of the MAC drop-down menus. The filter can be applied to either the Ethernet port, the radio ports, or both. You can also apply the filter to incoming traffic, outgoing traffic, or both.

Step 11. Click **Apply**.

NOTE: You need to restart the system, so that all clients are appropriately filtered.

IP Filtering

You can also limit access to your AP with IP filters. IP filtering can be applied based on IP address, IP protocol, and IP port. This allows or prevents the use of specific protocols through the AP's Ethernet and radio ports. Like MAC filtering, you can also set up the filter to allow or deny sending or receiving traffic from the AP based on IP address. You can set up IP filters to allow combinations of all three IP filtering components (address, protocol, and port).

IP filters are managed on the IP Filters page, shown in Figure 8-3.

Figure 8-3 *IP Filters Page*

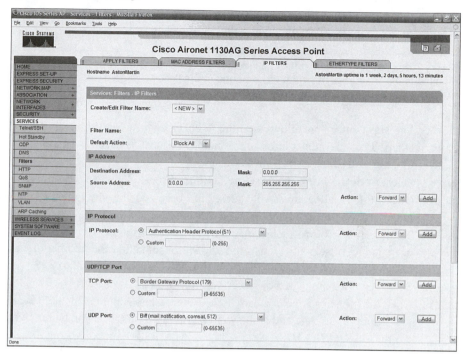

To reach the IP Filters page, follow these steps:

Step 1. On the AP's web page, click **Services** on the menu to the left of the page.

Step 2. Click **Filters** in the list of services.

Step 3. Click the **IP Filters** tab.

After you reach this page, you can enable IP filters.

Setting IP Filters

To configure an IP address filter, follow these steps:

Step 1. To create a new IP address filter, select **Create > Edit Filter Index > <New>**. To edit a filter, select the filter number from the menu.

Step 2. In the Filter Name field, identify the filter with a name.

Step 3. Select **Default Action > Forward All** or **Default Action > Block All** from the Default Action. You must establish the default action for this filter and it must be the opposite of the action for at least one of the IP filters. For example, if you chose **Forward** for several IP addresses, you should select **Block All** as the filter's default action.

Step 4. To filter a specific IP address, enter that address under the IP Address section. The Destination Address field is used to filter traffic going to an address; the Source Address filters filter traffic coming from a given IP address.

NOTE: If you intend to block traffic to all IP addresses except those specified, make sure you include the IP address of your own computer in the list of specified exceptions; otherwise, your computer is shut out from the AP.

Step 5. The Mask entry field allows the filter to check against certain bits, but not others. Type the subnet mask in this field. The mask is used if you are filtering everything to or from a subnet.

Step 6. Select **Action > Forward** or select **Action > Block**.

Step 7. Click **Add**. The IP address you entered has been added to the Filters Classes field. This address can be removed if you select it and click **Delete Class**.

Step 8. To filter an IP protocol, select one of the protocols from the IP protocol drop-down menu, or select the **Custom** radio button and enter the number of an existing ACL in the Custom field. Enter an ACL number from 0 to 255.

Step 9. Select **Action > Forward** or select **Action > Block**.

Step 10. Click **Add**. The protocol appears in the Filters Classes field. This field is at the bottom of the page and is shown in Figure 8-4. This filter can be removed if you click **Delete Class**.

Figure 8-4 *IP Filters Page with Filters Classes Field*

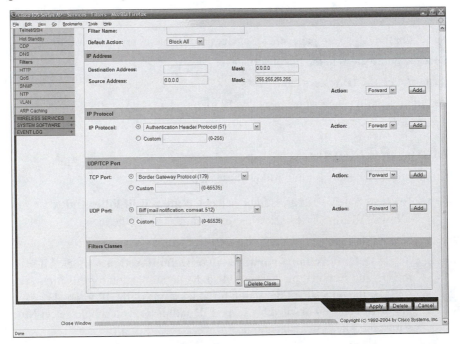

Step 11. To filter a TCP or UDP port protocol, select one of the common port protocols from the TCP Port or UDP Port drop-down menus, or you can select the
Custom radio button and enter the number of an existing protocol in one of
the Custom fields. Enter a protocol number from 0 to 65535.

Step 12. Select **Action > Forward** or select **Action > Block**.

Step 13. Click **Add**. The protocol appears in the Filters Classes field. This filter can
be removed if you click **Delete Class**.

Step 14. Click **Apply**.

Step 15. Click the **Apply Filters** tab.

Step 16. Select the filter names from one of the IP drop-down menus. The filter can be
applied to the Ethernet port, the radio ports, or both. You can also apply the
filter to incoming traffic, outgoing traffic, or both.

Step 17. Click **Apply**.

WPA

As noted in Chapter 4, "Wireless Security," Wi-Fi Protected Access (WPA) is the
replacement for WEP. It uses keys that automatically change, which enhances WEP.

First, open the Encryption Manager from the AP's home page (**Security > Encryption
Manager**) shown in Figure 8-5.

Figure 8-5 *The Encryption Manager Page Is Used to Manage WPA Settings*

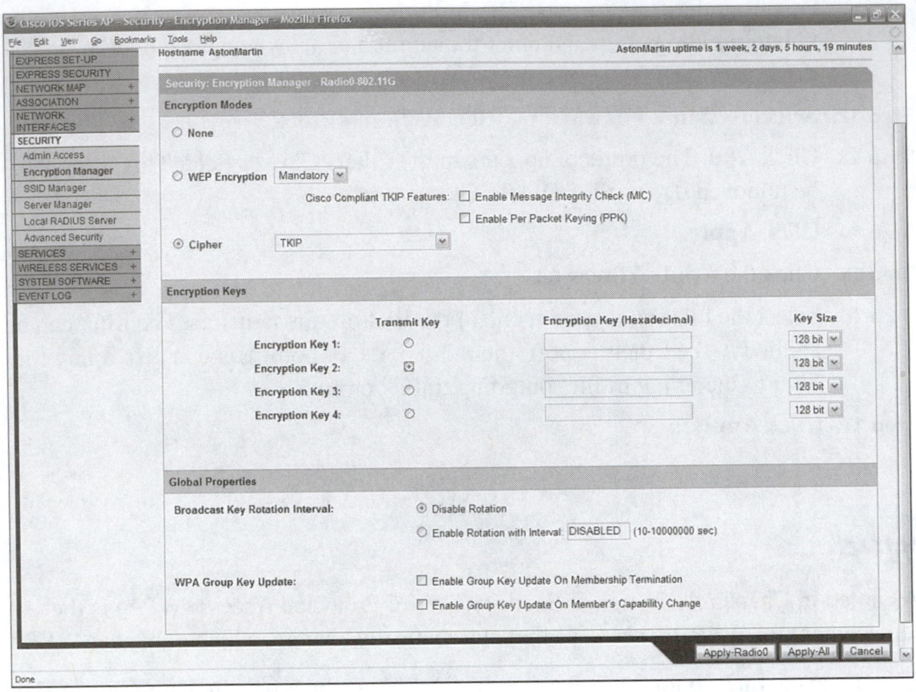

NOTE: This configuration assumes that you have a working LEAP, EAP, or PEAP configuration.

To configure WPA settings, follow these steps:

Step 1. Select the radio button next to Cipher and select **TKIP** from the drop-down menu.

Step 2. Clear the encryption key in Key 1.

Step 3. Enable Encryption Key 2 as the transmit key by selecting the **Transmit Key** radio button next to Encryption Key 2.

Step 4. Click the **Apply-Radio#** button.

Step 5. Next, you must set up the SSID manager. On the leftmost menu under SECURITY, select **SSID Manager** to bring up the screen shown in Figure 8-6.

Figure 8-6   *Making WPA Settings on the SSID Manager Page*

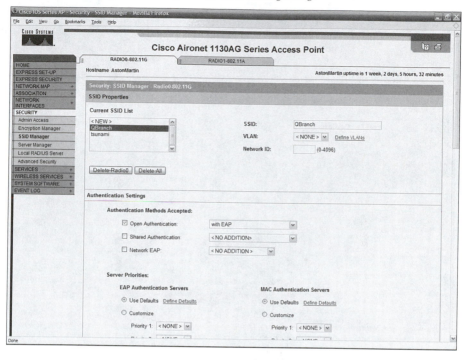

Step 6.   Select the appropriate SSID from Current SSID List.

Step 7.   Select the authentication method based on what type of clients you use. Use the authentication method listing in Table 8-1.

Table 8-1   *Select an Authentication Method Based on Your Clients*

Type of Clients	Authentication Method
Cisco clients	Use Network-EAP
Third-party clients, including Cisco Compatible Extension (CCX) clients	Use Open Authentication with EAP
Both Cisco and third-party clients	Use both Network-EAP and Open Authentication with EAP

NOTE: If EAP worked before you added WPA, you should not need to change this setting.

Step 8.   Under Authenticated Key Management, choose **Mandatory** from the drop-down menu, and then check the box to choose WPA. This is shown in Figure 8-7.

Figure 8-7   *Making Authentication Key Management Settings on the SSID Manager Page*

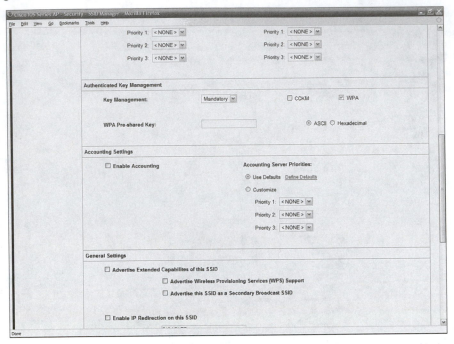

Figure 8-8   *Applying Settings on the SSID Manager Page*

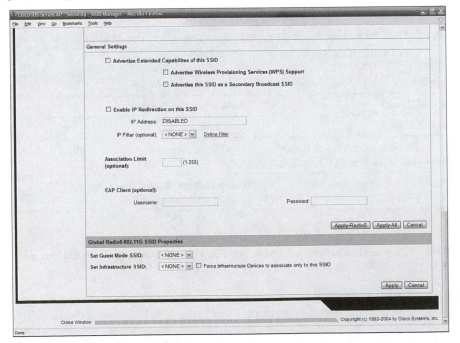

Step 9.   Click **Apply-Radio#**, as shown in Figure 8-8.

You can verify your WPA configuration if you click **Association** from the leftmost menu on the AP's homepage, and click the client's MAC address. Under Key Management, you can see if WPA has been properly enabled and if TKIP is used.

Connecting to a RADIUS Server

When you configure 802.1X authentication methods, the process requires three steps:

Step 1.   You must configure the AP to access the Remote Authentication Dial-In User Service (RADIUS) server.

Step 2.   You must configure the RADIUS server to use 802.1X.

Step 3.   You must configure the AP to use 802.1X authentication.

The sections that follow show how to make these configurations.

Configuring the AP for RADIUS Connection

The AP must be configured to connect to the appropriate RADIUS server. Open the Server Manager tab on the AP (this is done by following **Security > Server Manager**). Figure 8-9 shows the resulting Server Manager page.

Figure 8-9   *Configuring the RADIUS Server on the Server Manager Page*

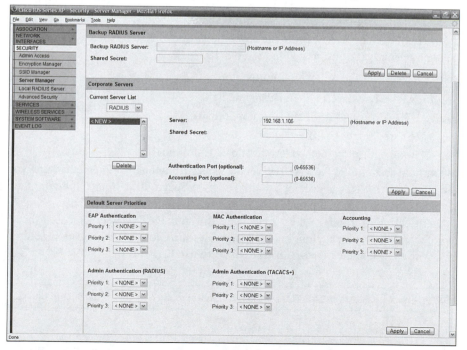

On this page, do the following:

Step 1. Enter the IP address of the authentication server in the Server field.

Step 2. Enter the shared secret password in the Shared Secret field.

Step 3. Enter the ports in the Authentication Port and Accounting Port fields (optional).

Step 4. Click **Apply**.

Step 5. Under Default Server Priorities, set the Priority 1 field under EAP Authentication to the RADIUS server's address. Click **Apply**.

Alternately, you can make this configuration from the command-line interface if you use the following commands:

```
AP# configure terminal
AP(config)# aaa group server radius rad_eap
AP(config-sg-radius)# server 192.168.1.105 auth-port 1630 acct-port 1631
AP(config-sg-radius)# exit
AP(config)# aaa new-model
AP(config)# aaa authentication login eap_methods group rad_eap
AP(config)# radius-server host 192.168.1.105 auth-port 1630 acct-port 1631
    key w@1th3r99k
AP(config)# end
AP# copy running-config startup-config
```

Configuring the RADIUS Server

The second step in connecting to a RADIUS server is to configure the RADIUS server to use the AP as an AAA client. The example in this section uses Cisco Secure ACS as the RADIUS server. If you use a different RADIUS server, you should refer to the server's documentation.

Setting up the AP as an AAA client in Cisco Secure ACS is done on the Network Configuration page, as illustrated in Figure 8-10.

On this page, enter the following information:

Step 1. AP's name (AAA Client Hostname field)

Step 2. IP address (AAA Client IP Address field)

Step 3. Shared secret key (Key field)

Step 4. Authentication method (Authenticate Using field)

You must also configure the RADIUS server to use the authentication method that you select for the AP. You can accomplish this in Cisco Secure ACS if you configure the Global Authentication Setup page (click **System Configuration > Global Authentication Method**). Again, if you use a different RADIUS server, check the manufacturer's documentation. Figure 8-11 shows the Global Authentication Setup page with the authentication server configured to use EAP-TLS.

NOTE: Enabling PEAP or EAP-TLS requires the installation of a server certificate on ACS.

Figure 8-10 *Configuring Cisco Secure ACS to Use the AP as a Client*

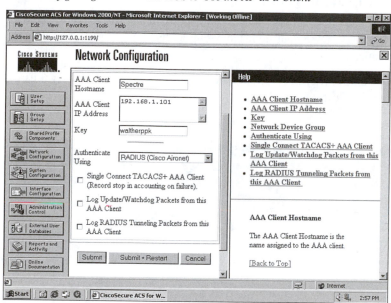

Figure 8-11 *Enabling EAP Authentication Methods on Cisco Secure ACS*

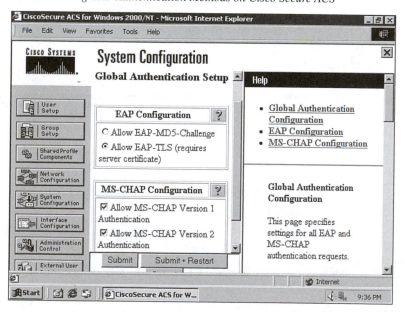

Defining Authentication

After the RADIUS server and the AP know they can talk to each other to share authentication data, the final step is to configure the AP to actually use 802.1X authentication methods.

First, open the Security Encryption Manager on the AP (select **Security > Encryption Manager**), as illustrated in Figure 8-12.

Figure 8-12 *Setting Up the AP to Use EAP*

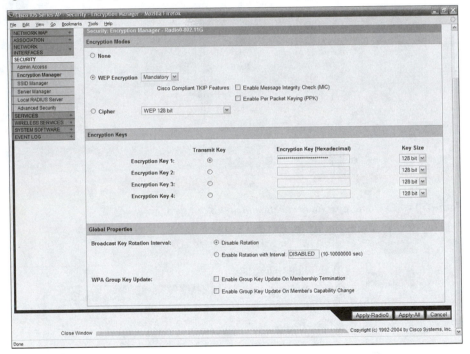

Next, do the following:

Step 1. Under the Encryption Modes section, check the **WEP Encryption** button and select **Mandatory** from the drop-down menu.

Step 2. Under the Encryption keys section, make sure the key size is set to **128 bit**.

Step 3. Click **Apply**.

You can also apply these settings from the CLI using the following commands:

```
AP# configure terminal
AP(config)# interface dot11radio 0
AP(config-if)# encryption mode wep mandatory
AP(config-if)# end
AP# write memory
```

The next settings are made on the AP SSID Manager tab (**Security > SSID Manager**), as illustrated in Figure 8-13.

Figure 8-13 *EAP Configuration Steps on the SSID Manager Page*

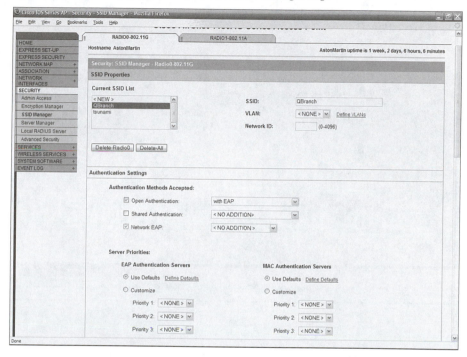

Enter the following settings:

Step 1.   Enter the SSID under SSID Properties. (Refer back to Figure 8-9.)

Step 2.   Under Authentication Methods Accepted, check the box labeled **Open Authentication**, and then select **with EAP** from the drop-down box.

Step 3.   Check the box labeled **Network EAP** if you have Cisco client adapters. Refer back to Table 8-1 for more information on this setting.

Step 4.   Click **Apply**, as shown in Figure 8-14.

Alternately, you can make these settings from the CLI using the following commands:

```
AP# configure terminal
AP(config)# interface dot11radio 0
AP(config-if)# ssid ssid qbranch
AP(config-if-ssid)# authentication open eap eap_methods
AP(config-if-ssid)# authentication network-eap eap_methods
AP(config-if-ssid)# end
AP# write memory
```

Figure 8-14 *EAP Configuration Steps on the SSID Manager Page (Cont'd)*

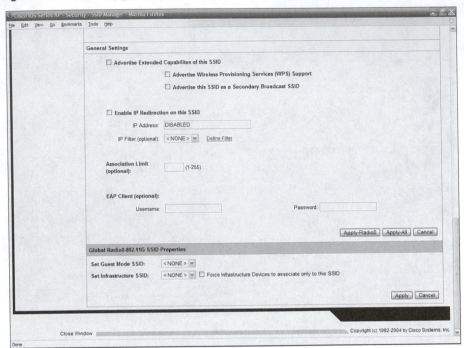

Building a Honeypot

If you have the time, inclination, and a touch of deviousness in you, you can thwart would-be attackers by simply giving them what they want. That is, let them break in.

But they won't get anything.

If you have a spare AP on hand—maybe you upgraded your WLAN equipment and have an unused AP—you can set up what is called a *honeypot*.

A honeypot is simply an AP that is set up to distract war drivers and attackers from your real AP. While the attackers are busy trying to access the honeypot, they might not even be aware of the real WLAN.

To set up a honeypot, you first need an unused AP—you can buy one, or if you are upgrading from older 802.11 equipment, you might have a spare one on hand. Next, do the following:

Step 1.   Set the SSID to something different from your real AP.

Step 2.   Use a channel at least five channels away from the channel you are using on the new AP. This avoids interference.

Step 3.   Place the AP and any antennas near an outside window.

Step 4.   Plug it into a power source, but do not connect it to your network.

Step 5.   Do not point any wireless computers or devices toward this AP.

A word of warning about a honeypot: Visitors with legitimate business on your WLAN might accidentally log on to your honeypot and not be able to access the WLAN. Because of this, you might want to ensure that the honeypot does not cover a visitor area.

That's all there is to building a honeypot. It probably won't deter someone who is really gunning for your network, but it should pacify casual and lazy snoops.

Chapter 9 Contents

CiscoWorks LAN Management Solution

Also important to the management of your WLAN is management of your LAN. Some devices on the LAN affect the WLAN and require monitoring and adjustment, so that they do not create problems for other devices. The CiscoWorks LAN Management Solution (LMS) is a suite of applications that allows you to manage your LAN.

This chapter is not meant to be an exhaustive exploration of this robust tool. Rather, it explains the various components of LMS and provides information about using its features. The "Other Resources" section at the end of this chapter can point you to more in-depth information about LMS.

CiscoWorks LMS Overview

CiscoWorks is a family of tools for network and device management. LMS is useful for providing switched network discovery, configuration, data path tracing, and LAN performance management on both device and network levels.

LMS comprises several applications. They are discussed in the following sections.

Campus Manager

Campus Manager is used for managing Cisco-based switched networks. Components of this application include:

- Intelligent discovery and display of Layer 2 networks.
- Configuration of virtual LAN, LAN Emulation, and asynchronous transfer mode (ATM) services.
- Path trace tool for diagnosing connectivity problems.
- Location of information on users is based on MAC address, IP address, NT or NetWare Directory Services login, and physical connections to the network.
- Tracking of phone handset to IP, MAC address, and switch port.

Device Fault Manager

The Device Fault Manager (DFM) gives real-time fault analysis. DFM monitors Cisco networks for numerous fault conditions. It then analyzes these conditions and notifies the network administrator when faults occur.

DFM monitors numerous problems at both the device and VLAN levels using Internet Control Message Protocol (ICMP) polling and the Simple Network Management Protocol (SNMP) Management Information Base (MIB) survey. It also analyzes Layer 2 and Layer 3 devices, checking to determine which ports are members of specific VLANs.

Resource Manager Essentials

Resource Manager Essentials (RME) simplifies network management by automatically performing a number of tedious tasks including:

- Building a network inventory.
- Monitoring and reporting hardware and configuration changes.
- Managing and deploying configuration changes and software updates to devices.
- Simplifying monitoring and troubleshooting of LAN resources.
- Managing the VPN with VPN-specific management tools.

CiscoView

CiscoView provides dynamic status, statistics, and configuration data for Cisco devices. CiscoView allows you to access detailed device information, examine graphical views of devices with color-coded status information, and utilize browser access to configuration and monitoring tools.

CiscoWorks Management Server

The CiscoWorks Server provides the essential management components, services, and security tools for the suite of CiscoWorks tools. It is also essential for integrating with other Cisco and third-party applications.

Common Services

CiscoWorks Common Services provides a universal collection of management services that are used by other CiscoWorks applications. Applications in CiscoWorks rely on Common Services for functionality. It allows them to share a common structure for services such as data storage, navigation, and security protocols. Common Services also allows information to be shared between CiscoWorks products.

Configuring CiscoWorks LMS

If you opt to use CiscoWorks LMS, configuration is a necessary step toward culling the functionality you want. This section examines what is involved in the configuration process and some of the major components of this step.

After it is installed, LMS is started by opening a web browser and entering the URL for your CiscoWorks Server. It uses this format:

http://*server_name:port_number*

NOTE: In HTTP mode, the default TCP port is 1741. When SSL is enabled, the default TCP port is 443.

LMS Homepage

After logging in, the CiscoWorks homepage comes up and shows the LMS applications installed.

The page is divided into sections, each with its own piece of LMS. Figure 9-1 shows these sections.

Figure 9-1 *CiscoWorks LAN Management Solution Homepage*

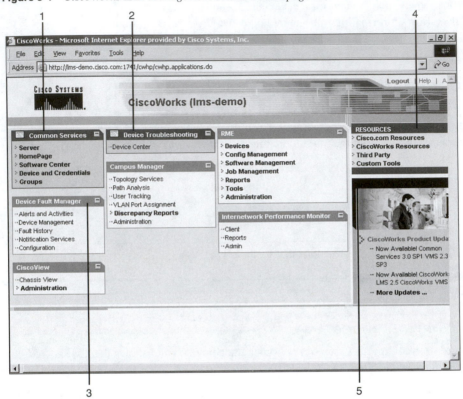

Following is an explanation of the numbered sections in Figure 9-1:

1. **Common Services Panel**—Shows all Common Services functions and is displayed in a collapsible pane.

2. **Device Troubleshooting Panel**—Allows you to launch the Device Center to view device details, perform troubleshooting, perform management tasks, and view reports for a given device. You can also manage device credentials and update the inventory.

3. **Application Panel**—Contains links to the LMS applications. Applications are presented in three columns, and the title of each application is displayed in the panel. When an application is clicked, that application's homepage is launched in a new window.

4. **Resources Panel**—This panel is in the top-right corner of the homepage. It is a launch point for CiscoWorks resources, Cisco.com resources, third-party applications, and custom tools.

5. **Product Updates Panel**—In the lower-right corner of the homepage is the Updates Panel. It shows information about CiscoWorks product announcements. Clicking the **More Updates** link creates a popup window with Cisco Product update details.

Initial Tasks

After the applications have been installed or upgraded, you should do a number of initial tasks:

Step 1. First, add devices to the system. This can be done in a number of ways:

- Automatically automatic device discovery can be configured on Campus Manager.

- Importing from a third party.

- Using the Add Device feature from the Device and Credential Admin (DCA).

- Importing from a flat file.

Step 2. The next step is to manage the devices. This is done by following **Common Services > Device and Credentials > Device Management**. Shown in Figure 9-2, this tool allows you to add, delete, edit, import, export, and view devices. Device Fault Manager automatically synchronizes its inventory with the Device and Credential Repository (DCR).

Figure 9-2 *Managing Devices with LMS*

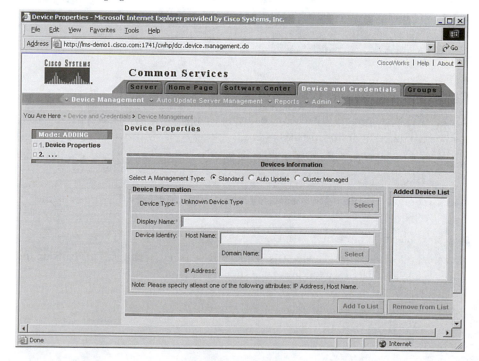

Step 3. The next step is to create new inventory jobs. Follow **RME > Devices > Inventory > Inventory Jobs**. This is shown in Figure 9-3.

Step 4. Next, configure DFM trap receiving.

Figure 9-3 *Jobs Are Tracked in the Inventory Jobs Window*

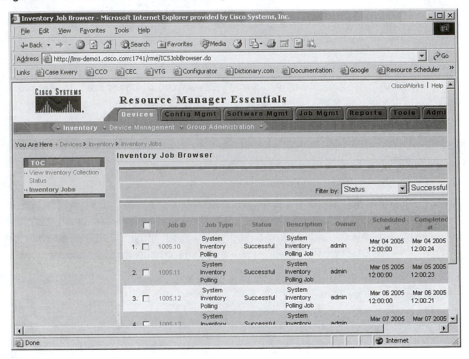

Automatic Device Discovery

Devices can be automatically discovered using Campus Manager. Campus Manager can be configured by following these steps:

Step 1. From the CiscoWorks homepage, follow **Campus Manager > Administration**.

Step 2. Follow **Admin > Device Discovery > SNMP Settings**. This calls up the SNMP Settings page.

Step 3. Enter the community strings.

Step 4. Follow **Admin > Device Discovery > Discovery Settings**. This calls up the Device Discovery Settings page shown in Figure 9-4.

Figure 9-4 *Device Discovery Settings*

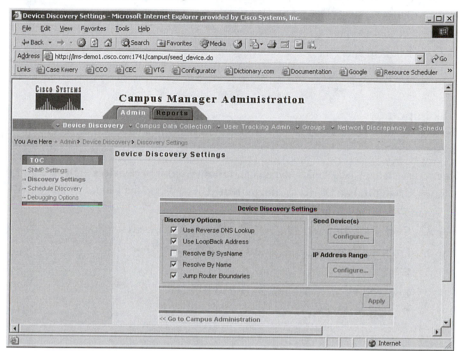

Step 5.   Enter Discovery options.

Step 6.   Follow **Seed Device(s) > Configure**. This calls up the Configure Seed Devices dialog box. *Seed devices* are devices used to start network discovery.

Step 7.   Click **Browse** to enter seed devices that will be stored. The list of seed devices must be separated by a single carriage return.

Adding Devices Using DCA

Another way to add devices to CiscoWorks is through the DCA. This helps manage the devices and their credentials. It also allows you to add devices to RME, Campus Manager, DFM, and Internetwork Performance Monitor (IPM).

Follow these steps to add devices to the list:

Step 1.   From the CiscoWorks homepage, follow **Common Services > Device and Credentials > Device Management**. This calls up the Device Management page.

Step 2. Click **Add**. This calls up the Device Properties page. There are three ways to perform device management:

Standard Type

Auto Update Type

Cluster Managed Type

Bulk Import

Devices can also be added as a "bulk import." To perform a bulk import, follow these steps:

Step 1. From the CiscoWorks homepage, follow **Common Services > Device and Credentials > Device Management**. This calls up the Device Management page.

Step 2. Click **Bulk Import**. This calls up the Import Devices window.

Step 3. From the drop-down list, select one of the following:

File

Local NMS (network management station)

Remote NMS

Collecting Data

You must configure Campus Manager to collect data to manage devices. This is initiated from the CiscoWorks homepage by following **Campus Manager > Administration**. Following are some of your options for data collection:

- Select **Campus Data Collection** to view a summary of data collection settings.
- Follow **Campus Data Collection > Schedule Data Collection** to schedule data collection. This is shown in Figure 9-5.
- Follow **Campus Data Collection > Data Collection Filters** to specify data collection filters.
- Follow **Campus Data Collection > Debugging Options** to indicate how to debug data collection.

Figure 9-5   *Scheduling Data Collection Using Campus Manager*

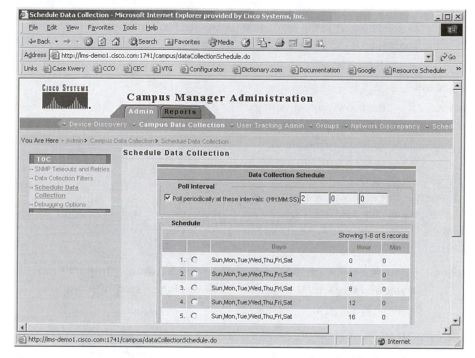

Performing Application Tasks

Specific tasks are accomplished in LMS by starting them from the LMS homepage. The following sections explain additional tasks you can perform and how to initiate them.

Campus Manager

To configure user tracking acquisition actions, follow **Campus Manager > User Tracking > Acquisition > Actions**. This allows you to track users based on how they are connected to the network. For example, you can track users based on whether they are currently connected to the network or if they use Windows or UNIX hosts.

RME

To configure the transport protocol for configuration management, follow **RME > Administration > Config Mgmt**. This allows you to select the protocol you prefer for transport, whether it is Telnet, TFTP, RCP, SSH, SCP, or HTTPS.

To view, create, and manage inventory jobs, follow **RME > Devices > Inventory**.

DFM

To prepare the DFM for use, you should configure these settings for which detailed steps can be found online in the user guide for Device Fault Manager 2.0 at http://www.cisco.com/univercd/cc/td/doc/product/rtrmgmt/cw2000/dfm/dfm20/:

❑ SNMP trap forwarding

❑ Notifications

❑ Adjust polling and threshold settings

❑ Adjust the rediscovery schedule

❑ Adjust the daily purging schedule

❑ Add views to the Alerts and Activities display

Internetwork Performance Monitor

To configure the Internetwork Performance Monitor, the first step is to import devices from the Device Credentials Repository as source or targets. Follow these steps to configure IPM:

Step 1. Follow **Internetwork Performance Monitor > Admin > Import From Device and Credential Repository**. The resulting screen is shown in Figure 9-6.

Figure 9-6 *IPM's Import from Device and Credential Repository Window*

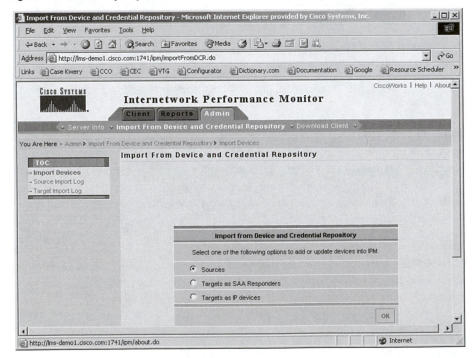

Step 2. When the Import from Device and Credential Repository page pops up, click **Import Devices**.

Step 3. Next, choose how to import the devices:

- **Sources** imports devices for use as source routers.

- **Targets as SAA Responders** imports data for use as SAA Responders target devices.

- **Targets as IP devices** imports devices for use as IP target devices.

More information on configuring the IPM can be found online in the user guide for Internetwork Performance Monitor, Release 2.5 at http://www.cisco.com/univercd/cc/td/doc/product/rtrmgmt/ipmcw2k/cipm26/.

Other Resources

- **LAN Management Solution—Version 2.5**

  http://www.cisco.com/univercd/cc/td/doc/product/rtrmgmt/cw2000/cw2000_b/lms/lms25/index.htm

Chapter 10 Contents

CiscoWorks Wireless LAN Solution Engine (WLSE)

Management is reasonably straightforward on a small wireless LAN (WLAN). If only a few access points (APs) exist, it's easy to see operations and how they perform configurations. However, when you have a large WLAN with dozens, hundreds, or even thousands of APs, management gets more complex. To help manage these environments, Cisco offers CiscoWorks Wireless LAN Solution Engine (WLSE).

The WLSE is a hardware and software solution to manage up to 2500 APs. The device is rack mounted, and you can collocate it with your other LAN hardware in a server room. You can manage WLSE through either a menu-based web browser or the command-line interface (CLI).

Reports in WLSE cover a broad range of information, and can include the number of users associated, a certain AP, and the use of radio interfaces. This allows you to map capacity, understand performance, and plan for expansion.

WLSE is the heart of Cisco Structured Wireless Aware Network (SWAN) solution. A bonus of SWAN is its ability to survey and map a site.

NOTE: Flip back to Chapter 3, "Cisco Wireless Technologies," for more information about SWAN.

Dashboard

The WLSE is managed from a *dashboard* on its home page. The dashboard is comprised of several tabs. The tabs give a brief explanation of what they manage. After you select a tab, other subtabs are shown. Table 10-1 explains each tab of the WLSE dashboard, tells its purpose, and includes a description of each subtabs.

NOTE: For this discussion, WLSE version 2.9 is used. If you use a newer or older version of WLSE, you might encounter some different options.

Table 10-1 *The Dashboard's Tabs and Subtabs*

Tab	Subtabs and Description
Faults	Used to display and manage fault information. Subtabs include: • **Display Faults**—Displays device-based faults. Manages fault settings. Sets and manages thresholds. • **Manage Network-Wide Profiles**—Establishes and manages network-wide profiles. • **Notification Settings**—Manages settings to send fault information.
Devices	Used to manage and discover devices on your WLAN. Subtabs include: • **Discover**—Runs device discovery, manages polling, manages devices, runs inventories, and views logs. • **Group Management**—Establishes and manages groups of devices.
Configure	Used for the configuration and configuration management of devices. Subtabs include: • **Templates**—Creates configuration templates for both IOS and non-IOS APs. • **Archives**—Manages and stores configurations. • **Jobs**—Sends templates to APs. • **Auto Update**—Automatically configures APs.
Firmware	Used to update and manage firmware updates. Subtabs include: • **Images**—Retrieves firmware for APs and bridges from the desktop or Cisco website. • **Jobs**—Sends the firmware to APs.
Reports	• Used to view reports about devices, radios, and clients. Also used to track trends. Subtabs include: • **Device Center**—Displays reports for a specific device. • **Radio Manager**—Displays radio management reports. • **Wireless Clients**—Displays client association information. • **Current**—Contains tools for viewing, exporting, and e-mailing current reports. • **Trends**—Contains tools to view, export, and e-mail WLAN trends. • **Realtime**—Provides detailed information on several APs. • **Scheduled Email Jobs**—Contains tools to manage e-mail functions.

Table 10-1 *The Dashboard's Tabs and Subtabs (Continued)*

Tab	Subtabs and Description
Radio Management	Used to manage radio features. Subtabs include: • **Radio Monitoring**—Monitors the WLAN and collects radio information used for configuration, rogues AP discovery, and interference detection. • **AP Radio Scan**—Enlists APs to characterize the radio environment that is used for RM-assisted configuration, preparing coverage maps, and rogue location. • **Client Walkabout**—Used with Cisco Compatible Extension (CCX) clients to walk a client around your location and gather radio data. This information is sent back to the client's AP for further analysis and transmission upstream to the WLSE. • **RM Assisted Configuration**—Configures APs and uses data collected from client walkabouts and AP radio scans.
Location Manager	Used to graphically display WLAN environments after existing, known APs are imported to the application. This includes the location of known APs and an estimation of where unknown APs might be placed. It also shows signal strength.
Administration	Used to manage the WLSE device. Subtabs include: • **Appliance**—Management tools for the WLSE system, including diagnostics, data backup, time settings, and NTP servers. • **System**—Displays information about firmware versions. • **User Admin**—Management tools for users and profiles. • **My Profile**—Management tools for your own profile. • **Links**—Manages links to other systems, including other WLSEs and CiscoWorks servers.

The WLSE is a robust management tool with many ways to configure, manage, and view the devices on your WLAN. It is not possible to explore every feature of the WLSE here. However, the following sections explain how to manage some of the more popular and useful features of the WLSE.

Managing WLANs

You can use the **Devices** tab to manage devices with WLSE. This tab contains the tools necessary to discover and manage devices, perform inventories, and organize devices into groups for easier management. After devices are discovered and managed, you can use the other WLSE features.

Configuring Devices

To manage the devices on your WLAN, you must set up the devices, configure WLSE, discover the devices, and then configure WLSE to manage those devices. This is accomplished following these steps:

Step 1. **Configure your devices**. Before WLSE can manage the devices, they must be configured correctly. Also, if you use WLSE radio management, you must configure IOS APs for wireless domain services (WDS) and LEAP authentication.

NOTE: The steps necessary to configure an AP for WDS are explained in Chapter 7, "Wireless and Wired LAN Integration Overview."

Step 2. **Log in to the WLSE**.

Step 3. **Enter device credentials on the WLSE**. Credentials depend on the type of device you configure. Table 10-2 lists the devices and the credential format for each. If you are confused about what to enter, the help screen can most likely tell you what information you need.

Table 10-2 *Device Credential Format*

Device	Description	Credential Format
All Managed Devices	WLSE uses SNMP community strings to discover devices and to enable other WLSE options, and includes firmware updates, configuration, and radio management.	SNMP Communities
Non-IOS APs	HTTP usernames and passwords are used on non-IOS APs. They are needed to download configuration files.	HTTP User/Password
IOS APs (HTTP ports)	HTTP port settings are needed for reports on IOS APs. These settings are used to link reports to the Web interfaces of APs.	IOS HTTP Port Settings
IOS APs (Telnet)	Telnet or SSH usernames and passwords are needed to configure IOS APs and for firmware upgrade.	Telnet/SSH User/Password
Wireless LAN Context Control Protocol (WLCCP) Credentials	If WLSE is used to monitor WDS, the WLCCP credentials must be provided.	WLCCP Credentials

You enter device credentials as follows: **Devices > Discover > Device Credentials**. Then select the type of credential you want to enter, as listed in the Credential Format column in Table 10-2.

Step 4. **Discover devices**. This is accomplished if you begin discovery from the WLSE or importing devices. To start the Discovery Wizard, follow **Devices > Discover > Discover > Discovery Wizard**. The Discovery Wizard offers three ways to introduce devices:

- **Automatic Device Discovery**—This runs an automatic discovery, based on the Cisco Discovery Protocol (CDP).

- **Import from File**—This imports devices from a pre-existing file.

- **Import from CiscoWorks**—This imports devices from a CiscoWorks server.

Step 5. **Verify discovery**. Follow **Devices > Discover > DISCOVER > Logs** to ensure your devices are added to the WLSE.

Step 6. **Set devices to the** *managed* **state**. You must tell the WLSE which devices you want to manage. This is accomplished if you set them to a managed state. Alternately, if you elect not to manage a device, it is said that those devices are set to an unmanaged state. To set devices to a managed state, do the following:

a. Follow **Devices > Discover > Managed Device > Manage/Unmanage**.

b. Three folders are presented: New (which contains newly discovered devices), Managed, and Unmanaged. Click the folder you wish to view, and then select the device you wish to manage.

c. Click **Manage** to set the device to a managed state.

Step 7. **Run an inventory**. After devices are added to the managed state, the WLSE performs an inventory to gather device information. You can also elect to run inventory if you poll on-demand. This is useful to do when there are configuration changes on network devices and you want those changes to reflect in the inventory reports.

Step 8. **Create users**. This step establishes which features of WLSE the user can access. This is accessed if you follow **Administration > User Admin > Manage Roles**. At this stage, you can add new roles or manage existing user roles.

Step 9. **Create device groups**. WLSE allows you to group managed devices as you see fit. This is useful if you configure several similar devices at the same time. Follow **Devices > Group Management**, and you call up the Group Details window. From here, you can view groups, create new groups, or manage existing groups.

Radio Management

The heart of WLSE's more interesting functionality comes from its radio management tools. These are the tools that allow you to search for rogue APs, detect interference, and automatically resurvey a site. Radio Manager also eases the deployment and daily management of your WLAN radio network. The subsequent sections explain how to configure Radio Manager.

Configuring the Network for Radio Manager

The information gathered from the **Radio Manager** tab is collected from the managed devices on your network. Before you can use radio management, you must properly configure the network. The following steps explain how to correctly configure the network to use radio management:

Step 1. Make sure all APs are managed. (See Step 6 in "Configuring Devices" earlier in this section.)

Step 2. At least one AP on each subnet must be configured with WDS (demonstrated in Chapter 7) or a central WDS, such as the WLSM or router.

Step 3. Enable LEAP authentication. This is a means to authenticate between the APs and the WLSE, and it is done separate from client authentication.

Step 4. Configure WLCCP credentials. (See Step 3 in the "Configuring Devices" section.)

Step 5. Verify that the active WDS appears on the device tree. Follow these steps:

    a. Select **Reports > Device Center**.

    b. Open the Wireless Domain Services folder.

    c. Open the Active WDS folder.

    d. Select the device.

    e. Select **WDS Summary Report**.

    f. Verify that the WLSE to WDS Authentication Status column contains the string "KeysSetUpWithWDS" or "Authenticate."

Step 6. Verify that the APs are managed with WDS. This is done if you perform the following steps:

    a. Select **Reports > Device Center**.

    b. Open the Wireless Domain Services folder.

    c. Open the Active WDS folder.

    d. Select the device.

    e. Select **WDS Registered APs**. A list of all the APs that are registered with this WDS AP is displayed.

Step 7. Configure the Access Control Server (ACS) server to support fast roaming and simultaneous logins.

Step 8. Configure the AAA server to allow multiple sessions.

Collecting Radio Location Data

The next step is to collect radio location data. This helps the WLSE "understand" the radio environment and provide information other Radio Manager features need. There are three ways the WLSE can collect this information:

- **AP Radio Scan**—The APs send beacons on the same channel to detect neighboring APs.
- **Client Walkabout**—The CCX client is walked throughout the area, detects APs, and then reports back to the WLSE.
- **Radio Monitoring**—RF statistics are periodically collected and their signal sources are identified.

You can select these methods if you click **Radio Manager**, and select **AP Radio Scan**, **Client Walkabout**, or **Radio Monitoring**.

Generating Radio Parameters

You can configure radio parameters in one of two ways, which depends on how you collected radio location data:

- **RM Assisted Configuration**—Used when data has been collected from AP radio scanning or a client walkabout. This is accessed if you follow **Radio Manager > RM Assisted Configuration**.
- **Assisted Site Survey**—Used when you want to step through AP radio scan, client walkabout, or radio parameter generation. This wizard is started from the Location Manager window, if you follow **Wizard > Assisted Site Survey**.

Radio Manager Features

After the aforementioned configuration steps have been accomplished, the WLSE is functional. This section explains how to perform three different management functions: perform an auto re-site survey, set up self healing, and detect interference.

Auto re-site survey and self healing require the following prerequisites, or the features cannot work:

- The network must be configured for radio management.
- An AP radio scan must be completed on all the APs on that floor.
- Radio monitoring must be enabled on all APs on that floor.

- Network-wide policies to detect network-performance degradation must be established.
- Buildings and floors must be created in Location Manager.
- APs must be placed on the floor images.

Auto Re-Site Survey

This feature is used to have Radio Manager examine the AP's current radio performance and compare it against historical data. If Radio Manager determines degradation in performance, a fault is generated.

Follow these steps to set up this feature:

Step 1. Follow **Radio Manager > Auto Re-Site Survey**. This calls up the Review Current form, which displays the building and frequency band of the AP that is currently enabled for Auto Re-Site Survey.

Step 2. Click **Select Floor** and choose a building from the Floors Selector list.

Step 3. Click on a floor, and then click the right arrows (>>) to add it to the Selected Floors list.

Step 4. Click **Set Base Values**.

Step 5. Click **Compute and Apply**. This calculates current performance data for each floor.

Step 6. Click **Finish** to complete the survey.

Step 7. Click **Save** to save these settings.

Each hour, the baseline data is compared against current performance. If there is 20 percent degradation or more, a fault is generated. The default value is 20 percent—you can set it to whatever value you choose.

Self Healing

The Self Healing feature on Radio Manager automatically adjusts radio parameters of APs to reduce loss of coverage in the event of network failure.

This feature works, however, only if two conditions are met: The APs run at less than full RF power when the survey and installation are done and they are placed such that the self healing function will be supported. If they are set at full power, there is no way that WLSE can turn power up to provide RF coverage for a failed AP.

When Radio Manager does not detect a radio interface on the selected floor for three report intervals, it adjusts power levels on neighboring APs to compensate for it.

This is set up by following these steps:

Step 1. Select **Radio Manager > Self Healing**. This calls up a display of currently selected floors that use self healing.

Step 2. Click **Select Floor** and choose a building from the Floors Selector list.

Step 3. Click on a floor, and click the right arrows (**>>**) to add it to the Selected Floors list.

Step 4. Click **Finish**.

Step 5. Click **Save** to save these settings.

NOTE: Self healing is a one-way process, and the administrator should perform another site survey after the fault is corrected.

Detecting Interference

One of the most impressive features of radio monitoring is its ability to monitor your WLAN and discover any interference. You can manage this setting if you follow **Faults > Manage Network-Wide Settings > Interference Detection**.

On this screen, you can set the threshold condition for which a fault is generated.

Security

Security is managed in many ways with the WLSE. First, basic security requirements are sent and used consistently throughout the WLAN. For example, the WLSE might require all APs in the organization to use a specific length of key. The WLSE also uses Radio Manager to locate and cut off rogue APs.

Managing Security

To configure security via WLSE depends on the security settings you wish to enable, as well as the type of radio you use. First, follow **Templates > Configure**, then select **Security**. Next, you are presented with a list of options. Table 10-3 lists those options and describes what you can do with them.

NOTE: Version 2.11 of WLSE includes a wizard for building templates.

Table 10-3 *Security Settings*

Security Setting	Description
Admin Access	Used to add users to the system, remove users from the system, and assign user privileges.
SSID 802.11b/g	Used to configure SSID 802.11b/g settings, including: • Authentication methods • Authentication servers • Key management • Proxy Mobile IP • Accounting
SSID 802.11a	Used to configure SSID 802.11a settings, including: • Authentication methods • Authentication servers • Key management • Proxy Mobile IP • Accounting
WEP 802.11b and 802.11g	Used to manage keys for 802.11b/g radio interfaces settings, including: • Key length • Ciphers • Send and receive keys • Key rotation
WEP 802.11a	Used to manage keys for 802.11a radio interfaces settings, including: • Key length • Ciphers • Send and receive keys • Key rotation
Server Manager	Used to select and configure the backup RADIUS server.
Advanced Security	Sets up the AP to authenticate client devices and uses a combination of MAC- and EAP-based authentication. If this is enabled, clients that use 802.11 open authentication first attempt authentication via MAC. If MAC fails, the AP waits for the client to try EAP authentication.
Local RADIUS Server	Used to configure the local RADIUS server.

Rogue AP Detection and Mitigation

WLSE's radio monitoring feature uses radio measurement capabilities of IOS-based Cisco APs and client adapters to discover unauthorized APs that send beacons. If beacons are detected, Radio Manager examines the beacon for the MAC address of the AP and sends that back to WDS to see if the address is one of the authorized APs in the WDS list. If not, WDS sends it up to the WLSE.

The administrator is given the opportunity to categorize the newly detected AP. They are placed into one of four AP types:

- **Managed AP**—An authorized AP that needs management from WLSE.
- **Unmanaged AP**—An authorized AP that does not need management from WLSE.
- **Friendly AP**—An AP that is not connected to the WLAN, although WLSE detects it. For example, your neighbor's AP can radiate into your office.
- **Rogue AP**—An AP that is detected and can or cannot be connected to the WLAN. It has not been identified as managed, unmanaged, or friendly. This is the default setting when a new AP is discovered and remains this way until the administrator reclassifies the AP.

The Fault Summary Table is the source of important information about rogue APs. When you click on the link in the Address, Description, or Timestamp fields, you are shown several pieces of information. Table 10-4 lists the information that you can learn about this device.

Table 10-4 *Rogue AP Detail*

Information	Description
BSSID	Basic Service Set Identifier.
State	The device's state.
Vendor	The name of the device's vendor.
Change to a Friendly AP	To reclassify this as a friendly device, click **Change to a Friendly AP**, and then refresh your browser.
Delete	To delete this notification, click **Delete**, and then refresh your browser.

In addition to basic information about the rogue AP, Table 10-5 lists information that can help you physically locate the rogue AP.

Table 10-5 *Rogue AP Location Details*

Information	Description
Location	Gives an estimated location of the AP.
Timestamp	Lists the date and time the AP was detected.
View in Location Manager	Click **View in Location Manager** for an approximate, graphical location of the rogue AP.

If the rogue AP is connected to a Cisco switch, you might identify the switch port to which it's connected if you use the Switch Port Location feature. Table 10-6 lists the information you can get from this feature.

Table 10-6 *Switch Port Location Details*

Information	Description
Switch IP	The IP address of the switch to which the AP is connected.
Switch port	The switch port to which the AP is connected.
Traced MAC address	The rogue AP's MAC address.
Timestamp	The date and time when the rogue AP was detected.
Re-Trace	Re-run the trace. This is useful if the AP moved to another switch port since its initial detection.

When a rogue AP fault is created, you can also configure the WLSE to suppress the port to which that rogue AP is connected.

The WLSE is a powerful piece of equipment and keystone of Cisco SWAN solution. To use the robust features of the WLSE, however, you must ensure that the network devices and the WLSE are all properly configured. Keep in mind that there is no substitute to plan and carefully implement WLSE. It pays dividends in the long run.

Chapter 11 Contents

Tuning AP Radio Parameters

Installing and configuring an access point (AP) is generally a straightforward affair. Plug in the unit, establish some basic configuration settings, and you are ready.

However, your environment might require you to tweak more settings for optimal performance. For example, in an effort to conserve laptop battery power, you might reconfigure transceivers to operate less frequently. You might also find the need to manually set radio channels or adjust the size of frames that are broadcast and received. Cisco APs provide a way to manage these settings.

Power Tuning

When people buy APs, they tend to purchase the unit with the most power. Although it's great to get the best range, there might be times when you need less, not more. For example, you might want to minimize a signal's interference with your neighbor's AP.

Power management has another useful purpose—it saves battery power. Many clients are likely installed on laptop computers and other mobile devices. By the nature of their design, these devices aren't generally plugged into the wall. Rather, they rely on battery power. If the 802.11 radio uses all the battery power, these devices cannot last long.

Managing Power Settings on the AP

The configuration steps for this section and chapter are located on the **Settings** screen. This page is reached from the AP's home page, then you click **Network Interfaces** from the menu on the left. Click the radio you want to change (**Radio0-802.11G** for the 2.4-GHz radio and **Radio1-802.11A** for the 5-GHz radio). Finally, click on the **Settings** tab.

Select the power level you wish, and then click **Apply** at the bottom of the screen. This portion of the Settings tab is shown in Figure 11-1.

Figure 11-1   *Within the Settings Tab You Can Manage the AP's Transmission Power*

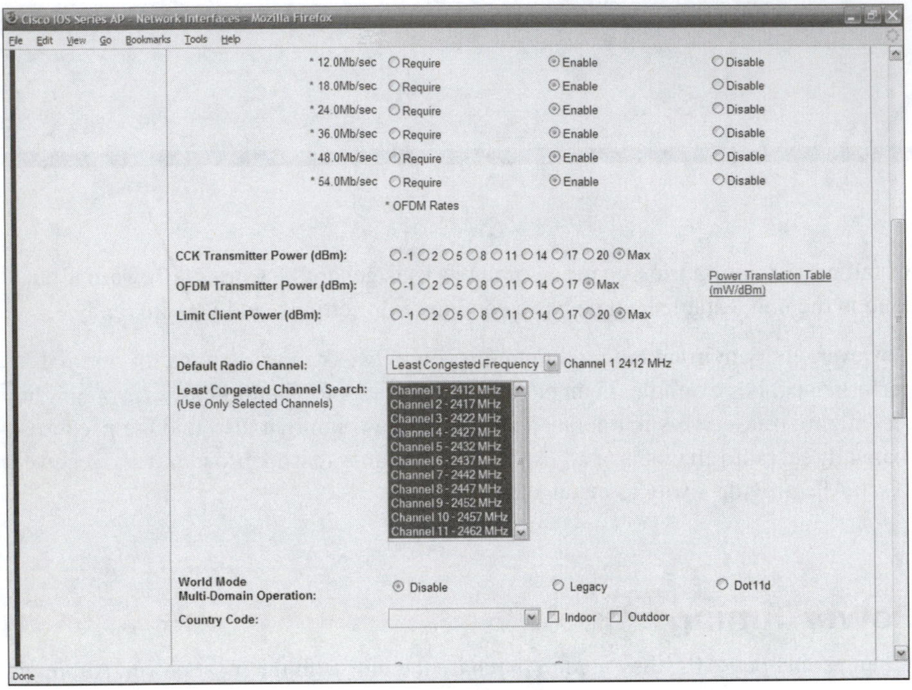

If you enter the commands described in Table 11-1, you can also adjust the AP's transmit power from the CLI. Use a console to access the CLI, or connect to the AP with a terminal program and log on with the AP's IP address.

Table 11-1   *Configuring Transmit Power*

Command	Description
configure terminal	Enters global configuration mode.
interface dot11radio {0 | 1}	Enters configuration mode for the radio interface. The 2.4-GHz radio is radio **0**, and the 5-GHz radio is radio **1**.
power local Power levels (expressed in milliwatts [mW]) available for the 2.4-GHz radio: {**1 | 5 | 20 | 30 | 50 | 100 | maximum**} Power levels available for the 5-GHz radio: {**5 | 10 | 20 | 40 | maximum**}	Sets the transmit power to one of the powers allowed in your regulatory domain.
end	Returns to privileged EXEC mode.

In Table 11-2, the power values are expressed in milliwatts (mW). However, if you use the web interface to change the settings, they are made in decibels referenced to one milliwatt (dBm). Table 11-2 shows the conversion between these values.

Table 11-2 *Converting Between mW and dBm*

dBm	−1	2	5	6	7	8	9	10	11	12	13	14	15	16	17	18	19	20	21	22	23	24
mW	1	2	3	4	5	6	8	10	12	15	20	25	30	40	50	60	80	100	125	150	200	250

To reset the power settings to their default, use the **no** form of the **power** command.

Managing Power Settings on the Client

You can enable the AP to tell Cisco clients how much power to use. When a client associates to the AP, the AP sends the maximum power setting to the client.

Stations associated with an AP listen for beacon frames. The longer the time between the frames, the longer a station can power down the radio; consequently it saves power and extends battery life. The downside to this, however, is that when the client radio is powered down, frames are buffered on the AP, and traffic does not reach the client as expeditiously as if the radio were constantly on.

NOTE: You must enable Aironet extensions to allow the AP to dictate power usage to clients. The 802.11d standard provides a way to do this, and does not require a Cisco proprietary extension. However, for our purposes, this setting is also found as a radio button on the Settings tab.

This setting is managed on the Settings tab, and uses the radio buttons adjacent to **Limit Client Power (dBm)**. Select the power level you wish, and then click **Apply** at the bottom of the screen. This is shown in Figure 11-1.

Table 11-3 lists and describes the CLI commands to manage client power settings.

Table 11-3 *Managing Client Power Settings from the AP*

Command	Description
configure terminal	Enters global configuration mode.
interface dot11radio {0 ǀ 1}	Enters configuration mode for the radio interface. The 2.4-GHz radio is radio **0**, and the 5-GHz radio is radio **1**.

continues

Table 11-3 *Managing Client Power Settings from the AP (Continued)*

Command	Description
power client For 2.4-GHz clients: {**1	5	20	30	50	100	maximum**} For 5-GHz clients: {**5	10	20	40	maximum**}	Sets the maximum power level allowed on client devices that associate to the AP. (All settings are in mW.)
end	Returns to privileged EXEC mode.

Similar to the power commands on the AP, to configure power in the CLI uses power expressed in mW. In the web interface, power is expressed in dBm. Refer back to Table 11-2 to convert these values.

NOTE: You can also use the Cisco Wireless LAN Solution Engine (WLSE) to set the power levels for a group of APs. Flip back to Chapter 10, "CiscoWorks Wireless LAN Management Solution Engine," for more information about Engine (WLSE).

Radio Tuning

When you set up your APs, you might encounter interference, the grouping of several APs in one location. You might also need to change the configured AP channel. The sections that follow show how to manage these settings through both the web browser interface and the CLI.

NOTE: In this chapter, settings are configured on an Aironet 1130AG AP. Your AP might differ, although this device uses both 2.4- and 5-GHz radios, so you can make the settings on your own devices.

Determining Optimal Channel and Frequency

There are 11 channels available on the 2.4-GHz radio and 23 channels available on the 5-GHz radio. The best settings for the 2.4-GHz radio are channels 1, 6, and 11. This is because these channels do not overlap and provide the best performance. Because of this, you can configure three APs to work in the same environment and not interfere with each other. However, keep the APs at least 5 feet apart. Even on different channels, the broadcasting APs can still interfere with one another.

Bandwidth for the 5-GHz radio, on the other hand, overlaps slightly. You can lessen the impact of this overlap, however, by selecting channels that are not adjacent to each other for neighboring APs.

Tuning to the Optimal Channel and Frequency

When first powered up, Cisco APs scan the airwaves and use the **Least Congested Frequency** setting for channel selection. That is, the AP listens to the airwaves, and then selects the channel with the least amount of traffic on it. To configure the radio to your own settings, select the **Settings** tab from the web interface, as shown in Figure 11-2.

Figure 11-2   *The Settings Tab Is Home to Various Radio Settings*

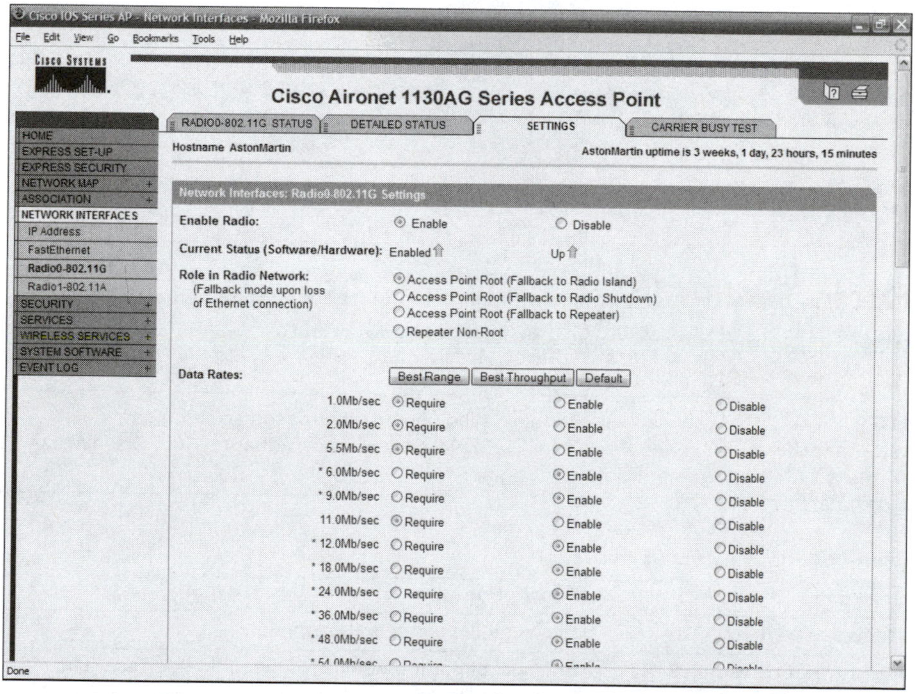

Scroll farther down this page and you can find the settings for channel and frequency settings as illustrated in Figure 11-3. Select the channels and frequencies you wish from the **Least Congested Channel Search** list, and then click **Apply** at the bottom of the screen.

Figure 11-3 *Setting Channel and Frequency Values on the Settings Tab*

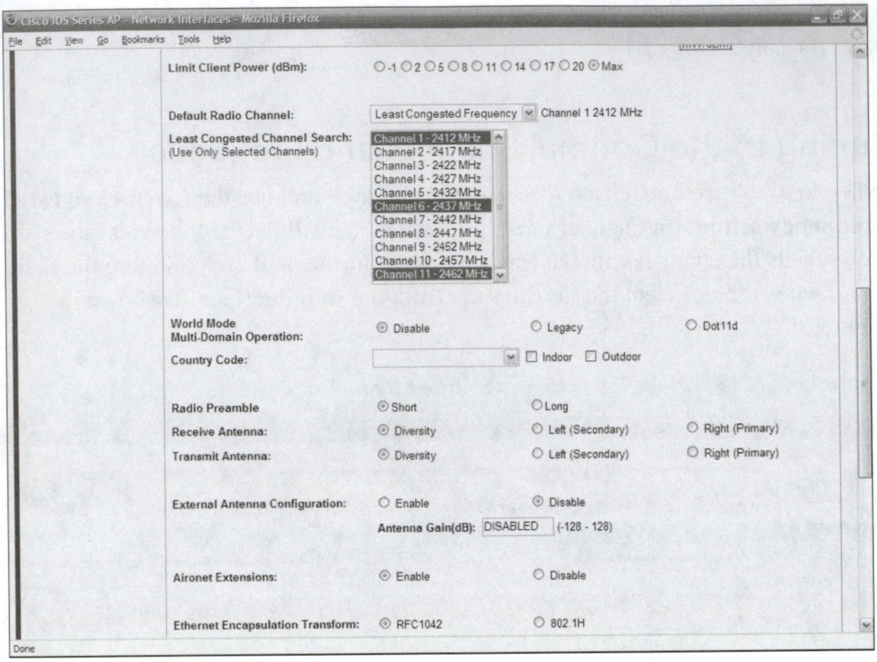

Table 11-4 lists and describes the commands to configure the channel and frequency settings if you elect to use the CLI instead of the web interface.

NOTE: The WLSE can also set channels. Also, a controller-based solution can automatically assign channels. Again, WLSE was examined in Chapter 10, "CiscoWorks Wireless LAN Management Solution Engine."

Table 11-4 *Configuring Channels*

Command	Description
configure terminal	Enters global configuration mode.
interface dot11radio {0 I 1}	Enters configuration mode for the radio interface. The 2.4-GHz radio is radio **0**, and the 5-GHz radio is radio **1**.
channel *frequency* I **least-congested**	Establishes the default channel. If you enter **least-congested**, you select the least congested channel available.
	The following are the channels and frequencies for the 2.4-GHz radio:
	Channel 1—2412
	Channel 2—2417
	Channel 3—2422

Table 11-4 *Configuring Channels (Continued)*

Command	Description
channel *frequency* | **least-congested** *(continued)*	**Channel 4**—2427
	Channel 5—2432
	Channel 6—2437
	Channel 7—2442
	Channel 8—2447
	Channel 9—2452
	Channel 10—2457
	Channel 11—2462
	Channel 12—2467 (EMEA and Japan only)
	Channel 13—2472 (EMEA and Japan only)
	Channel 14—2484 (Japan only and only for 802.11b)
	The following are the channels and frequencies for the 5-GHz radio:
	Channel 34—5170 (Japan only)
	Channel 36—5180
	Channel 38—5190 (Japan only)
	Channel 40—5200
	Channel 42—5210 (Japan only)
	Channel 44—5220
	Channel 46—5230 (Japan only)
	Channel 48—5240
	Channel 52—5260
	Channel 56—5280
	Channel 60—5300
	Channel 64—5320
	Channel 100—5500
	Channel 104—5520
	Channel 108—5540
	Channel 112—5560
	Channel 116—5580
	Channel 120—5600
	Channel 124—5620
	Channel 128—5640

continues

Table 11-4   *Configuring Channels (Continued)*

channel *frequency* | **least-congested** *(continued)*	**Channel 132**—5660
	Channel 136—5680
	Channel 140—5700
	Channel 149—5745
	Channel 153—5765
	Channel 157—5785
	Channel 161—5805
end	Returns to privileged EXEC mode.

Data Configuration

To further manage your AP, you can adjust numerous settings to govern the data transmission. You can adjust how fast data is sent, the size of packets, and several other variables.

Data Rates

Although your AP might work at speeds up to 54 Mbps if you use an 802.11a or 802.11g radio (11 Mbps if you use an 802.11b radio), you might find it advantageous to limit your transmission rates because you can get greater distances from the AP. On the other hand, if you enforce limits on the bottom end, it's better for everyone connecting because there's less time on the air.

Each data rate in an Aironet AP is configured to one of three settings:

- **Basic**—This allows transmission at this rate for both unicast and multicast packets. At least one of the AP's data rates must be set to basic.

NOTE: On the web interface, "Basic" is referred to as "Required."

- **Enable**—Unicast packets are sent at this rate only.
- **Disable**—The AP cannot send traffic at this rate.

The **Data Rates** setting is useful when you set up specific data rates for specific devices.

Figure 11-4 shows where to adjust the Data Rates settings in the web browser interface. Enter the value you wish, and then click **Apply** at the bottom of the screen.

Figure 11-4 *Configuring Data Rates on the Settings Tab*

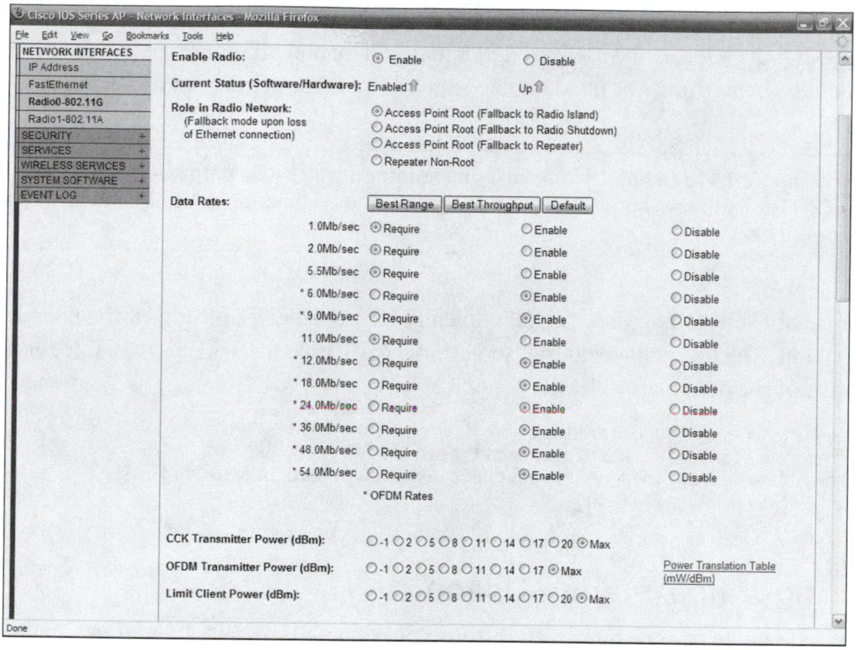

Table 11-5 explains the function of each line of the CLI configuration.

Table 11-5 *Configuring Data Rates*

Command	Description
configure terminal	Enters global configuration mode.
interface dot11radio {0 | 1}	Enters the configuration mode for the radio interface. The 2.4-GHz radio is radio **0**, and the 5-GHz radio is radio **1**.
speed For the 2.4-GHz radio: **{[1.0] [11.0] [2.0] [5.5] [basic-1.0] [basic-11.0] [basic-2.0] [basic-5.5] | range | throughput}** For the 5-GHz radio: **{[6.0] [9.0] [12.0] [18.0] [24.0] [36.0] [48.0] [54.0] [basic-6.0] [basic-9.0] [basic-12.0] [basic-18.0] [basic-24.0] [basic-36.0] [basic-48.0] [basic-54.0] | range | throughput}**	Each data rate is set to enabled or basic. Alternately, you can enter the range to optimize range and enter throughput to optimize throughput. If you enter just the number, it sets these data rates to enabled. Entering basic- plus the rate sets the rate to basic.
end	Returns to privileged EXEC mode.

In addition, you can configure the AP to select data rates that automatically deliver either the best range or the best throughput. When you configure the data rate, enter **range** and the AP sets the 1-Mbps data rate to **basic** and all other rates to **enabled**. If you enter **throughput** for the data rate setting, all data rates are set to **basic**.

NOTE: For 802.11g radios, be careful if you automatically select data rates when you have any 802.11b clients that connect. If you require 802.11g connection rates, the 802.11b clients cannot connect.

You can disable certain data rates completely if you use the **no** form of the **speed** command. The following example shows how to disable the 1-Mbps data rate, and set the rest of the data rates to **basic**:

```
AstonMartin# configure terminal
AstonMartin(config)# interface dot11radio 0
AstonMartin(config-if)# no speed basic-2.0 basic-5.5 basic-11.0
AstonMartin(config-if)# end
```

Configuring Antenna Usage

The best way to resolve multipath distortion (explained in greater detail in Chapter 2, "Cisco Antennas") is through the use of diversity antennas; however, you aren't locked into that configuration. With two antennas on your AP, you can select which one to use. This is especially useful if you use detachable antennas that you can position to your needs. Your options are as follows:

- **Diversity**—This is the default setting on Aironet APs. It tells the AP to use the antenna that receives the best signal. This is the optimal setting for fixed antennas.

- **Right**—If your AP has removable antennas and you install a high-gain antenna on the right antenna port, you should use this option to receive and transmit.

- **Left**—If your AP has removable antennas and you install a high-gain antenna on the left antenna port, you should use this option to receive and transmit.

Figure 11-5 shows where to adjust the Receive Antenna and Transmit Antenna settings in the web browser interface. Enter the value you wish, and then click **Apply** at the bottom of the screen.

Figure 11-5 *Configuring Antenna Receive/Transmit Settings*

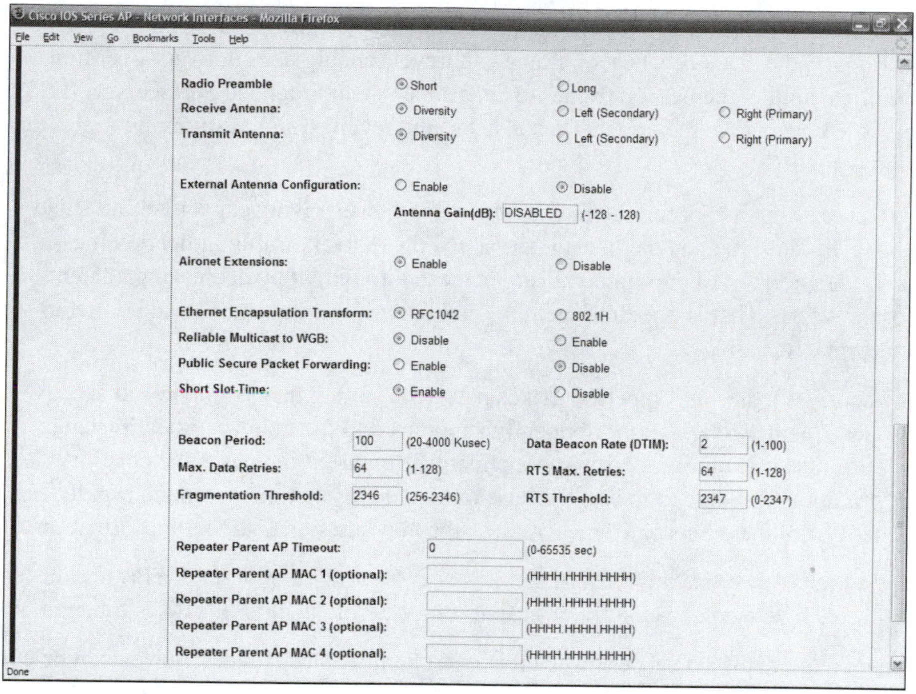

You can also configure the antenna setting if you use the CLI commands listed and described in Table 11-6.

Table 11-6 *Configuring Antennas*

Command	Description
configure terminal	Enters global configuration mode.
interface dot11radio {0 | 1}	Enters configuration mode for the radio interface. The 2.4-GHz radio is radio **0**, the 5-GHz radio is radio **1**.
antenna receive {diversity | left | right}	Configures which antenna to use for reception.
antenna transmit {diversity | left | right}	Configures which antenna to use for transmission.
end	Returns to privileged EXEC mode.

Configuring the Beacon Period and DTIM

Communications in a wireless LAN are centered on the AP. Because APs are stationary, the distance a beacon frame can travel reliably does not vary over time. Stations monitor the beacon frames to determine which Extended Service Sets (ESSs) provide coverage in their area. They also use the received signal strength to monitor signal quality.

An increase in the beacon interval increases the power-saving capacity of attached nodes, because it alters the listen interval and the delivery traffic indication message (DTIM) interval. A larger interval can increase throughput by decreasing contention for the signal. That is, the time spent to send beacon frames can instead be used to transmit data.

A decrease in the beacon period makes passive scanning more reliable and speedy because the network is more frequently announced to the radio. Further, a smaller beacon interval makes mobility more effective because it increases the coverage information available to nodes. Because of this, nodes that move around rapidly can benefit from these beacon frames because they update signal strength information.

DTIM tells power-saving stations that a packet waits for them. The DTIM period indicates how many beacon frames can transmit before another DTIM is transmitted.

An increase in the DTIM period count allows clients to sleep longer; however, it delays the delivery of multicast and unicast packets. Because the packets are buffered, large DTIM period counts can cause a buffer overflow.

NOTE: Beacon period is expressed in kilomicroseconds (kμsec). This unusual measurement of time is used to express some software application time. One kμsec is equivalent to 1024 microseconds, whereas one kμsec is close to a millisecond (1000 microseconds). It's just a bit longer, so gets its own unusual moniker.

You can manage the Beacon Period and Data Beacon Rate (DTIM) settings from the Settings tab, as shown previously in Figure 11-5. Enter the value you wish, and then click **Apply** at the bottom of the screen.

Table 11-7 lists and describes the CLI commands to manage the beacon period and DTIM settings.

Table 11-7   *Configuring the Beacon Period and DTIM via the CLI*

Command	Description
configure terminal	Enters global configuration mode.
**interface dot11radio {0	1}**	Enters configuration mode for the radio interface. The 2.4-GHz radio is radio **0**, and the 5-GHz radio is radio **1**.

Table 11-7 *Configuring the Beacon Period and DTIM via the CLI (Continued)*

Command	Description
beacon period *value*	Sets the beacon period in kµsec.
beacon dtim-period *value*	Sets the DTIM in kµsec.
end	Returns to privileged EXEC mode.

Configuring the RTS Threshold

Request to Send (RTS) indicates the size of a frame that requires an RTS control message sent before it. You must keep a few considerations in mind when you set this parameter.

RTS packets are sent more often because of smaller values. In addition, more bandwidth is consumed, therefore reducing the amount of throughput on the network. However, the more RTS packets sent, the quicker the system can recover from interference or collisions, which occurs in large, busy networks.

RTS is also helpful when two clients cannot hear each other (for instance, they are on opposite sides of a cell), although they can hear the AP.

The RTS Threshold setting is between 0 and 2339 bytes. The default value is 2312.

The RTS Max. Retries setting dictates the number of times the AP issues an RTS before it quits. This setting is a value between 1 and 128. The default value is 32.

You can manage the RTS Threshold and RTS Max. Retries settings from the Settings tab, shown previously in Figure 11-5. Enter the values you wish, and then click **Apply** at the bottom of the screen.

Table 11-8 lists and describes the CLI commands to manage the RTS settings.

Table 11-8 *Configuring RTS Retries and Threshold via the CLI*

Command	Description
configure terminal	Enters global configuration mode.
**interface dot11radio {0	1}**	Enters configuration mode for the radio interface. The 2.4-GHz radio is radio **0**, the 5-GHz radio is radio **1**.
rts threshold *value*	Enter the RTS threshold (a value between 0 and 2339).
rts retries *value*	Enter the number of RTS retries (a value between 1 and 128).
end	Returns to privileged EXEC mode.

Configuring Data Retries

When packets are sent, they can be lost. As such, the AP resends the packets to ensure the packets are received by the client. You can tell the AP how often to resend packets by configuring the maximum amount of data retries.

You can manage the maximum amount of data retries on the SETTINGS web page, shown previously in Figure 11-5. In the Max. Data Retries box, enter the number of retries you wish, then click **Apply** at the bottom of the screen.

You can also use the CLI to configure this setting as described in Table 11-9.

Table 11-9   *Configuring Data Retries*

Command	Description
configure terminal	Enters global configuration mode.
interface dot11radio {0 | 1}	Enters configuration mode for the radio interface. The 2.4-GHz radio is radio **0**, the 5-GHz radio is radio **1**.
packet retries *value*	Enters the number of data retries (value between 1 and 128).
end	Returns to privileged EXEC mode.

Configuring the Fragmentation Threshold

The fragmentation threshold establishes the level that traffic fragments. When an AP sends a transmission, the traffic *fragments*, or divides into smaller pieces. Smaller frames result in fewer collisions. When the station receives those pieces, it sends an acknowledgement to the AP. Pieces that are not received are resent. The benefit is that with more pieces sent, there is a better chance that the entire transmission is received. The downside is obvious—more fragmentation means more throughput consumed with acknowledgement messages.

A good rule of thumb for the fragmentation threshold setting is that if few collisions are occurring (less than 5 percent), don't bother to use fragmentation. The extra overhead created by the headers reduces throughput.

On the other hand, if you see a good deal of collisions, you can attenuate them, set the fragmentation threshold to around 1000 bytes, and adjust it up or down from there. You have to strike a balance between throughput and collisions.

Fragmentation can also be useful in high-interference environments, environments with high multipath distortion, and environments where clients rapidly move.

You can set the fragmentation threshold between 256 and 2346 bytes. The default setting is 2338 bytes and can be adjusted up or down.

NOTE: These fragmentation threshold values are interchangeable between the 2.4-GHz and 5-GHz radios.

You can manage the fragmentation threshold on the Settings tab, as shown previously in Figure 11-5. In the Fragmentation Threshold box, enter the threshold you wish, and then click **Apply** at the bottom of the screen.

You can also use the CLI to configure the fragmentation threshold settings as described in Table 11-10.

Table 11-10   *Configuring the Fragmentation Threshold*

Command	Description
configure terminal	Enters global configuration mode.
interface dot11radio {0 | 1}	Enters configuration mode for the radio interface. The 2.4-GHz radio is radio **0**, the 5-GHz radio is radio **1**.
fragment-threshold *value*	Enters the fragmentation threshold (values in the range of 256 to 2346 bytes).
end	Returns to privileged EXEC mode.

Although your Aironet AP functions nicely right out of the box, the settings discussed throughout this chapter can help fine tune the device to fit in with the rest of your wireless LAN.

Chapter 12 Contents

Network Tuning Tools and Resources

Tuning your network is a balancing act among a number of variables. The task is tricky on a wired network; however, it's even more complex a wireless LAN (WLAN), where radio broadcasts and reception play an important part.

This chapter looks at some tools you can use to ensure that your WLAN operates at peak efficiency. After we discuss signal strength, we give an overview of the popular Windows tuning application, Perfmon, and how you use it to monitor your WLAN. Then we discuss quality of service (QoS), why it is useful to improve your WLAN's performance, and how you enable it.

To conclude this chapter, we look at some third-party tuning applications that you might consider to help your WLAN work at peak efficiency.

Signal Strength

To assess how much signal strength a client receives is not difficult, especially when you use Cisco clients. Each Cisco client is equipped with Cisco Aironet Desktop Utility (ADU). (We covered these utilities in more detail in Chapter 6, "Configuring Clients.")

If you open the tool and select **Site Survey**, ADU shows two important metrics—signal strength and signal quality, as illustrated in Figure 12-1. The most important part of this screen is Overall Link Quality, which gives you a simple assessment of your connection to the WLAN.

Figure 12-1   *ADU's Site Survey Tool*

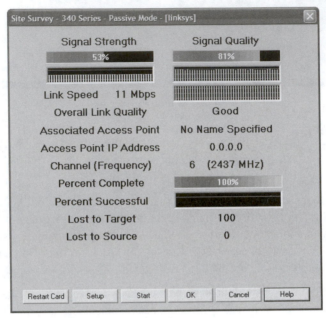

The site survey tool is helpful not only when you analyze a client's ability to connect to the WLAN; it also helps when you perform a site survey. It's easy to find the best (and worst) reception by carrying around your organization a laptop equipped with a wireless interface and ADU.

You can use the Site Survey component of ADU to help monitor your WLAN's performance and better position APs and clients. This is accomplished with two different site survey modes:

- **Passive mode** — The site survey does not send out traffic. It simply listens to other RF network traffic, and displays signal strength and quality.
- **Active mode** — The site survey exchanges packets with the AP.

The default action for the site survey is in passive mode. However, to engage active mode, click **Setup** to configure active mode, and then click **Start** to run the test. When the test has ended, the site survey tool returns to passive mode (or you can click **Stop**). This can help you assess your client's transmitting and receiving abilities.

The site survey tool using ADU is covered in more depth in Chapter 5, "Installing and Configuring Access Points."

Using Perfmon

You probably already have one of the best network performance tools installed on your network. Microsoft includes System Monitor (formerly known as Performance Monitor and synonymously referred to as Perfmon) since the days of Windows NT. Perfmon provides current, accurate information on thousands of different attributes of your network, and you can easily draft it for WLAN performance monitoring.

To start Perfmon, either select its snap-in from the Microsoft Management Console (MMC) or enter **Perfmon** in the command line.

You might already use Perfmon to keep an eye on your wired network. The tool makes it easy to monitor both your wired network and WLAN. Figure 12-2 shows how Perfmon looks when it is first started.

Figure 12-2   *Perfmon's Opening Display: Ready for Action*

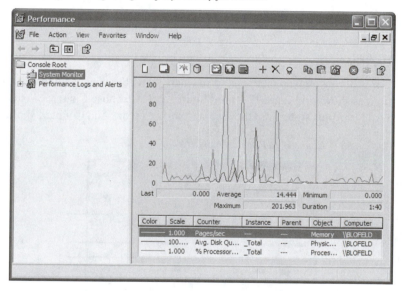

Views

Perfmon tracks the data you choose to monitor, and then it offers four ways for you to manage that data. Think of Perfmon as an application with four different tools. These tools are known as *views*. Each view allows you to display, perform actions, store, and generate reports on the data monitored by System Monitor. Table 12-1 explains the Perfmon views in more detail.

Table 12-1 *Perfmon Views*

View	Description
Chart	Displays monitored system data in line graph or histogram formats.
Alert	Used to create alerts based on counter thresholds. Alerts can perform actions when a counter exceeds or drops below a specified threshold. Actions can process a certain application or notify the system administrator.
Log	Create a new file or open an existing log file. This file can create reports in Report view. Data can be exported in .tsv and .csv formats (tab- or comma-separated values) for analysis in applications, such as Microsoft Excel.
Report	You can list objects and their associated counter data in a report that uses values derived from current activity or a log file.

Perfmon can track thousands of metrics. This chapter focuses on network performance in Perfmon.

Chart View

To begin monitoring a given metric, start in Chart view (the view when you start the application, as shown in Figure 12-2). In Figure 12-3, we chose Chart view, and then selected Add (the plus sign) from the toolbar to bring up the Add Counters dialog box.

Figure 12-3 *Adding Counters to Perfmon's Chart View*

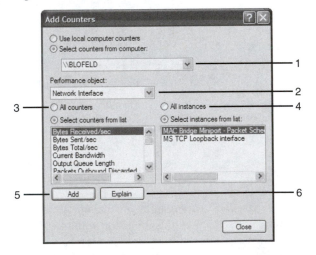

NOTE: You could also click on the icon that looks like a plus sign at the top of the window.

The following explains the settings selected for this window, as marked in Figure 12-3.

1. This is used to select which computer in your network you monitor. In this case, the computer BLOFELD is chosen.

2. This provides a list of performance objects that you can monitor. These objects include memory, network interface, and server, among many other categories. In this case, Network Interface is chosen.

3. Within the performance object category, you can track certain instances. If you want, you can click the **All counters** radio button immediately above the list. However, this example tracks only the bytes received by the client computer. Therefore, Bytes Received/sec is chosen.

4. Because the computer BLOFELD has different network interfaces installed, you have the option to select which network interface you want to monitor. The interface you choose is the interface to the wireless network. (Here, the connection is bridged so it shows as **MAC Bridge Miniport**, although it contains the Wi-Fi connection.) Again, the option to monitor all interfaces is presented with a radio button (**All instances**).

5. When the monitored items are selected, click the **Add** button.

6. If you need an explanation of what the counter monitors, click **Explain** for a brief description.

If you care to add more instances to your monitor, use the aforementioned steps. When you finish, click the **Close** button.

After you select the items you wish to monitor, Perfmon looks like the image in Figure 12-4. When Perfmon runs for a short time, you can see how well your client devices fare. If they do not receive all the data, you should reposition the client. Remember, that even under ideal circumstances you cannot see an 802.11g client that receives traffic at 54 Mbps. You should expect about half the 802.11 data rate if data comes from a local source.

Figure 12-4 *Checking the Client's Performance*

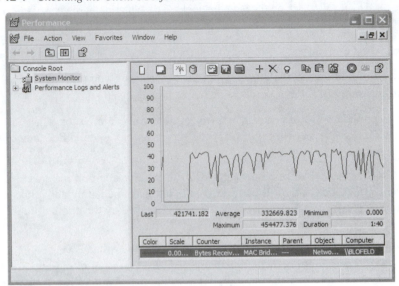

You can set up Chart view to display information from saved log files or you can display information in real time. The uses for the Chart view range from network performance spot checks to long-term analysis of data. The information bar below the graph provides the last, average, minimum, maximum, and duration data on the selected counter. When the information is captured to a log file, it is stored with the ability to read it later.

Alert View

If you actively monitor your network, Chart view is an excellent tool. However, if you need another option, alert view is helpful.

For example, you can set up Alerts to notify you when packet errors exceed a given threshold. If that threshold is breached, you can run a command-line executable.

You can add alert counters the same way you do in the Chart view. The Alert view is located in the left pane of the MMC while the System Monitor snap-in runs. Right-click the **Alert** icon, and then select **New Alert Settings** from the context menu. A window pops up and asks for you to name the alert. For this example, the Alert is called Client Notification. The window looks like the one in Figure 12-5.

Figure 12-5   *Adding an Alert and Sampling Rate*

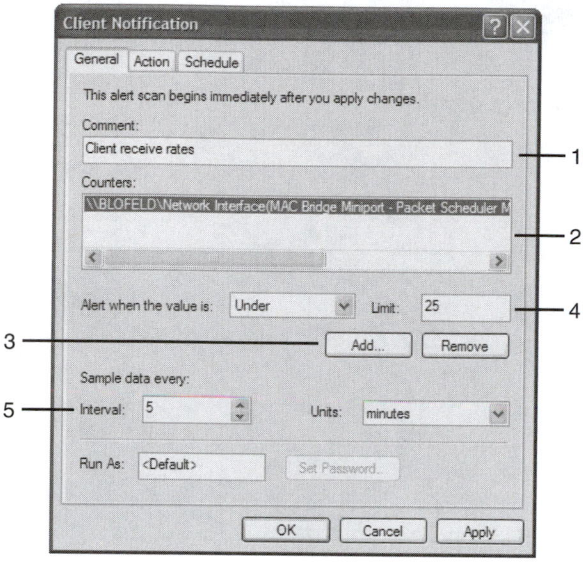

The following are important aspects of this window, as marked in Figure 12-5:

1. Add a brief comment that describes the purpose of this alert.

2. View the counters that are monitored.

3. Click **Add** to add counters using the same method used for the Chart view. If you no longer want a counter monitored, click the **Remove** button.

4. Establish your threshold. The pull-down menu allows you to select either **Over** or **Under**. Next to it, you enter your chosen value. For this example, the value is set at 25.

5. These settings allow you to determine how often data is sampled. You can select a given amount of seconds, minutes, hours, or days to check the data.

After you select the data to monitor, click on the **Action** tab. The result is shown in Figure 12-6.

Figure 12-6 *The Action Tab Is Used to Specify a Behavior to Process When an Alert Is Tripped*

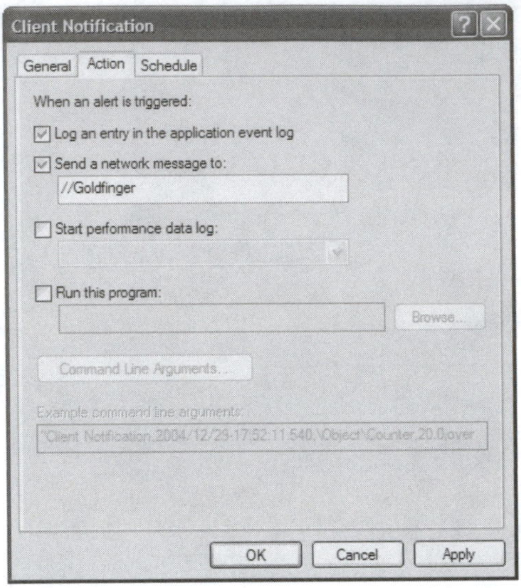

As Figure 12-6 shows, when the threshold is surpassed, you can select one or more of the following actions:

- Log an entry in the application event log
- Send a network message
- Start performance data log
- Run this program

For Perfmon to send an alert message, it must be sent to a registered NetBIOS name, and the Alerter and Messenger services must run. In this example, the computer's Net Name is GOLDFINGER, so you do not have to establish a name. However, you can register a NetBIOS name at a specific computer if you enter **net name Goldfinger / add** at the Windows command prompt. After the name is registered, the alerts are displayed on that computer, which you can view by selecting the Schedule tab. Figure 12-7 illustrates the Schedule tab.

To set up the time when the scan begins and ends, use the Schedule tab. You can start the scan at an exact time, and it can end either at an exact time, or after a certain period of time.

Log View

You can collect your performance data at predetermined intervals for analysis later. The other views can then read the log file and perform their various functions as if the logged data were in real time.

Each selected object is monitored, then the data written to the log. To start the view, right-click on the log in the leftmost pane of the MMC, then select **New Log Settings** from the context menu. Figure 12-8 shows the resulting window.

Figure 12-7   *Scheduling Start and End Times for a Performance Scan*

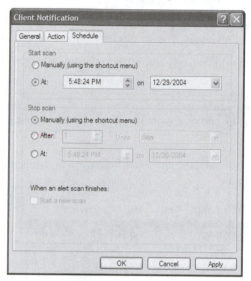

Figure 12-8   *Defining Which Network Performance Metrics to Log*

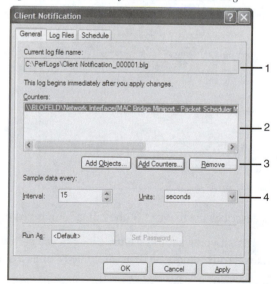

By now you should understand how to add information to this log. The following explain the features of the General tab of the Log view, as numbered in Figure 12-8:

1. The file name of the current log.

2. A list of the counters that are logged.

3. Click **Add** or **Remove** to change counters and objects. The process is identical to the methods used Previously to add counters to the Chart and Alert views.

4. Use the **Units** drop-down list to establish how often data is sampled for the log.

NOTE: Be careful when you establish the time interval. Some objects can generate a huge amount of data for the log, and you might find yourself running out of hard drive space.

The Log Files tab, illustrated in Figure 12-9, helps you to manage some housekeeping attributes.

Figure 12-9 *The Log Files Tab Is Used for File Management*

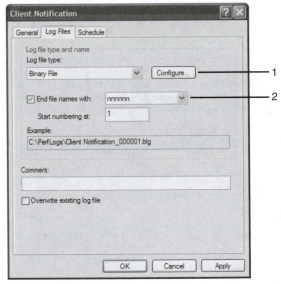

The list that follows describes the features of the tab, as numbered in Figure 12-9.

1. Determine what format you want to save the file. You can choose from binary, binary circular, text (both comma- and tab-delimited), or as a SQL database file.

2. The **End file names with option** is used to name your log files. You can end log files with a sequential number or with a timestamp and date stamp.

The Schedule tab for Log view is similar to that shown for Alert view in Figure 12-6, and it is used to tell when to start and end the log. You can also tell Perfmon what to do when logging has ended; for example, it can start a new log file or application.

Report View

The Report view displays the same counter information available from the Chart view; however, rather than showing performance data graphically, the information displays in a tabular format.

Useful Perfmon counters for WLAN performance tuning come from the Network Interface performance object and include:

- Bytes Received/sec
- Bytes Sent/sec
- Bytes Total/sec
- Current Bandwidth
- Output Queue Length
- Packets Outbound Discarded
- Packets Outbound Errors
- Packets Received Discarded
- Packets Received Errors
- Packets Received Non-Unicast
- Packets Received Unicast/sec
- Packets Received Unknown
- Packets Received/sec
- Packets Sent Non-Unicast/sec
- Packets Sent Unicast/sec
- Packets Sent/sec
- Packets/sec

QoS

In addition to the radio tuning techniques discussed in Chapter 11, "Tuning AP Radio Parameters," another way to ensure complete packets arrive at their destinations is to employ quality of service (QoS). In essence, QoS sends packets before it sends other traffic—they are a higher priority. QoS is especially useful in environments that use the WLAN for voice or video applications. QoS is a popular way to prioritize traffic on a wired network, although you can also implement it in a wireless environment.

NOTE: You must also consider range when you diagnose performance problems. Even with QoS, you cannot mitigate problems for a client who is out of range or on the periphery of the AP's cell.

QoS Overview

QoS enables you to use congestion management and avoidance tools, which prevent traffic from slowing down your WLAN.

In a wired network, routers or switches primarily enforce QoS. In a WLAN, however, the AP manages the QoS duties for traffic to wireless clients.

NOTE: You might not notice the effect of QoS on small WLANs with light traffic loads. However, the effect of QoS is more apparent where APs manage heavy loads.

If you already employ a QoS mechanism on your network, your AP assigns QoS policies in the following order:

1. Packets that have already been classified by a switch or router. Existing classification takes priority over all other QoS policies on the AP.

2. QoS Element for Wireless Phones setting. If this setting is enabled, voice traffic takes precedence over other traffic.

3. Policies created on the AP.

4. Default classification for packets.

Configuring QoS

To configure QoS on your Cisco AP, follow these steps:

NOTE: If you use VLANs on your WLAN, make sure the VLANs are properly configured before you continue.

Step 1.   Open the Cisco AP's web browser interface.

Step 2.   Click **Task > Services** on the left side of the browser.

Step 3.   Click **QoS**. This calls up the QoS Policies page, shown in Figure 12-10.

Figure 12-10 *Cisco AP QoS Screen*

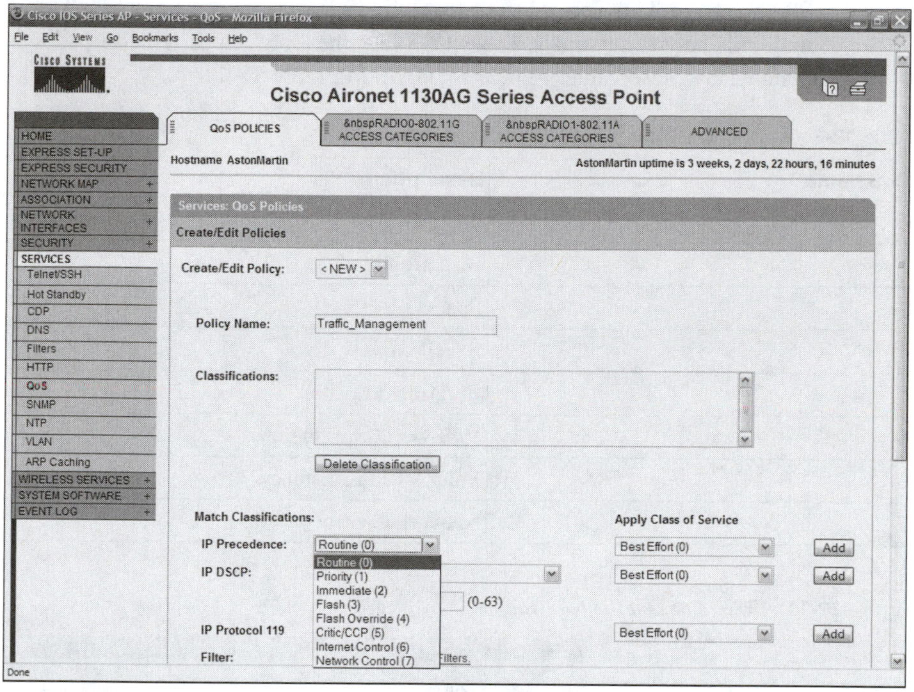

Step 4. Select **<NEW>** in the **Create/Edit Policy** field, then type in a name for the new policy.

Step 5. If the packets you prioritize contain IP precedence information in the IP header Type of Service (ToS) field, select an IP precedence classification from the IP Precedence drop-down menu. This value is between 0 and 7. Table 12-2 lists the ToS values. Figure 12-10 shows the ToS values in a drop-down menu.

Table 12-2 *ToS Values When Enabling QoS on a Cisco AP*

ToS Value	Description
0	Routine
1	Priority
2	Immediate
3	Flash
4	Flash Override
5	Critic/CCP
6	Internet Control
7	Network Control

Step 6. Use the Apply Class of Service drop-down menu to select the CoS that the AP gives to packets you selected from the IP Precedence drop-down. This number is between 0 and 7. Table 12-3 lists the CoS values. The drop-down menu where these values appear is shown in Figure 12-11.

Table 12-3   *CoS Values When Enabling QoS on an Cisco AP*

CoS Value	Description
0	Best Effort
1	Background
2	Spare
3	Excellent
4	Controlled Load
5	Video <100ms Latency
6	Voice <100ms Latency
7	Network Control

Figure 12-11   *CoS Values on the QoS Tab*

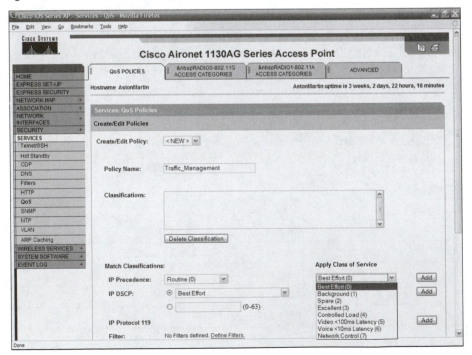

Step 7.   Click the **Add** button next to the Class of Service menu for IP Precedence. This adds the classification in the Classifications field. You can delete previously defined classifications if you highlight the classification and click the **Delete** button.

Step 8.   If these packets contain IP Differentiated Services Code Point (DSCP) information in the header ToS, select a classification from the IP DSCP drop-down menu. The drop-down menu looks similar to the one in Figure 12-11.

Step 9.   The Apply Class of Service drop-down menu is used to select a CoS that the AP applies to packets that you select from the IP DSCP menu.

Step 10.   Click the **Add** button next to the Class of Service menu. This classification is added to the Classifications field.

Step 11.   The IP Protocol 119 selections are used to prioritize packets from Spectralink phones. Specify a CoS, and then click the **Add** button to add this to the Classification field.

Step 12.   You can establish a default classification for all packets on the VLAN if you select a CoS, then click **Add**.

Step 13.   After you add classifications to this policy, click the **Apply** button under the CoS drop-downs. If you want to delete the entire policy, click **Delete**.

Step 14.   The next portion of the browser shows the **Apply Policies to Interface/VLANs** drop-down menu, as shown in Figure 12-12. This is used to apply policies to the AP Ethernet and radio ports. If VLANs are configured on the AP, drop-downs appear for each VLAN's virtual ports. If VLANs are not configured, drop-downs for each interface disappear.

Step 15.   Click the **Apply** button at the bottom of the page to finalize your settings and to apply them to your AP.

Step 16.   To give voice traffic priority over other traffic on your WLAN, click the **Advanced** tab, and select the radio button to enable this policy.

The QoS values you select for your network depend largely on your organization's policies, as well as what traffic you deem to be more important than others.

Figure 12-12 *Policies Are Applied Using the Drop-Down Menus at the Bottom of the QoS Tab*

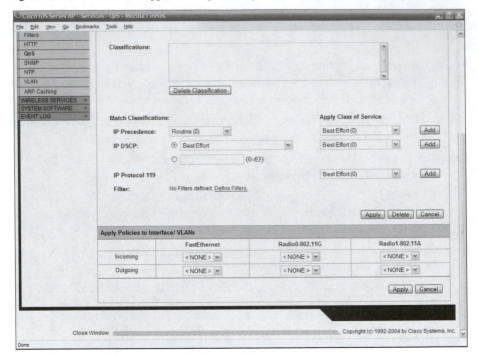

Using Third-Party Tools

After you build your WLAN, you need to continue ongoing performance tuning. You can make tuning significantly easier if you use tools, such as Perfmon, or establish and use a QoS plan.

Third-party vendors offer several tools to tune a WLAN. These applications often mix performance and tuning tools; they detect radio signals; analyze individual broadcast packets; and offer a suite of security measures.

As with QoS, you need to change your thought processes when you use these sorts of wireless performance tools. If you know how to use network analyzers in a wired network, remember that you cannot manage or track anything outside the RF range of these tools, even if it's still part of the WLAN. Therefore, be sure to move around your network to get optimal results.

NetStumbler

NetStumbler is a freeware tool for Windows that allows you to detect WLANs with 802.11a, 802.11b, and 802.11g technologies. The tool has numerous uses, including:

- Ensures your WLAN operates properly
- Finds locations with poor coverage in the WLAN
- Locates other networks that might cause interference
- Detects rogue APs

After it's activated, NetStumbler goes to work and detects all APs in the area. Figure 12-13 shows NetStumbler has detected an AP with the SSID linksys.

Figure 12-13 *NetStumbler Locates and Analyzes All APs It Can Hear*

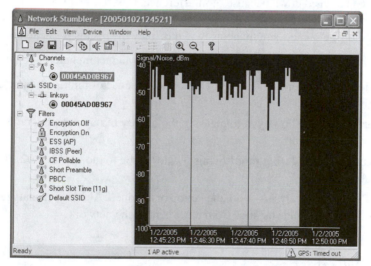

NetStumbler enables you to examine the detected APs based on the channel they use by SSID, or via several different filters (for instance, by which APs have WEP keys activate and which do not). If you refer back to Figure 12-13 and select the AP with the MAC address of 00045AD0B967, it results in the display of statistics that show the AP's broadcast signal to noise ratio.

This is useful when you locate your own APs because you can find where the signal strength is best, and where it needs improvement.

AirMagnet

The AirMagnet laptop and handheld analyzers can diagnose and troubleshoot WLANs from any Windows-based laptop or pocket PC. The analyzers can track security issues (such as policies, rogue devices, and network vulnerabilities) and performance problems. AirMagnet monitors WLAN performance with over 40 alerts for various situations, including:

- RF problems
- Traffic problems
- Configuration issues
- Overloaded infrastructure
- Hardware failures

Each alert is accompanied with a detailed description of the problem and diagnostic data and suggestions for correcting the problem.

Additionally, AirMagnet can track performance for individual channels. For example, if channel 6 is bogged down because of interference, broadcast storms, and low transmission rates, the application can alert users to the situation. Additionally, you can monitor multiple channels simultaneously and display the results for analysis.

Other WLAN performance-enhancing features of AirMagnet include:

- **Multipath detection**—It can alert you to the presence of multipath interference at a given location.
- **Coverage tool**—Allows you to measure the quality of network coverage against desired service levels.
- **Concurrent 802.11a/b/g monitoring**—Allows you to monitor all 802.11 bands, concurrently.
- **Mobile WLAN analysis**—With the laptop or handheld AirMagnet analyzers, you can cull readings and statistics from anywhere in the network.

Sniffer Wireless

Network General offers Sniffer Wireless application, a third-party WLAN performance monitoring tool.

Sniffer can identify security concerns, as well as network performance problems. It is used with Windows-based laptops and handheld PCs, and it's compatible with Cisco wireless cards.

The following outlines Sniffer's features:

- Automatic channel surfing provides an overview of network traffic and hosts, which allow you to identify the traffic on your WLAN.
- Real-time and post-capture WEP decryption helps to troubleshoot traffic at upper network layers.
- Real-time expert analysis identifies potential network performance problems.

- Dashboard view shows statistics for 802.11 traffic. It includes the rate and the number of packets sent.

- Host Table displays information on each station that Sniffer monitors. You can examine transmission speeds, extend service set IDs per AP, and signal strength per station.

- Analysis of 802.11 frames from network to application layer.

- Automatic detection of problems.

- Identification of problems (such as bottlenecks, duplicated IP addresses, misconfigured routers, and so forth) are identified before they are problematic.

In addition to its WLAN performance duties, Sniffer Wireless can also identify security concerns, to include rogue AP detection.

If you want to keep your WLAN running optimally, it requires periodic examination and adjustment. If you use tools, such as Perfmon, the Cisco site survey tool, or any of the other tools examined in this chapter, your WLAN can perform optimally.

Other Resources

- **AirMagnet**

  http://www.airmagnet.com

- **Sniffer Wireless**

  http://www.sniffer.com

- **The NetStumbler survey tool**

  http://www.netstumbler.com

- **A Mac version of NetStumbler**

  http://www.macstumbler.com

- **WaveStumbler, a Linux tool that locates APs and assesses their strength**

  http://www.cqure.net/tools.jsp?id=08

Chapter 13 Contents

Diagnosing Client Connection Problems

Tracking down problems in a wired network is tough enough. The project gets more complex in a wireless network, where not only are the issues of network configuration at play, but so are the issues that affect radio transmission and reception.

This chapter explains how to troubleshoot your wireless network. Not only does the chapter discuss common problems related to Cisco wireless LAN (WLAN) configuration, but also topics relevant to Windows WLAN environments.

Troubleshooting Access Points (AP)

When tracking down client connection issues, the problem often is either a misconfigured client or access point. First, however, you should make sure that there is not a physical problem with your AP or APs.

AP Problems

When you are in an environment with multiple clients and APs, finding out what is wrong can be a chore. For example, if you have many users — some of whom are able to connect to the WLAN, others who are not — your most likely culprit is a misconfigured AP. How do you know which AP to fix?

You can look around your office and make a good guess about which AP is malfunctioning. If the users who cannot access the WLAN work in the same area, you should look at the AP servicing that area.

NOTE: Don't overlook the obvious.

Sometimes an AP gets unplugged or the circuit breaker has been turned off. It sounds obvious, but make sure there is power to the AP.

In addition, a client adapter that is not Wi-Fi certified is a good sign of trouble ahead. Vendors who are eager to ship product don't always ensure that their products are compatible with other manufacturers' devices. As such, if an adapter has not been Wi-Fi certified, it might not work with other companies' APs. Cisco products are Wi-Fi certified.

It has been mentioned previously, but bears repeating—Is there any radio interference? (For example, a new cordless telephone or a new WLAN might have been installed in the neighboring office.) Don't overlook the potential for bad wiring between your AP and the switch. Also don't miss such simple issues as a power cable coming loose from the AP.

Check the AP

Perform a communications test to see if the AP responds. You can do this with the basic **ping** command. You should attempt the communications test twice—once on the wired network and once on the wireless network. If you are not familiar with the test, it is an easy, two-step process:

Step 1.   Open a command prompt window.

Step 2.   Enter **ping 192.168.1.101** (where *192.168.1.101* is the AP's IP address).

Begin by pinging the AP from a PC on the wired network. If the AP does not respond to the ping test, there is a break in the communications link or the AP is misconfigured. You can determine which is the problem by repeating the ping test on a wireless client. If the wireless client can successfully ping the AP, then you know there is a communications link problem between the AP and the wired network. You might have to run new Category 5 cabling to the AP.

If the ping from a wireless client is unsuccessful, the AP might be faulty. Unplug the AP to reset it, and then reconnect the power. If you can do it without affecting users, reset the switch the AP is connected to. Give the AP a few minutes before you try to ping it again; this gives the network time to recognize the AP. Run the ping test from both wired and wireless networks again. If both tests fail, the problem might be either a faulty AP or a misconfigured AP.

Faulty APs

The best way to determine if your AP is damaged is to plug it into a jack you know works using a patch cable you know is not damaged. Also verify the AP's TCP/IP configuration. The AP's IP address can be found on the Express Setup page. When you have done this, try to ping the device from a wired client. If the test still fails, the AP is probably damaged and should be replaced.

APs tend to be reliable devices, so before calling your AP's vendor with your warranty in hand, take a closer look at the AP's configuration. This tends to be where the bulk of the problems exist.

Configuration Issues

Most often the source of connection problems stems from a misconfigured client or AP. This section explains some of the more prevalent configuration issues and how you can correct them.

In a Windows XP environment, right-clicking the wireless networking icon in the taskbar, and then selecting **View Available Wireless Networks** results in the window shown in Figure 13-1.

Figure 13-1 *Windows XP Shows You Which Wireless Networks Are Available*

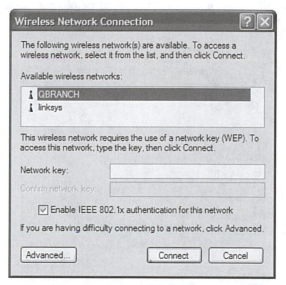

You see the Wireless Network Connection dialog box. This dialog box shows the Service Set Identifier (SSID) of wireless networks on your channel to which you are not currently connected. If the network you want to connect to is shown on this list, but you are unable to connect, the connection is good; however, there is a configuration issue.

The sections that follow detail some of the more common issues related to AP configuration problems.

Signal Strength

Ideally, you should perform a site survey before planning and deploying your WLAN. A site survey helps locate the best (and worst) spots for signal reception. If you have problems connecting, it's time to revisit this practice and perform a signal strength test.

Most client adapters (including the Cisco product line) have a signal strength application.

If your ping test on the wired network is successful, try to run the Cisco Aironet Client Utility Site Survey Utility and move around the office. You might be located in a spot that gets poor reception. This utility tests for signal strength and quality.

With Cisco devices, you can determine signal strength by going to the Aironet Desktop Utility (ADU) and clicking the **Link Status** icon. Third-party client adapters usually have a similar tool. Check your adapter's documentation for usage information.

Figure 13-2 shows the resulting graphic representation of your signal's strength and quality from the Aironet Desktop Utility Link Status option.

Figure 13-2 *Checking Signal Strength Between an AP and Client*

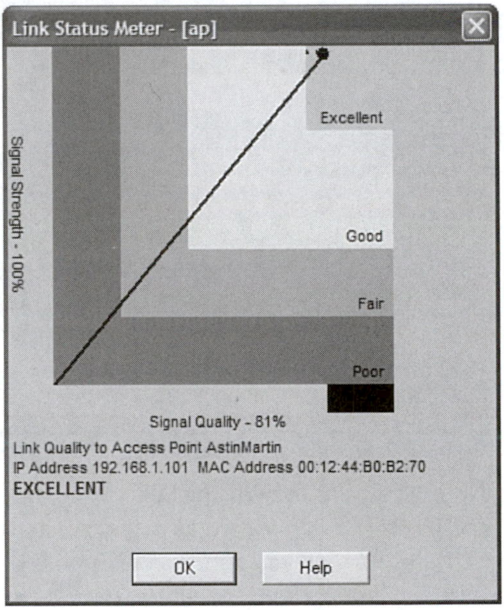

Change Channels

If you discover a weak or poor quality signal, but nothing has changed in your organization, try to change the channels on your AP and the wireless client. Again, sources of interference can creep in when you don't expect them (a new cordless phone in an adjacent office or a leaky microwave oven, for example) and to respond to that interference, channel changes can be helpful.

NOTE: Remember that best practices dictate that you should have at least five channels among adjacent APs to keep interference to a minimum. Because 802.11b and 802.11g networks operate on 11 channels in the 2.4-GHz frequency, you can safely use channels 1, 6, and 11. In 5-GHz 802.11a networks, however, 23 nonoverlapping channels work.

Wi-Fi channels are explained in more detail in Appendix A, "802.11 Protocols."

If you can eliminate the source of interference (get rid of an interfering cordless phone or switch the phone to a 900-MHz model, for example), you can save yourself the trouble of reconfiguring to a new channel. However, changing channels might be the best solution. If the neighboring office has recently installed its own WLAN that uses the same channel, it might be easier to simply change channels rather than changing the neighbor's channel.

Check the SSID

Your WLAN likely has its own SSID. However, if the SSID on the client does not match the SSID of the AP, the two cannot connect. If an SSID doesn't specify the correct network, you cannot ping the AP while the client searches for a network with the correct SSID.

For example, assume the client is to associate with an AP that has an SSID of QBRANCH. However, the AP has an SSID of SPECTRE. As such, the client ignores SPECTRE as it searches for QBRANCH.

Check this setting on both the AP and the client. Users who fiddle with their laptops might alter this setting. Or, if the client has recently associated with a different WLAN, this setting might have been changed, but not reset for use in your network.

WEP Keys

Although WEP keys do not provide an ideal level of WLAN security, using them is better than nothing. If WEP is not correctly configured, you cannot ping the AP from a wireless client.

Be cognizant of how you need to enter your WEP key, as mentioned in Chapter 5, "Installing and Configuring Access Points." Some wireless adapters require you to enter the key in hexadecimal format, whereas others require it to be in ASCII format. You should also be aware of the differences between 64- and 128-bit encryption. It is important that the settings on both the AP and client match precisely.

WEP key misconfigurations are responsible for many configuration problems. The symptoms of a WEP key mismatch sometimes mirror those of more serious problems.

For instance, if a WEP key is incorrectly entered, wireless clients won't be able to get an IP address from the Dynamic Host Configuration Protocol (DHCP) server. This is great to keep people out of your network, but not so great if a WEP key misconfiguration disrupts legitimate, authorized clients.

Wi-Fi Protected Access (WPA)

The troubleshooting process can be even more complex if you use an 802.1X solution for your security. Chapter 8, "Wireless Security: Next Steps," explains the process of enabling WPA in greater detail.

802.1X authentication has three components:

- The client
- The AP
- The RADIUS server

You can check three places for misconfigurations.

You must ensure that the AP is a client of the RADIUS server. If the AP is not configured to talk to the RADIUS server, the client cannot log on to the network.

Next, check for misconfigurations between the AP and client WPA settings, such as the authentication method (EAP, LEAP, and so on).

If you use Windows, you might run into a conflict between the Cisco ADU and Windows because each might attempt to manage the WPA duties. You can disable this feature on Windows XP (other versions of Windows are similar) by following these steps:

Step 1. Choose **Start > Control Panel > Network and Internet Connections**.

Step 2. Click **Network Connections.**

Step 3. Right-click **Wireless Network Connection**.

Step 4. Click **Properties**.

Step 5. Click the **Wireless Networks** tab.

Step 6. Clear the **Use Windows to configure my wireless network settings** check box.

Step 7. Click **OK** to save your settings.

IP Address Duplication

For many networks, it makes good sense to offload DHCP services to a dedicated network server. Consider an environment that has multiple APs assigning IP addresses. If the APs assign addresses in the 192.168.0.x range (with no coordination between the two APs), it won't be long before two clients are issued the same IP address, with trouble sure to follow.

There are two ways to solve this problem:

- Disable the APs' DHCP servers, and then forward the client DHCP requests so that they can obtain IP addresses from the network's DHCP server.
- Assign IP addresses in unique scopes. That is, set each AP's DHCP server so that it issues its own set of IP addresses that does not overlap.

DHCP Misconfiguration

Depending on the size of your network and your resources, your network might or might not have a DHCP server. Many APs come with their own built-in DHCP servers.

By default, these AP-based DHCP servers typically assign IP addresses in the 192.168.0.x/24 range, the public Class-C address space. Many DHCP APs do not connect with clients for which they did not issue IP addresses. A problem is that the 192.168.0.x range of IP addresses might be incompatible with your network's IP addressing scheme.

There are two ways to solve this problem:

- You can change the IP address range by changing the AP's DHCP server from the 192.168.0.x block to a block of addresses in line with your organization's addressing scheme.
- You can disable the AP's DHCP server, allowing wireless clients to obtain an IP address from the network's DHCP server.

MAC Filtering

Chapter 8 discussed MAC filtering lists, which, when used properly, are another weapon in your arsenal to keep unauthorized people out of your network. If a user's MAC address is not on the list of permitted MAC addresses, he cannot access the AP. This can work the other way, however, if misconfigured.

If you don't normally use MAC filtering, it can be a source of headache if it is accidentally turned on, as Figure 13-3 shows. Unless the clients are on that list, they cannot connect to the WLAN, regardless of other configuration settings.

Figure 13-3 *Accidentally Activating MAC Filtering Can Keep Authorized Users off the WLAN*

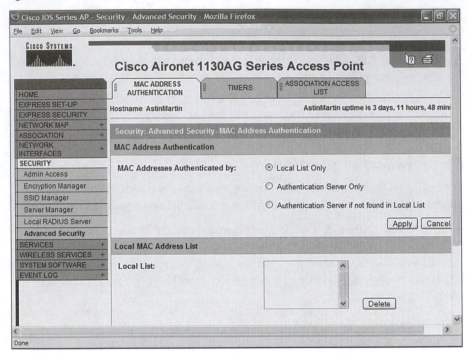

NOTE: MAC filtering can also be a problem in environments that have multiple APs. Just because the administrator enters the MAC address into one AP doesn't mean that the address is propagated to other APs. A client might connect with one AP, but if it roams away from that AP, it cannot connect to an AP that isn't on its MAC list. A central RADIUS server can manage MAC addresses in an environment that has multiple APs.

Misconfigurations are the most likely sources for your connectivity problems. You must be thorough and check for the previously discussed issues when resolving network problems.

Troubleshooting and Conflict Resolution Tools

Troubleshooting a WLAN is sometimes more complex than double-checking WEP keys. Cisco includes with its client devices a helpful utility known as the Client Troubleshooting Utility. This section examines that tool and provides information about resolving common sources of client problems in a Windows environment.

Client Troubleshooting Utility

As with APs, there are some useful places to check first. Check to ensure that the radio is turned on. Many laptops use both hardware and software switches to turn off the radio. Do you also see a Link Status icon that indicates whether or not you have a connection? The problem might not have anything to do with an RF connection; it's more than likely a configuration issue.

Cisco includes a useful troubleshooting tool with its client utilities package. The Troubleshooting Utility enables you to find and fix problems on the client computer.

NOTE: The Troubleshooting Utility is meant for use only when the computer is in infrastructure mode and not ad hoc mode. This is because the utility is used to evaluate the connection between the client and an AP.

The following explains how you can use the Troubleshooting Utility. Again, the steps might vary depending on the model of wireless card you use. However, this should give you an idea of what to do and what to look for when using the tool:

Step 1. Start the utility by opening ADU.

Step 2. Click the **Diagnostics** tab, and then click **Troubleshooting.** The Trouble-shooting Utility window appears.

Step 3. Click **Run Test**. The utility performs seven tests to check client operation and connectivity:

- Driver installation test
- Card insertion test
- Card enable test
- Radio test
- Association test
- Authentication test
- Network test

The utility runs, and then it shows the results for each test.

For each of the seven Troubleshooting Utility tests, different messages can appear in the Troubleshooting Utility window:

- **Test passed**—The test was successful.
- **Test bypassed**—The test was skipped because it was not necessary for the current operation.
- **Test failed**—If the test failed, click **View Report** to show detailed information about the test and why it was unsuccessful. Figure 13-4 shows an example of a report.

Figure 13-4 *The Cisco Client Troubleshooting Utility's Detailed Report View*

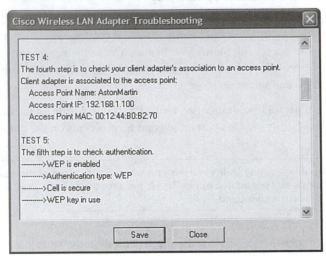

TIP: If you choose to, you can save the report for later review by clicking **Save**.

Prioritizing Connections

If the client computer has more than one network adapter installed (for example, the client might have an Ethernet adapter in addition to an Aironet client card), you can establish which connections are attempted first by assigning priority to your network connections.

The following steps, used with Microsoft Windows, show how to prioritize network connections:

Step 1. Right-click the **My Network Places** icon. This icon can be found either on your desktop or from the Start menu.

Step 2. Click **Properties**.

Step 3. Select **Advanced** from the menu at the top of the screen.

Step 4. Click **Advanced Settings**. This shows your network connections in the Connections box on the Adapters and Bindings tab, as illustrated in Figure 13-5.

Figure 13-5 *Client Network Adapters Can Be Prioritized on Systems with More Than One Adapter*

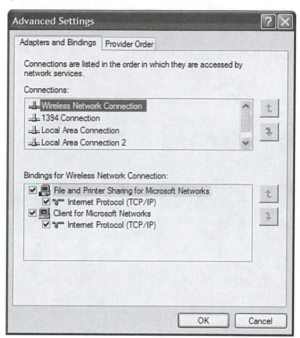

Step 5. Use the arrow buttons next to the Connections box to prioritize your connections.

Step 6. Click **OK**.

NOTE: Windows XP users might think there are problems with their connection when no problem exists. If a client adapter was configured using ADU, the Windows Wireless Network Connection icon in the system tray might be marked with a red *X*. This shows that the connection is unavailable. However, it is likely that the connection does, in fact, exist. This is caused by a conflict between the wireless network settings of ADU and Windows XP. You can ignore the Windows icon and instead use the Aironet System Tray Utility icon to verify the status of your wireless client adapter's connection. This seems to be much less of a problem with Service Pack 2, but it is still something to be mindful of.

Windows Resource Conflicts

You might run into trouble with a client adapter running on a Windows-based computer. You might occasionally encounter a situation in which a different interrupt request (IRQ) is necessary because of a device conflict. By default, IRQ 10 is used, which might not be compatible with all systems. To change the IRQ setting, follow these steps:

NOTE: The following steps are used on Windows XP. The process is similar, but somewhat different, with different flavors of Windows.

Step 1.   Double-click **My Computer** and then click **Control Panel > System**.

Step 2.   Click the **Hardware** tab, and then click **Device Manager**. The resulting window is shown in Figure 13-6.

Figure 13-6   *Windows Device Manager*

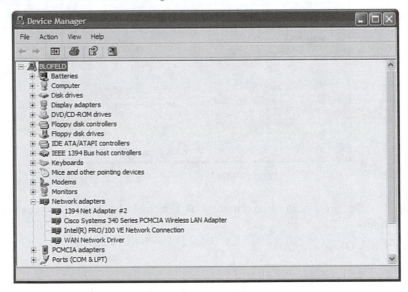

Step 3.   Under **Network Adapters**, double-click the **Cisco Systems Wireless LAN Adapter**. This is shown in Figure 13-7.

Figure 13-7   *Details of the Cisco Wireless Adapter*

Step 4.   The **Device Status** field shows if there are any resource problems. If one exists, click the **Resources** tab. This is shown in Figure 13-8.

Figure 13-8   *The Resources Tab Can Be Used to Resolve Hardware Conflicts*

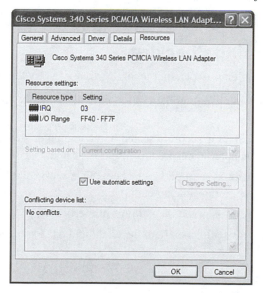

Step 5.   Uncheck the **Use automatic settings** check box.

Step 6.   Under **Resource Settings**, click **I/O Range.**

Step 7.   In the **Conflicting Device** list, check to see if the range is used by another device, and then click the **Change Setting** button.

Step 8.   Choose a range that does not conflict with the device. The **Conflict Information** pane at the bottom of the window shows if the range is already being used.

Step 9.   Click **OK**.

Step 10.   Under **Resource Settings**, click **IRQ**.

Step 11.   Examine the Conflicting Device list at the bottom of the window. If an IRQ setting is used by another device, click the **Change Setting** button.

Step 12.   Choose an IRQ in the **Value** dialog box and select one that does not conflict with the device. The **Conflict Information** pane at the bottom of the window shows if the IRQ is already being used.

Step 13.   Click **OK**.

Step 14.   Reboot your computer. (This is required.)

As you have seen in this and previous chapters, wireless networks combine many of the issues germane to a wired network, along with the specialized characteristics of radio transmission and reception. Successfully troubleshooting these networks requires you to balance the two disciplines.

Troubleshooting Checklist

If your client has problems associating to any of your APs, try the following:

- ❑ If the client is a laptop, palmtop, or other portable device, try to move it closer to the AP.
- ❑ Make sure the adapter is securely seated in the computer's adapter slot. Remove and reinsert the adapter to ensure it is properly seated.
- ❑ Make sure the antenna is properly attached. (This is especially important for desktop PCs with a removable antenna.)
- ❑ Confirm that the AP is turned on and runs properly.
- ❑ Double-check your settings on both the client and AP. Parameters to check include:
  - — SSID
  - — EAP authentication

— WEP activation

— The correct WEP key (Remember that WEP keys are lengthy, and if even one character is incorrect, the key won't work.)

❑ Confirm network settings.

❑ Confirm that TCP/IP is installed on the AP and clients.

❑ Confirm that the AP and client use the same channel.

Other Resources

• **Windows XP Troubleshooting Tips**

http://www.microsoft.com/technet/prodtechnol/winxppro/maintain/wifitrbl.mspx

• **Wi-Fi Alliance Certified Products List**

http://www.wi-fi.org/OpenSection/certified_products.asp

• **Practically Networked Troubleshooting Tips**

http://www.practicallynetworked.com/support/troubleshoot_wireless.htm

Chapter 14 Contents

Diagnosing Performance Problems

Performance problems in a wireless LAN (WLAN) occur at many points—the radio, access points (APs), device configuration, connectivity to the wired network, and even on individual clients. This chapter examines common sources of performance problems and explores steps to fix those problems.

Connection Problems

When clients cannot connect to the WLAN, it is often difficult to find the problem, whether the problem affects one client or the entire site. Table 14-1 lists some common scenarios and resources to check so your WLAN runs optimally.

Table 14-1 *WLAN Connectivity Issue Scenarios*

Problem	Probable Cause(s)	Resolution
A single client cannot connect to the WLAN.	Computer misconfiguration or problem with user or computer account. Defective client card.	❑ Check the computer account. ❑ Check the user account. ❑ Check the client computer. ❑ Verify security credentials. ❑ Check the client card.
Multiple clients at a single site cannot connect to the WLAN.	Misconfigured AP. Defective AP. Defective antenna.	❑ Check AP configuration. ❑ Check to ensure the AP is working. ❑ Check the antenna to ensure it is functional.
An entire site is unable to connect to the WLAN.	Misconfigured RADIUS server.	❑ Check the RADIUS server's configuration ❑ Check the AP's configuration as it relates to RADIUS functions.
No client at any site can connect.	Organization-wide configuration issue.	❑ Check network directory services (such as Microsoft Active Directory). ❑ Check the RADIUS server(s).

Authentication and Re-Authentication Problems

To authenticate to an AP (or to re-authenticate when a client roams from one AP to another) can also cause problems. Table 14-2 lists some common authentication performance problems and how to resolve the issues.

Table 14-2   *Authentication Performance Issues*

Problem	Probable Causes
Slow authentication affects users.	The RADIUS server might be heavily loaded.
	The WAN link might be slow, which causes slow authentication.
	The Dynamic Host Configuration Protocol (DHCP) server that issues IP addresses is slow to respond to address issuance.
Re-authentication delay when roaming between APs.	The AP might not be aware of the client's presence. The time it takes to re-authenticate depends on how often the client probes the AP.
	Misconfigured Wireless Domain Services (WDS), AAA server, or a slow WAN link.
WLAN throughput is slow.	Too many clients overburden the APs.
	APs might be poorly placed or experience weak radio signals because of obstructions, interference, or because they are out of range.
	Multicast applications, broadcast storms, interference, misconfigurations, and data rates can also cause slow throughput.

Hardware Issues

Hardware can play a major issue in poor WLAN performance. This can range from outdated system software on your APs to loose cabling on your antennas.

Firmware

Out-of-date firmware is an often overlooked problem with radio performance.

Sometimes the firmware on your AP becomes out-of-date as new features are added. You can update the firmware if you load the firmware image from the manufacturer.

You can try to reset the AP's configuration. Disconnect power for a few minutes, and then reconnect. Alternately (as in the case of the Cisco 1100 APs), press the MODE button for 30 seconds. This resets the firmware image to its default settings.

You can also update your AP's firmware if you download the newest version from the Cisco website. Follow these steps to install it onto your AP:

Step 1. Navigate to the Software Upgrade screen (follow **System Software > Software Upgrade**).

Step 2.   Click the tab at the top of the screen to pick an upgrade method. Figure 14-1 shows the **HTTP Upgrade** tab selected, although you can also upgrade via TFTP.

Figure 14-1   *Upgrading an AP's Firmware*

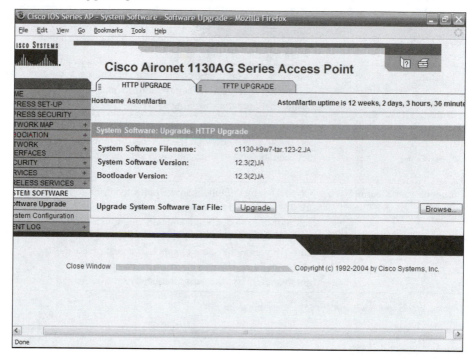

Step 3.   Click the **Browse** button to select the updated firmware file.

Step 4.   Click **Upgrade** to install the system software.

Don't overlook the firmware on your client devices, too. You should make sure to upgrade AP firmware and adapter firmware. Also check release notes on firmware. This can tell you what the firmware updates, including any bug fixes.

Configuration

Many performance and connectivity problems stem from configuration issues. If you have problems with WLAN performance and connectivity, check this place first.

You can spread out these settings through various screens in your AP's configuration screens or you can manage them via the command-line interface. Table 14-3 lists and explains the usual sources of configuration problems.

Table 14-3 *Common Configuration Problems*

Setting	Description
Service Set Identifier (SSID)	Unless the AP and client use the same SSID, they cannot communicate with one another.
Data Rate	If devices are configured to use different data rates, they cannot communicate. Check the setting on all devices to ensure that they use the same data rate.
Distance*	For bridges, the Distance setting is important to set because it lets the bridges know that there is a given amount of lag time between the bridge's transmission and the receiving bridge's reception.
Frequency and Channel	Cisco APs, by default, scan the radio spectrum to locate an ideal channel and radio frequency to use. However, if this setting is disabled, clients and APs might use different frequencies. For best results, check to ensure that the clients and APs are on the same channel. The best practice is to ensure that the APs and clients are configured to automatically use the same frequency.

*This setting is commonly made in kilometers, not miles.

Signal Problems

Radio signals are disrupted for several reasons. The most common include interference, which we discuss in preceding chapters. Interference comes from other RF sources (cordless telephones or neighboring WLANs, for instance) or from electromagnetic interference (from non-communications equipment, such as microwave ovens).

Other factors, however, can have an impact on your WLAN's performance. Although you might blame typical problems on radio interference, you might check the cabling, instead.

Cable Type

When you connect bridges or APs that are situated far from their antennas, it's best to keep the antenna cabling as short as possible, because signal strength degrades on long runs of cabling. Cisco provides a tool to help determine the maximum distance over which two bridges can communicate. The link to the *Antennae Calculation Spreadsheet* is contained in the "Other Resources" section in this chapter.

Installation Issues

When cables connect your antennas to your wireless devices, problems can occur. Check your cabling, with a special eye for the following:

- **Loose connections**—Poorly seated connector cables can cause poor signal quality.

- **Exposed connectors**—Seal connectors that are exposed to the elements.

- **Damaged cables**— Bent, crimped, or otherwise mutilated cabling can cause signal degradation.

- **Power cables**— Electromagnetic interference that comes from nearby power cables can cause signal degradation.

Slow WLAN Network Throughput

Ideally, you should construct your WLAN to please all your users. However, as time passes, it is likely that the network will start to slow down. This section examines some common sources of throughput deterioration in WLANs.

Cisco APs are robust, little machines. Each one can handle dozens of wireless clients. Unfortunately, it's easy to take for granted how many clients each one can handle. Each time another client associates to an AP, performance drops a little. If clients transfer large amounts of data, performance takes another hit.

How do you know if you have too many devices on your WLAN? The first step is through some preventive efforts. A solid site survey can help you understand how many APs you need to handle the load.

Another issue comes from the understanding of the radio channels available. For example, in 802.11b and 802.11g networks, there are 11 channels available in the U.S. Therefore, you might think that you can have a total of 11 networks that run in a given area. In theory, that is correct. In practice, however, it is a different story. Although there are 11 channels, you can use only three of them (channels 1, 6, and 11). This is because neighboring frequencies overlap and interfere with one another.

Of course, capacity is somewhat of a moving target. It is likely that when more clients are added to your environment, they will use more bandwidth. Therefore, it is important to watch your WLAN and know the demands placed upon it.

Bridged Networks

To diagnose problems with bridges can cause issues. The following helps to address those issues.

Line-of-Sight Networks

If you employ a bridging technology to connect two sites, you are likely to use line-of-sight to forge that connection. Line-of-sight is a technology that requires the transmitter and the receiver to point at and have a clear view of each other. Although it's useful to connect two remote sites, wirelessly, several things can cause performance problems or complete outages.

First, line-of-sight antennas are difficult to align. Many bridges (such as the Cisco 1300) come with self-aligning features. For example, the Cisco 1300 uses numerous light emitting diodes (LEDs) to indicate whether the bridge associates to another bridge. If the unit associates to a root bridge, the LED turns amber. If the unit does not associate to a root bridge in the first minute, the LED blinks green.

If you notice performance problems between your remote sites, check the antenna alignment. You might run into trouble with performance, especially on windy days because antenna masts tend to sway. Although the disparity between antennas might be a few inches only, those few inches cause connection problems.

NOTE: Towers cause problems. Avoid mounting your antennas on poles, which can sway dramatically.

Fresnel Zone

Although antennas that broadcast in a line-of-of sight configuration are best if they point directly at each other, it is also important to consider the Fresnel Zone. The *Fresnel Zone* is the area around the line-of-sight radio waves that spread out after they leave the antenna. This is illustrated in Figure 14-2. This area must be at least 60 percent clear, or else the signal weakens.

Figure 14-2   *The Fresnel Zone*

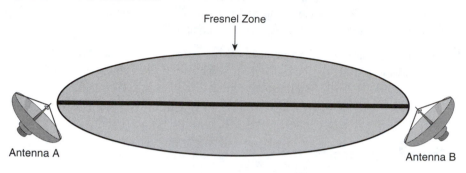

2.4-GHz wireless signals pass through walls, although they have trouble passing through organics, such as trees. This is because walls are dry and trees contain a lot of water—water absorbs the 2.4-GHz radio waves.

NOTE: Microwave ovens are a source of interference for WLANs because they cook food on the same 2.4-GHz band. The water in food resonates to cook the food.

In addition to the water content of materials between antennas, the density and composition of other materials between antennas can cause problems. Table 14-4 lists some materials you might encounter—indoors or outdoors—and explains what makes it problematic.

Table 14-4   *Effect of Various Materials on RF Signal Performance*

Material	Explanation
Paper and vinyl	Negligible impact on signal propagation.
Concrete (solid)	The signal can penetrate one or two walls without serious coverage degradation. However, some walls have steel reinforcement that blocks radio signals.
Concrete (block)	The signal can penetrate three or four walls without serious coverage degradation.
Metal	Causes the signal to reflect.
Wood	The signal can penetrate five or six walls without serious coverage degradation.
Mesh fences	Fences (such as chain-link) with 1- to 1.5-inch spacing can block a 2.4-GHz signal.

Check to ensure that the Fresnel Zone is not obstructed. If it is, reposition the antenna to clear the Fresnel Zone. Also, if the antennas are more than 6 miles apart, the curvature of the Earth might interfere with the connection.

Performance problems can frustrate the network users, as well as the technology professionals who try to fix the problem. If you examine your equipment and its configuration, you probably can resolve a great deal of your performance issues.

Other Resources

- **Fresnel Zone Calculator**

  http://gbppr.dyndns.org/fresnel.main.cgi

- **Antennae Calculation Spreadsheet**

  www.cisco.com/warp/public/102/us-calc.xls

Appendix A Contents

802.11 Protocols

The technology behind Wi-Fi networking is the 802.11x protocol. In your environments—and using popular Cisco gear—you are likely to come into contact with three prevalent versions of this protocol: 802.11a, 802.11b, and 802.11g.

Like other computing and networking technologies, wireless started with slow and nonstandardized equipment. When wireless networking came into its own in the late 1990s, 802.11b was the standard. It was popular for a number of reasons, not the least of which was that it operated in the unlicensed, 2.4-GHz band. That meant anyone could buy it, deploy it, and use it without worrying about governmental permission. The standard also brought decent range (up to 120 meters) and a workable amount of throughout (11 Mbps). However, anyone who has been around computers in the past 20 years can tell you that what's "workable" today is substandard tomorrow. 802.11a and 802.11g have taken the limelight as the prevalent Wi-Fi standards.

NOTE: Look for the 802.11n standard in the future. This standard promises speeds of at least 100 Mbps. At this point, 802.11n is still a prestandard—that is, nothing is formalized and vendors are putting out their own versions of 802.11n equipment. 802.11n builds on existing standards by adding multiple-input, multiple-output (MIMO) technology. Additional transmitter and receiver antennas allow increased throughput and increased range.

These protocols offer something different and should be adopted based on performance and environmental needs. This appendix examines these protocols and provides more insight into their functionality, helping you determine which protocols might be best suited for your environment.

Bands and Channels

802.11g's big benefit is that it operates in the same unlicensed, 2.4-GHz band in which 802.11b lives. This allows backward compatibility with existing 802.11b gear. Rather than discard old Wi-Fi equipment, you can use old equipment if you opt to move to the 802.11g standard. Unfortunately, many consumer products also use this band, and you can experience interference from a number of sources, including cordless telephones and microwave ovens.

802.11a also operates in the unlicensed 5-GHz band, which is largely uncluttered and offers many more nonoverlapping channels (assuming you use both indoor and outdoor channels) in which to operate than 802.11b and 802.11g.

NOTE: There is a tradeoff in range when it comes to the frequency band in which a radio broadcasts. 802.11b and 802.11g get a better range because they operate at a lower frequency than 802.11a. Lower frequencies propagate farther than higher frequencies. Longer waveforms also have an easier time penetrating obstacles, such as walls.

Throughput

Both 802.11a and 802.11g offer data rates up to five times faster than 802.11b (54 Mbps versus 11 Mbps), and they also promise to transmit signals more cleanly and with fewer lost packets. This means an improvement in overall throughput. Throughput, compared to simple data rates, is the actual rate achieved after you factor in hardware limitations, network congestion, buffering, transmission errors, and so on.

This is possible thanks to improved modulation technologies in the guise of Orthogonal Frequency Division Multiplexing (OFDM). OFDM is a more efficient means of transmission than Direct Sequence Spread Spectrum (DSSS) transmission, which 802.11b uses.

802.11a and 802.11g also offer more throughput than 802.11b. Table A-1 compares throughput for the various network technologies.

Table A-1   *Approximate Throughput Comparison of 802.11a, 802.11b, and 802.11g Technologies*

Protocol	Data Rates (Mbps)	Approximate Throughput (Mbps)
802.11b	11	6
802.11g (with 802.11b clients)	54	14
802.11g (with no 802.11b clients)	54	22
802.11a	54	25

Notice the throughput hit 802.11g access points (AP) take when 802.11b clients are associated with them. This is because 802.11g was designed for backward compatibility with 802.11b, which nicely leverages an existing investment. When an 802.11b client associates, the slower traffic takes up more air time at a slower speed to communicate with that client. Because of this, the 802.11g clients have to wait longer.

Network Capacity

Another consideration when selecting a protocol is its overall capacity. Network capacity can be expressed as the throughput multiplied by the number of available channels. Because 802.11g has access to the same three nonoverlapping channels, the only way to increase total capacity is to increase throughput on individual channels. Table A-2 shows approximate network capacities for different Wi-Fi technologies.

Table A-2   *Network Capacity Comparison*

Protocol	Throughput (Mbps)	Channels	Capacity (Mbps)
802.11b	6	3	18
802.11g (with 802.11b clients)	14	3	42
802.11g (with no 802.11b clients)	22	3	66
802.11a	25	23 (assumes the use of both indoor and outdoor channels)	575

As you can see, 802.11b clients have the lowest capacity, whereas 802.11a clients have almost 32 times as much capacity. As you can see in the next section, however, there is a tradeoff in ranges when it comes to these technologies.

Range

Range is a key consideration when selecting your Wi-Fi solution. Although it is often desirable to have the gear that operates with the longest range, don't get stuck in the mindset that the longest range is the best.

A longer range solution (such as 802.11g) reduces costs in that you do not need to buy extra APs to reach distant clients; however, a shorter range technology (such as 802.11a) makes it easier to segment users and reduces interference between neighboring APs.

A discussion of range involves an approximation at best. Don't take Table A-3 into your organization and expect the ranges to be exactly as they are described in the table. Range is greatly affected by your environment, including the materials used in your building and any sources of interference. Table A-3 shows the types of ranges you can expect at differing speeds from the 802.11 protocols.

Table A-3   *Data Rates and Ranges*

Data Rate (Mbps)	802.11a	802.11g	802.11b
54	90 ft (27 m)	90 ft (27 m)	–
48	225 ft (69 m)	95 ft (29 m)	–
36	300 ft (91 m)	100 ft (30 m)	–
24	350 ft (107 m)	140 ft (42 m)	–
18	400 ft (122 m)	180 ft (54 m)	–
12	450 ft (137 m)	210 ft (64 m)	–
11	–	220 ft (67 m)	160 ft (48 m)
9	475 ft (145 m)	250 ft (76 m)	–
6	500 ft (152 m)	300 ft (91 m)	–
5.5	–	310 ft (94 m)	220 ft (67 m)
2	–	350 ft (107 m)	270 ft (82m)
1	–	410 ft (124 m)	410 ft (124 m)

802.11b and 802.11g

Because 802.11b and 802.11g share the same range, it is not necessary to perform another site survey to locate the new APs. They can be installed in the same locations that existing 802.11b APs were placed.

Although the advantage of compatibility between 802.11b and 802.11g cannot be denied, the fact that both technologies use the 2.4-GHz band poses some problems. As noted throughout this book, the 2.4-GHz band is unlicensed and is crowded. Interference can come from cordless phones, microwave ovens, and Bluetooth devices. Interference from these devices can be mitigated, but if it persists, serious problems for Wi-Fi networks can result. Because 802.11b/g networks offer only three nonoverlapping channels, there are few places to run.

Performance also takes a hit, due to the commingling of 802.11b and 802.11g. When 802.11b legacy devices use an 802.11g network, the 802.11g clients suffer from AP congestion.

Consider a conference room full of people using an AP at 54 Mbps. When the guy down the hall with the legacy 802.11b client adapter logs on to the AP, not only will the client experience 1 or 2 Mbps of throughput (simply because of the distance from the AP), but it will also absorb more of the radio's time, robbing it from other users.

In addition, to prevent 802.11g clients from getting preferential treatment over 802.11b clients, a mechanism is in place that adds bulky overhead to packets.

802.11g also uses the speedy OFDM modulation scheme; however, to support its older brother 802.11b, it must also support Complementary Code Keying, which takes a bite out of throughput.

802.11b

Does this mean that 802.11b has no place in today's Wi-Fi networks? This is not the case. If you have 802.11b equipment, it can be put into low-powered devices, such as scanners or cameras. In addition, you might find some clients or groups of clients that simply don't need 54-Mbps access, and you can give them all the legacy 802.11b devices. It keeps them wirelessly connected, but you don't have to buy new equipment—at least not for a while. That said, 802.11b has a place in the network only if you have legacy 802.11b equipment sitting around and need a home for it. If you buy wireless gear, you are better off getting the 802.11g equipment, assuming you can find it for sale.

The pros of 802.11b are:

- Least expensive.
- Long signal range.
- Not easily obstructed.

The cons of 802.11b are:

- Slowest maximum speed.
- Supports fewer simultaneous users.
- Common appliances can interfere.

802.11g

It's easy to see why 802.11g is so popular. Both the price of this high-speed, Wi-Fi solution and its compatibility with 802.11b devices make it a desirable choice, especially in environments in which both technologies are deployed.

Deploying an 802.11g solution not only makes sense for the environments over which you have control (that is, you've selected the clients and know what to expect in your

WLAN), but it's also a safe way to hedge your bets in environments in which you don't know what the client adapters will use. For instance, if you offer up a hotspot at a local restaurant, 802.11g is a good choice because it's more likely that 802.11b or 802.11g will be used.

In addition, there's a comfort level for network professionals who have already lived and worked with the 2.4-GHz band. Upgrading to 802.11g is the same, easy graduation as the move from 10-Mbps Ethernet to Fast Ethernet.

Ideally, if you upgrade from 802.11b to 802.11g, your best bet is to also upgrade your clients. Although it's best to make this upgrade, it's not necessary.

The pros of 802.11g are:

- Fastest maximum speed.
- Support for more simultaneous users.
- Longest signal range.
- Not easily obstructed.

The cons of 802.11g are:

- Common appliances can interfere.
- Fewer nonoverlapping channels than 802.11a.

802.11a

If 802.11g is so great, why bother with 802.11a? The answer comes down to one word: performance.

As Wi-Fi networks become larger and more complex, performance takes a serious hit. To address this problem, 802.11a uses OFDM to offer a data rate of 54 Mbps and operates in the reasonably uncluttered 5-GHz band.

802.11a offers many more channels in which to operate than 802.11b or 802.11g. With as many as 23, nonoverlapping channels, you can have up to 12 APs set to different channels in the same area without interfering with each other.

802.11a is popular in certain industries. Environments in which large data transfers are necessary might be wise to consider 802.11a because of the improved performance.

The pros of 802.11a are:

- Fastest maximum speed.
- Support for more simultaneous users.

- Less interference because the radios are more expensive and are not found in popular consumer products.

The cons of 802.11a are:

- Highest cost (though costs are coming down).
- Shorter range signal that is more easily obstructed.

Multiband Solutions

The solution offering the most flexibility and future-proofing is to buy multiband equipment. For example, the Cisco Aironet 1130AG AP offers AP services for devices that use 802.11a, 802.11b, and 802.11g. Although multiband technology can be pricey, costs might come down as more multiband products are produced.

Future-proofing is an important factor when considering this option. After you install a multiband device, it'll be a while before you have to touch it again. In addition, as Wi-Fi networks grow, you might find 802.11b's and 802.11g's three channels quickly used up, making 802.11a's 23 channels appealing.

As WLANs grow, these multiband networks can find channels used for specific functions. For instance, a large company with a robust WLAN might assign users to different channels and bands based on their use. For example, an engineer who needs access to large technical files might be assigned wireless access using 802.11a, whereas someone who accesses the network for e-mail might be assigned to one of the 802.11b channels.

Ultimately, selecting a technology boils down to the following:

- 802.11b and 802.11g offer the best cost and are the most popular deployments.
- 802.11a offers an easier deployment with 23 nonoverlapping channels.
- Multiband 802.11a, 802.11b, and 802.11g offer high performance and great compatibility, but are also the most expensive options. On the other hand, you might save money in the long run because they decrease the likelihood of having to upgrade equipment in the future.

Although it can be somewhat difficult to figure out which wireless technology to support, look for 802.11n to make it even more challenging. 802.11n—still a couple of years off—promises speeds in excess of 100 Mbps.

Index

D

dashboards
  Sniffer Wireless, 219
  WLSE, 171–173
Data Encryption Standard (DES), 79
data
  transfer rates
    802.11b vs. 802.11g, 4
    APs, 11–15, 192–195
    bridges, 23
    client adapters, 29
    repeater/parent APs, 95
    throughput problems, 238–240
  transfer retries, 198
database authentication, 76
DCA (Device and Credential Admin), 165
decibel scale, 36–37, 187
decryption dictionaries, 68
defense agencies, 30
delivery traffic indication messages (DTIMs), 196–197
design
  See network design
Dell, 32
DES (Data Encryption Standard), 79
Device and Credential Admin (DCA), CiscoWorks LMS, 165
Device Troubleshooting panel, CiscoWorks LMS, 162
DFM (Device Fault Manager), 160, 168
DHCP (Dynamic Host Configuration Protocol)
  misconfiguration, 227
  relay, 134
  servers, 133
dipole antennas, 37
directional antennas
  alignment, 48
  function, 35
  remote sites, 49

discovery
  devices, CiscoWorks LMS, 164
  network, 105
distance, bridges, 240
distortion, multipath, 41, 194
diversity antennas
  configuring multiple, 42–43
  function, 35
  optimal placement, 43–45
driver installation tests, 229
DTIMs (delivery traffic indication messages), 196–197
dual mode, 7

E

EAP (Extensible Authentication Protocol)
  Aironet 1130AG, 7
  Cisco Wireless EAP, 72
  Cisco Wireless Security Suite, 5
  EAP FAST, 75–76
  EAP-GTC (EAP-Generic Token Card), 90
  EAP-MD5 (Message Digest 5), 5, 114
  EAP-SIM (EAP-Subscriber Identity Module), 90, 114, 120
  EAP-TLS (EAP with Transport Layer Security), 71–72, 90, 114, 119
  EAP-TTLS (EAP-Tunneled TLS), 90
  LEAP (Lightweight EAP), 72, 90, 115–116
  PEAP (Protected EAP), 73–75, 90, 114, 119
  Windows, 117–118
encryption
  AES, 78–79
  bit significance, 86–87
  CLI, 88
  DES, 79
  RC4, 78
  strong encryption, 79
  WPA, 78, 147
Encryption Manager, WPA, 147